Sibling Loss Across the Lifespan

Sibling Loss Across the Lifespan brings together researchers, clinicians, and bereaved siblings to explore sibling loss. Unique in both form and content, the book focuses on loss within five key age ranges – childhood, adolescence, emerging adulthood, adulthood, and late adulthood – and losses within a special topics section that addresses areas of interest across multiple age groups. In addition to chapters from researchers and clinicians, the book includes personal stories from bereaved siblings who describe the lived experience of this loss.

Brenda J. Marshall, PhD is a well-known speaker, facilitator, coach, and founder of the Solacium Group and FLOW Learning Group in Ontario, Canada.

Howard R. Winokuer, PhD is the founder of the Winokuer Center for Counseling and Healing in Charlotte, North Carolina, and a well-known author and internationally renowned speaker.

The Series in Death, Dying, and Bereavement

ROBERT A. NEIMEYER, CONSULTING EDITOR

For a complete list of all books in this series, please visit the series page at: www.routledge.com/series/SE0620

Balk – Dealing with Dying, Death, and Grief during Adolescence
Beder – Voices of Bereavement: A Casebook for Grief Counselors
Berger – Music of the Soul: Composing Life out of Loss
Buckle and Fleming – Parenting after the Death of a Child: A Practitioner's Guide
Davies – Shadows in the Sun: The Experiences of Sibling Bereavement in Childhood
Doka and Martin – Grieving beyond Gender: Understanding the Ways Men and Women Mourn, Revised Edition
Harris – Counting Our Losses: Reflecting on Change, Loss, and Transition in Everyday Life
Harris and Bordere – Handbook of Social Justice in Loss and Grief: Exploring Diversity, Equity, and Inclusion
Harvey – Perspectives on Loss: A Sourcebook
Hedtke and Winslade – The Crafting of Grief: Constructing Aesthetic Responses to Loss
Jeffreys – Helping Grieving People – When Tears Are Not Enough: A Handbook for Care Providers, Second Edition
Jordan and McIntosh – Grief after Suicide: Understanding the Consequences and Caring for the Survivors
Katz and Johnson – When Professionals Weep: Emotional and Countertransference Responses in Palliative and End-of-Life Care, Second Edition
Kissane and Parnes – Bereavement Care for Families
Klass – The Spiritual Lives of Bereaved Parents
Kosminsky and Jordan – Attachment-Informed Grief Therapy: The Clinician's Guide to Foundations and Applications
Leenaars – Lives and Deaths: Selections from the Works of Edwin S. Shneidman
Leong and Leach – Suicide among Racial and Ethnic Minority Groups: Theory, Research, and Practice
Lester – Katie's Diary: Unlocking the Mystery of a Suicide
Marshall and Winokuer – Sibling Loss Across the Lifespan: Research, Practice, and Personal Stories

"This is a timely, groundbreaking contribution by an eminent group of scholars with a wide range of perspectives that results in a treasure trove of useful lessons, penetrating insights, and practical approaches for managing sibling grief. *Sibling Loss Across the Lifespan* is a unique, valuable resource!"
      Gerry R. Cox, PhD, *professor emeritus, Center for Death Education & Bioethics, The University of Wisconsin–La Crosse*

"*Sibling Loss Across the Lifespan* is a unique contribution to our understandings of bereavement, incorporating as it does both developmental perspectives and contributions from researchers, clinicians, and individuals who describe their personal encounters with the death of a brother or sister. *Sibling Loss Across the Lifespan* is an invaluable resource for researchers, educators, and counselors, one that will spark further interest in additional dimensions of this woefully understudied subject area."
      Charles A. Corr, PhD, *member, board of directors, Suncoast Hospice Institute, an affiliate of Empath Health, Clearwater, Florida*

"The death of a brother or sister has a unique impact on a sibling, particularly at a young age but also throughout life. Profound feelings, including neglect, guilt, and vulnerability, can persist and impact one's view of the world. *Sibling Loss Across the Lifespan* addresses this understudied area with insight, depth, and compassion. It is essential for the library of anyone seriously interested in grief and loss."
      Stephen R. Connor, PhD, *executive director, Worldwide Hospice Palliative Care Alliance*

"While children have been called the 'forgotten grievers,' perhaps the least recognized are those bereaved by the death of a sibling. Given that more than 80% of us have brothers or sisters, we're increasingly likely to experience the loss of one or more throughout our lifetime. Blending research, theory, and personal experience, this book captures the uniqueness of sibling loss from varied perspectives."
      Donna L. Schuurman, EdD, FT, *senior director of advocacy & training, executive director emeritus, The Dougy Center*

"When my only sister was diagnosed with triple negative breast cancer, my heart sank and I lost 10 pounds while she was undergoing treatment. Sibling loss is a neglected area that touches many people deeply and yet is seldom discussed or acknowledged. This book is truly inspiring and educational, and it beautifully integrates research, practice, and personal stories of sibling loss across the lifespan. I strongly recommend it to everyone."
      Cecilia L. W. Chan, BSocSc, MSocSc, PhD, RS, JP, *Si Yuan Professor of Health and Social Work, The University of Hong Kong*

"This is an important book with helpful insights. It will be of value to anyone working with grieving individuals and families or studying to do so. It has much to commend it."

Neil Thompson, PhD, DLitt, *author of Grief and Its Challenges and board member of the International Work Group on Death, Dying, and Bereavement*

Martin and Doka – Men Don't Cry…Women Do: Transcending Gender Stereotypes of Grief

Neimeyer – Techniques of Grief Therapy: Creative Practices for Counseling the Bereaved

Neimeyer – Techniques of Grief Therapy: Assessment and Intervention

Neimeyer, Harris, Winokuer, and Thornton – Grief and Bereavement in Contemporary Society: Bridging Research and Practice

Nord – Multiple AIDS-Related Loss: A Handbook for Understanding and Surviving a Perpetual Fall

Rogers – The Art of Grief: The Use of Expressive Arts in a Grief Support Group

Roos – Chronic Sorrow: A Living Loss

Rosenblatt – Parent Grief: Narratives of Loss and Relationship

Rosenblatt and Wallace – African American Grief

Rubin, Malkinson, and Witztum – Working with the Bereaved: Multiple Lenses on Loss and Mourning

Silverman – Widow to Widow, Second Edition

Tedeschi and Calhoun – Helping Bereaved Parents: A Clinician's Guide

Thompson and Neimeyer – Grief and the Expressive Arts: Practices for Creating Meaning

Werth – Contemporary Perspectives on Rational Suicide

Werth and Blevins – Decision Making near the End of Life: Issues, Developments, and Future Directions

Sibling Loss Across the Lifespan

Research, Practice, and Personal Stories

Edited by
Brenda J. Marshall and
Howard R. Winokuer

LONDON AND NEW YORK

First published 2017
by Routledge
711 Third Avenue, New York, NY 10017

and by Routledge
2 Park Square, Milton Park, Abingdon, Oxon, OX14 4RN

Routledge is an imprint of the Taylor & Francis Group, an informa business

© 2017 Brenda J. Marshall and Howard R. Winokuer

The right of the editors to be identified as the authors of the editorial material, and of the authors for their individual chapters, has been asserted in accordance with sections 77 and 78 of the Copyright, Designs and Patents Act 1988.

All rights reserved. No part of this book may be reprinted or reproduced or utilised in any form or by any electronic, mechanical, or other means, now known or hereafter invented, including photocopying and recording, or in any information storage or retrieval system, without permission in writing from the publishers.

Trademark notice: Product or corporate names may be trademarks or registered trademarks, and are used only for identification and explanation without intent to infringe.

Library of Congress Cataloging in Publication Data
Names: Marshall, Brenda J., 1963– editor. | Winokuer, Howard Robin, editor.
Title: Sibling loss across the lifespan : research, practice, and personal stories / edited by Brenda J. Marshall and Howard R. Winokuer.
Description: New York, NY : Routledge, 2016. |
Series: Death, dying, and bereavement |
Includes bibliographical references and index.
Identifiers: LCCN 2016014098|
ISBN 9781138927285 (hardback : alk. paper) |
ISBN 9781138927292 (pbk. : alk. paper) | ISBN 9781315672861 (ebook)
Subjects: LCSH: Brothers and sisters. | Brothers and sisters–Death. | Grief.
Classification: LCC BF723.S43 S484 2016 | DDC 155.9/370855–dc23
LC record available at https://lccn.loc.gov/2016014098

ISBN: 978-1-138-92728-5 (hbk)
ISBN: 978-1-138-92729-2 (pbk)
ISBN: 978-1-315-67286-1 (ebk)

Typeset in ScalaSans and Frutiger
by Out of House Publishing

For my brother Brent who is with me always.

BJM

To my clients and colleagues who have inspired me and motivated me to be the best grief professional that I can be.

HRW

Contents

Series Editor's Foreword	xiv
ROBERT A. NEIMEYER	
Foreword	xvi
KENNETH J. DOKA	
Preface	xix
BRENDA J. MARSHALL AND HOWARD R. WINOKUER	
Editor Biographies	xxii
List of Contributors	xxv
Theoretical Models Guiding Our Understanding of Sibling Bereavement	1
David W. Kissane and Nadine A. Kasparian	

PART I: Childhood (Birth–11) — 15

1. Shadows in the Sun: Towards Understanding the Grief of Young Siblings — 17
   Betty Davies

2. Why Did My Sister Have to Die? Helping Children with Sibling Death — 25
   Linda Goldman

3. Growing Up Grieving — 37
   Alicia Sims Franklin

4. A Brother's Loss — 42
   Christopher Lourenco

PART II: Adolescence (12–17)	47
5. Adolescent Sibling Loss *David E. Balk, Corinne Cavuoti, and Anne M. Smith*	49
6. Bereaved Adolescent Siblings: The Forgotten Mourners *Jennifer Kaplan Schreiber*	58
7. Michelle's Story *Rose Planer*	65
8. Losing My Brother at 14 *Elizabeth DeVita-Raeburn*	68
PART III: Emerging Adulthood (18–30)	73
9. Living the Moment...Envisioning the Future *Ann Laverty*	75
10. Making Clinical Sense of Sibling Bereavement: *Ordinary People* as a Case Study *Simon Shimshon Rubin*	83
11. The Happiness of Moving Forward: Sibling Suicide Loss 20 Years Later *Michelle L. Rusk*	91
12. Brother And Sister Always *Rayna Vaught Godfrey*	94
PART IV: Adulthood (31–59)	99
13. Sibling Loss in Adulthood: Narrative Reflections *Brenda J. Marshall*	101
14. While the World Mourned a Hero, I Mourned My Murdered Brother: The Case of Barbara, a Bereaved 9/11 Sibling *Cori Bussolari and Heidi Horsley*	110
15. Honoring Donna *Lyn Prashant*	118
16. On My Only Brother's Death *H.D. ("De") Kirkpatrick*	123

PART V: Late Adulthood (60 Plus)	127
17. Clinical Issues Related to Sibling Loss in Older Adulthood *Jason M. Holland and Vincent Rozalski*	129
18. A Letter to My Brother *Carol L. Sachs*	141
19. The Death of a Sister and a Brother *Gloria Horsley*	144
PART VI: Special Topics	149
20. Sibling Grief after Suicide *Diana C. Sands*	151
21. Sibling Grief and Its Effect on the Family System *Kathleen R. Gilbert and Rebecca J. Gilbert*	159
22. The Impact on Siblings When a Parent Dies *Howard R. Winokuer*	167
23. Disappearance, Not Death: The Ambiguous Loss of a Missing Sibling *Pauline Boss and Patty Wetterling*	174
24. The Dirt on Sibling Grief: A Look at Bereavement Camps *Tina Barrett and Molly Murphy*	184
25. Epilogue *Brenda J. Marshall and Howard R. Winokuer*	193
Index	201

Series Editor's Foreword

One cold winter morning ten days before my twelfth birthday, my younger brother and I awoke to the panicked voice of our mother saying, "Boys, boys, I can't wake your father!" Stumbling alarmed from beneath our cowboy comforters, we trundled timidly to the door of our parents' bedroom, where we saw our mother once more shake our father's unresponsive body, then pull back in horror with a scream that I can hear to this day. With that shriek, one world ended, and another began.

    In the jumbled months that followed we packed what we could in a U-Haul truck, left the rest, and moved from the small town in Ohio in which we had always lived to Orlando, Florida, as our mother sought to flee the memories of our father's death – and in the process to leave behind everyone and everything we had ever known or loved. Thus began a long course of complicated grief for her, and tumultuous transition for my brother, my little sister, and myself, the reverberations of which continue to be felt in our current lives, for both better and worse. This much of the story I have acknowledged previously in print, and occasionally in professional workshops. I am particularly likely to do so when the conversation turns to suicide loss, as my pharmacist father ended his encroaching blindness, business debt, and very likely private pain I will never fully know with a lethal mix of barbiturates and alcohol to ensure that he would not awaken into another day of darkness and shame. Unquestionably, in the clarity of hindsight, this fateful turn of events planted the seeds of receptivity to my pursuit of a career as a psychologist and grief therapist in the decades that followed.

What I have not previously acknowledged – and scarcely recalled, frankly – was a tragic footnote to our father's suicide, which has uncanny relevance to the topic of this book. Toward the end of my adolescence, when I began to find the words to speak to my mother and others about the circumstances of Dad's death, I inquired about a particularly perplexing interval of some weeks in which Mom simply disappeared from the house, and ancient Aunt Mamie, actually the sister of our deceased paternal grandmother, came to stay with us. At the time we three children – then 12, 9, and 7 – were told simply that our mother "had to go to the hospital." Years later I learned that the precipitant to that psychiatric admission was Mom's miscarriage of the child no one knew she was carrying at the time of our father's death, as she struggled with the overwhelming stress and stigma of his suicide. The "nervous breakdown" that followed triggered her own long struggle with suicide ideation and attempts, each of which sent shock waves through a shattered family system with few resilient resources beyond our aging aunts to buffer them.

My thoughts drifted back to those dark years and their brighter aftermath as I read the pages that follow. Although we never knew (and scarcely knew of) the brother we never had, his brief presence and long absence compounded an already anguishing shared passage, and no doubt carried complicating meaning for our mother that she harbored as a silent story for the rest of her life. This is of course only one of the many forms of sibling loss, each of which leaves its mark on surviving brothers and sisters, however unconsciously. One of the great strengths of *Sibling Loss Across the Lifespan* is that it not only acknowledges this marginalized form of bereavement, but also sensitively and systematically explores its meaning and consequences for siblings of all ages, in chapter contributions that are by turns personally evocative, empirically informed, and clinically astute. This structure, with its grounding in attachment, developmental and systems theories, and its felicitous blend of case studies, authoritative research reviews, and descriptions of interventions, offers much to the practitioner looking for insight and guidance, as well as to the scholar seeking more nuanced acquaintance with a loss that is too often unrecognized and uninvestigated. In editing this book, Marshall and Winokuer have opened this unique form of grief to a fuller reading, in a way that invites our deeper engagement with a loss that commonly stands in the shadow of our practice, our research programs, and our lives. I have no doubt that it will prove to be a milestone in the further development of clinical scholarship on sibling bereavement.

Robert A. Neimeyer
University of Memphis

Foreword

Sibling relationships are among the most important relationships we are likely to have in our lives. They are likely to be the longest lasting. I have known my sister and brother for all near seven decades of my life – longer than I have known my partner, my parents, or my child. Since I am the youngest, I have never known a time when they were not around me. And they have to reach way into the recesses of their childhoods to remember a time when I was not around.

In fact, siblings frame our own identity. Part of who I am, who I will ever be, is how I was defined growing up – Frankie and Dot's kid brother. Our sibling position, as well researched, carries its own imprint as we consider the unique characteristics of older, younger, and middle children. Yet, sibling position is only part of that critical constellation. Age spacing and gender also play a role. For example, the fact that my sister was the middle child – and only girl – mitigated the inevitable anonymity sometimes assigned to the child betwixt the eldest and youngest.

Indeed, the experiences inherent in the sibling dynamic forge our personality. My sister – eight years older than me – became an almost surrogate mother to me, her younger brother, through my Mom's bouts with multiple sclerosis. That experience of caring for a younger brother through periods of her adolescence has forged the kind and compassionate mother and wife that are a mark of her individuality.

Siblings have a unique relationship. Siblings are family, tied through life by that kinship. Yet, unlike most family relationships, sibling relationships are more equal and less hierarchical. Siblings may differ in the authority they hold over their other siblings, dependent on culture, gender, and age spacing. Whatever authority they may hold is likely to be more tentative – and more challenged – than those of parents, grandparents, or even aunts and uncles. They are more likely to be our models and playmates.

Siblings share a secret language, a private code that unlocks common experiences. Some are mundane yet important – the smell of Grandma's house or damp summer mornings in Maine. Siblings retain their distinct memories and shared encounters. I can make my sister laugh at any time. All I need to do is to sidle up to her and ask her in a whisper if she has had a BM today. Though I am in my 60s and my sister now in her 70s, the comment still never fails to engender a smile. It brings us back to a long time past – a scary time when my mother was struggling with her illness. My sister and I were cared for in that summer by an aunt. I was 5 years old, my sister 13. We clung together as we sought both to cope with Mom's relapse and our time away. My aunt, for whatever reason, valued regularity. A negative answer meant that she would give us a spoonful of a foul-smelling and even fouler-tasting tonic. Moreover, the question was embarrassing, especially to two children from a home where private functions stayed private. The question today brings up all those emotions – the fear and anxiety, the embarrassment, the conspiracy of support we lent one another, the closeness that has always characterized our relationship, and the shared humor that allowed us to cope.

Yet, sibling relationships also can have a dark side. Not all sibling relations are positive. Sometimes siblings can abuse one another – physically, psychologically, or sexually. Sibling relations can be hostile as each sibling battles to retain their place in the family. Helen Rosen (1986) once characterized sibling relationships as having a number of dimensions. One dimension she called closeness-distance. Some siblings are in constant contact with each other. Others seldom speak. Another dimension was warmth-hostility. Some siblings have warm, supportive relationships. Others constantly argue and fight or consciously choose to limit contact.

Naturally, then, we grieve the deaths of siblings – no matter what the relationship. After all, we have likely lost our longest relationship, even a part of ourselves. We grieve their loss even when relationships may be strained or absent. Rosen (1986) notes that the more relationships veered toward the end of the continuum that is the very close or distant, the very warm or hostile, our grief is likely to be more intense. Thus it is not only the close, warm relationships we grieve. The sister who angrily fought with a brother may be filled with remorse and grief should that person die.

We grieve our siblings whether they are 9, 19, or 90 years old when they die. There is, however, one difference. When a 9-year-old dies, families and friends may be very aware of the effect of that loss on a brother or sister. Yet when we are older, our grief is more likely to be disenfranchised. Especially as we move into adulthood, support may be more focused on other survivors – the sibling's partner or spouse, children, and even parents. The grieving sibling is easily forgotten – their grief ignored, disenfranchised.

That is why Brenda J. Marshall and Howard R. Winokuer's *Sibling Loss Across the Lifespan* is so helpful. They offer a comprehensive perspective of sibling loss. This comprehensive quality includes but is not limited to assessing the impact of sibling loss throughout the lifespan – from the youngest children to older adults. Here they not only include the integration of sound research with clinical practice but also the personal accounts of siblings recounting the impact of their losses of siblings at varied points in their lives.

Moreover, *Sibling Loss Across the Lifespan* acknowledges the varied circumstances and conditions of loss such as death by suicide. Marshall and Winokuer also acknowledge the varied ways we can lose siblings – including disappearances and fractured relationships. They acknowledge the impact that the loss can have on the family system. They understand the varied complications that can arise from the loss of a lifelong, sometimes highly intense, and ambivalent relationship.

In short, *Sibling Loss Across the Lifespan* will be a standard reference for death educators, grief counselors, family therapists, and researchers. Hopefully, it will enfranchise sibling loss – whenever it is experienced within the lifecycle. It will remind clinicians – as well as offer theoretical insights, clinical tools, and directions for research – of the importance of sibling relationships in our lives. For when we lose a sibling, we may lose a lifelong friend, a sharer of our memories, and most importantly, whatever the relationship, someone who shaped us. We have lost our sibling.

Kenneth J. Doka

Reference

Rosen, H. (1986). *Unspoken grief: Coping with childhood sibling loss.* Lexington, MA: Lexington Books.

Preface

"Did having a sister make any difference?" the psychologist asked Rebecca. She straightened a trace. Spreading her parchment hands palms up and shrugging quickly, she flashed a glance of irritation to let the interviewer know that he had missed the obvious. "Of course it makes a difference! I know I have a sister! She's my flesh and blood. And I don't even have to see her all the time. To have a brother, to have a sister" – she paused, groping for the right words for her deep feelings. "To know they're just – around – that's all I need to know."

(Bank & Khan, 1982, p. 3)

"I don't feel like I'm finished writing about this topic quite yet," I remember saying to my colleague. It was 2013, and I had just published my book on adult sibling loss (Marshall, 2013) and yet still felt drawn to the topic, but in a different way. I'd recently come into possession of some letters exchanged between my great aunt Allison and her beloved brother Alex, as he traveled across the country during the 1920s. The letters were newsy and loving and demonstrated such deep care between the two. But what made them especially poignant for me was that Alex had died on that trip. And my great aunt had kept those letters until her death some nearly 70 years later. Growing up, I knew a little of Alex's story. My grandmother (his sister) would sometimes talk about him, but then get teary, and almost always finish with the words, "it's just so sad." Allison would fall silent or leave the room. She could not speak of her brother. I never understood the depth of their loss until the sudden death of my own brother. Finding those letters felt like a sign to keep writing but I wasn't sure in which direction to go. The colleague I shared my musings with was Howard Winokuer.

As I (HW) listened to Brenda share her story about her great aunt Allison and her beloved brother Alex, it became clear that the area of sibling death, which impacts most people, had proportionally very little written about the topic. Articles such as Balk (1990), Packman, Horsley, Davies, and Kramer (2006), and Marshall and Davies (2013), and classic books such as Davies (1999) pointed to the need for more study. Upon consulting with my friend and colleague Bob Neimeyer, we decided that a book on sibling loss could fill a major void in the grief literature.

The idea for a lifespan perspective was appealing. In speaking with many bereaved siblings over the years, I (BM) knew that age played a role in how the loss rippled through their lives. Building off the approach used by our colleagues Neimeyer, Harris, Winokuer, and Thornton (2011), whereby both clinicians and researchers came together to write from multiple lenses, we thought a similar approach would work well here. And we also decided to add a twist by including personal stories from bereaved siblings. Finally, we opted to seek out writers with varied interests and styles and leave each free to explore the topic in any way they chose.

The book is organized into six sections, loosely based around the age groupings associated with Erikson's (1950) stages of development. Parts I–V follow a similar pattern. Each opens with a research-oriented chapter, a clinical chapter which concludes with two or three "best practice" ideas, and then closes with two personal stories from bereaved siblings. The personal stories come from individuals whose siblings died when they (the individual) was in this age group and provide a retrospective on how the loss impacted their life moving forward. Part VI includes chapters we felt presented topics that were applicable to all age groups. Finally, to help ground the book and provide a context for readers, we invited our colleagues (Kissane and Kasparian) to write an introductory chapter outlining several dominant models of grief along with commentary on their broad implications in sibling bereavement.

Our goal with this text was to provide a forum for varied lenses, writing styles, and perspectives in a format that was appealing to multiple audiences. And in so doing, we hoped to "illuminate" a loss that impacts so many yet receives little attention. We wanted to invite readers into these stories in a way that allowed each to formulate their own connections to the material. The inclusion of personal stories was a way to connect research, practice, and experience in a unique way, not typically part of a text. We are excited to share the wonderful chapters of our contributors and hope that this collection shines a light on a topic that impacts so many.

Brenda J. Marshall
Howard R. Winokuer

References

Balk, D.E. (1990). The self-concepts of bereaved adolescents: Sibling death and its aftermath. *Journal of Adolescent Research*, 5, 112–32.

Bank, S. & Kahn, M. (1982). *The sibling bond*. New York: Basic Books.

Davies, B. (1999). *Shadows in the sun: The experiences of sibling bereavement in childhood*. Philadelphia: Taylor & Francis.

Erikson, E.H. (1950). *Childhood and society*. New York: Norton.

Marshall, B.J. (2013). *Adult sibling loss: Stories, reflections and ripples*. New York: Baywood Publishing.

Marshall, B.J. & Davies, B. (2011). Bereavement in children and adults following the death of a sibling. In R. Neimeyer, D. Harris, H. Winokuer, & G. Thornton (Eds.), *Grief and bereavement in contemporary society: Bridging research and practice* (pp. 107–16). New York: Routledge.

Neimeyer, R.A., Harris, D.L., Winokuer, H.R., & Thornton, G.F. (Eds.). (2011). *Grief and bereavement in contemporary society: Bridging research and practice*. New York: Routledge.

Packman, W., Horsley, H., Davies, B., & Kramer, R. (2006). Sibling bereavement and continuing bonds. *Death Studies*, 30, 8, 17–841.

Editor Biographies

Brenda J. Marshall, PhD, CT is a speaker, facilitator, and executive coach and founder of two professional consulting firms – the Solacium Group and FLOW Learning Group, a corporate talent-development firm. Her interest in grief work came after the sudden death of her younger brother in 2006. At the time, she was a senior-level business consultant at a busy management consultancy. Recognizing the challenges she faced grieving her brother's death while continuing a busy professional life, she created Solacium as a resource to help others.

Marshall's eclectic background includes work in corporate, consulting, and academic environments as well as time off to play and write. Passionate about personal growth and development, she loves to ignite the spark for change in others. Audiences relate to and remember her for her authenticity, humor, and ability to bring ideas to life with powerful real-life stories.

Marshall now splits her time between FLOW Learning Group, Solacium, and a busy writing and speaking schedule. In her work with FLOW, she's led large-scale talent-development initiatives, team interventions, and coached scores of emerging and established leaders. Under Solacium, she's a sought-after consultant in the field of Adult Sibling Loss and Grief in the Workplace, speaks at events across North America, and consults with professionals and individuals dealing with loss. She has been interviewed on radio and video and is a contributing author to the Open to Hope Foundation. Her first book, *Adult Sibling Loss: Stories, Reflections and Ripples* (2013), continues to receive high praise. Her most recent project, Conversation Starters, is a cartoon series of cards illustrating the various challenges bereaved siblings face and will launch later this year.

Marshall holds a PhD in Adult Education from the University of Toronto Canada, an MEd in Teaching and Learning from Brock University, a BSc in Psychology and Criminology from the University of Toronto and has advanced training in solution-focused and narrative approaches to coaching and counseling. In addition, she is certified in Thanatology: Death, Dying, and Bereavement.

Read more about Marshall and her work at www.solaciumgroup.ca and www.flowlearninggroup.ca.

Howard R. Winokuer, PhD, FT is the founder of the Winokuer Center for Counseling and Healing in Charlotte, North Carolina where he maintains a full-time clinical practice. He completed his PhD in 1999 at Mississippi State University where he developed the first course in Grief Counseling Skills. As the founder of TO LIFE, a not-for-profit educational and counseling organization, he was the associate producer of seven PBS specials, and helped pilot one of the first teen suicide-prevention programs in the southeast. He has taught numerous courses and been a guest lecturer at many colleges and universities, including New York University, Rochester University, the University of North Alabama, Queens University, Appalachian State University, the University of North Carolina, and Hong Kong University.

Winokuer has conducted workshops and seminars throughout the United States as well as nine foreign countries including programs for St. Christopher's Hospice and St. George's Medical Centre, London, UK, the National Assistance Board, Barbados, and the United States Embassy at The Hague, Netherlands. He wrote a bi-monthly column in *The Concord Tribune* entitled "Understanding Grief" and hosted a regular radio show on WEGO entitled *Life Talk*. He was a consultant to WBTV, the local CBS affiliate in Charlotte, NC, after the tragedy of 9/11 and has been the mental health "professional on call" for Fox TV's news show "The Edge." He has recently appeared on the radio show "Healing the Grieving Heart" and has been interviewed by the *ACA Journal, Counseling Today*, as well as in the *Staten Island Advance, Houston Chronicle, Charlotte Observer, Detroit Free Press*, and the *Chicago Tribune*. Winokuer also led an international delegation of funeral directors to Russia and Holland to study death and funeral practices in those countries.

Winokuer has been actively involved in the field of dying, death, and bereavement since 1979. He has presented workshops and seminars to many organizations, including the National Funeral Directors Association, the University of North Carolina's Department of Neurological Surgery, the Tennessee Health Care Association, and Presbyterian Hospital. He also developed the crisis-management plan for the Cabarrus County School System. Howard has been an active member of the Association for Death Education and Counseling (ADEC) for almost three decades and has served in numerous leadership positions. In his almost 30 years of membership, he has chaired the national public relations committee, co-chaired the 2000 and 2003 national conferences, served on the board of directors, co-chaired the 2011 international conference that ADEC co-hosted with the International Conference on Grief and Bereavement in Contemporary Society, was the president of the Association for Death Education and Counseling, and was one of the co-editors for the recently released book *Grief and Bereavement in Contemporary Society: Bridging Research and Practice* (2011). He is also the co-author of *Principles and Practices of Grief Counseling* (2012) and *Principles and Practices of Grief Counseling* (Second Edition, 2016).

Contributors

David E. Balk, PhD is a professor at Brooklyn College, chair of the Department of Health and Nutrition Sciences, and director of Graduate Studies in Thanatology. His research has examined adolescent bereavement over the deaths of family members and friends. He and colleagues at different universities have collaborated to establish the prevalence and severity of college student bereavement. Balk is Associate Editor and Book Review Editor of the peer-reviewed journal *Death Studies*, and wrote both *Dealing with Dying, Death, and Grief during Adolescence* (2014) and *Helping the Bereaved College Student* (2011). His doctoral dissertation examined *Sibling Loss during Adolescence: Self-Concept and Bereavement Reactions*.

Tina Barrett, EdD, LCPC, a licensed counselor, has specialized in outdoor-based therapies since 1994. Co-founder and Executive Director of Tamarack Grief Resource Center, Barrett focuses on best practices of nature-based support with trauma survivors and family systems. She has worked with bereaved youth, adults, and families in individual, group, camp, and workshop settings, pulling from her background in residential treatment, wilderness therapy, schools, group homes, and private practice. A graduate of the University of Montana's Department of Educational Leadership and Counseling, Barrett's doctoral research explored bereavement camp benefits.

Pauline Boss, PhD coined the term "ambiguous loss" and is Professor Emeritus, University of Minnesota; Fellow, American Psychological Association and American Association of Marriage and Family Therapy; and the former president of the National Council on Family Relations. Her acclaimed book, *Ambiguous Loss* (Harvard Press, 1999), was followed by *Loss, Trauma, and Resilience* (Norton, 2006) with guidelines for treatment based on over 30 years of work with families with loved ones gone missing in body or mind. Her 2011 book, *Loving Someone Who Has Dementia* (Jossey-Bass), offers hope for families coping with Alzheimer's disease and other cognitive impairments.

Cori Bussolari, PsyD is a licensed psychologist and a credentialed school psychologist. For most of her professional clinical career, she has worked with individuals and families with illness, death, or significant life experiences. In addition to her clinical work in private practice in San Francisco, Dr. Bussolari is an Associate Professor at the University of San Francisco in the Counseling Psychology Department. While her current research involvement is in the area of pet loss and grief, she has always been immersed within the area of bereavement and trauma, especially in regards to positive and lifelong coping. Dr. Bussolari is an active consultant for schools, families, and community mental health clinics related to illness, bereavement, and learning difficulties. She also facilitates the San Francisco SPCA Pet Loss Support Group.

Corinne Cavuoti, MA graduated in Community Health with a concentration in Thanatology from Brooklyn College of the City University of New York. Her thesis addressed the question "Do Elderly Nursing Home Residents Experience Disenfranchised Grief?" She previously worked as a patient facilitator, counseling patients experiencing loss at a women's clinic in New York City. In addition to facilitating bereavement groups and developing an online support program for adolescents dealing with loss and bereavement, she is currently teaching thanatology courses at Brooklyn College.

Betty Davies, RN, PhD is Adjunct Professor, School of Nursing, University of Victoria and Professor Emerita, Department of Family Health Care Nursing, University of California San Francisco. Her career has focused on pediatric palliative care and bereavement following a child's death. Funded by regional and national agencies (NIH and CIHR), her research is reported in nearly 200 professional and popular publications. Dr. Davies has contributed to various professional organizations and is the recipient of numerous awards, most recently an Alumni Honor Award from the University of Alberta.

Elizabeth DeVita-Raeburn is an author and journalist who specializes in health and medicine. She has written for *Discover*, *Psychology Today*, *The Washington Post*, *The New York Times*, and others. She is the author of *The Empty Room: Understanding Sibling Loss* (Scribner, 2004). Her most recent book, co-authored with her father, is *The Death of Cancer: After Fifty Years on the Front Lines of Medicine, a Pioneering Oncologist Reveals Why the War on Cancer Is Winnable – and How We Can Get There*. She lives in New York City with her husband, writer Paul Raeburn, and their two sons.

Kenneth J. Doka, PhD is Professor of Gerontology at the Graduate School of the College of New Rochelle and Senior Consultant to the Hospice Foundation of America. Dr. Doka has written 30 books including with Terry Martin *Grieving beyond Gender: Understanding the Ways Men and Women Mourn* (2010) and more than 100 articles and book chapters. Dr. Doka is the editor of both *Omega: Journal of Death and Dying* and *Journeys*. He is a former president of the Association for Death Education and Counseling and chair of the International Work Group on Dying, Death, and Bereavement.

Alicia Sims Franklin, LICSW, GMS is a bereaved sibling, licensed clinical social worker, and a grief-management specialist. Her younger brother and only sibling, Austin, died of a brain tumor when she was four years old. She is the author of *Am I Still A Sister?* (2005) and a contributing author in *Dear Parents* and *The Dying and Bereaved Teenager* (1986). She co-authored *A Place For Me: A Healing Journey for Grieving Kids, Footsteps through Grief, the Other Side of Grief* and *Finding Your Way through Grief* with Darcie D. Sims. She has worked in the field of mental health for over 20 years.

Kathleen R. Gilbert, PhD is Professor Emerita in the Department of Applied Health Science at Indiana University. Her scholarly and academic background has been focused on individual and family resilience in the face of sometimes overwhelming stress. Much of her research has addressed strength-based ways in which individuals and families cope with and make sense of both death and non-death losses. Kathleen's research interests are varied and include loss and bereavement in the family, especially parental bereavement; stress and resilience in the family; and qualitative approaches to grief research.

Rebecca J. Gilbert, PhD earned her doctorate in leisure behavior at Indiana University, with a specialization in therapeutic recreation. Previously, she worked as a mental health therapist with children and their families. She currently works as Assistant Director of Wellness and Recreation at the Indiana University Health Center and School of Public Health while continuing research in health and wellness and the family.

Rayna Vaught Godfrey, PhD is a licensed psychologist in private practice. Specializing in grief and loss, she provides individual therapy for adolescents and adults. Godfrey has presented at workshops and conferences around the country on sibling loss. She was an adjunct professor in the master's and doctoral counseling psychology programs at the University of Denver and has taught undergraduate psychology courses at the

Metropolitan State College of Denver. Godfrey holds a PhD in counseling psychology from the University of Denver, where her doctoral dissertation explored the experience of *Losing A Sibling in Adulthood*.

Linda Goldman, FT, MS, LCPC, NBCC has served as a teacher and counselor in the school system, grief therapist for children and adults, and lecturer and professor at many institutions, including Johns Hopkins Graduate School. She is the author of several books, including *Life and Loss: A Guide to Help Grieving Children* (Third Edition, 2014), *Children Also Grieve* (2005), *Lucy Lets Go: Helping Children Love a Pet through Death and Dying* (2014), and *Great Answers to Difficult Questions about Death* (2009).

Jason M. Holland, PhD is a licensed clinical psychologist and assistant professor at William James College. He graduated with his Doctorate in Clinical Psychology in 2008 from the University of Memphis and completed his internship at the Palo Alto VA (PAVA), specializing in geropsychology. Upon graduation, he worked as a postdoctoral fellow at PAVA and Stanford University. His program of research focuses on stressful late-life transitions, such as bereavement, caregiving, and coping with a debilitating illness. Holland has published more than 60 peer-reviewed articles on these topics and currently serves as the associate editor for *Death Studies*.

Gloria Horsley, RN, MFT, PhD is an internationally recognized grief expert, licensed marriage and family therapist and clinical nurse specialist. She is the founder and president of Open to Hope, the world's largest multimedia web-based resource for the bereaved. Dr. Gloria is an award-winning author who has co-authored eleven books. She is a clinical member of the American Association of Marriage and Family Therapy and is a past faculty member of the University of Rochester School of Nursing and the Academy of Intuition Medicine. She is a certified Reiki master and Enneagram teacher, and has taught for Byron Katie, Carolyn Myss, and Helen Palmer. She also serves on the advisory board for the Elisabeth Kubler-Ross Foundation.

Heidi Horsley, PsyD, LMSW, MS is a licensed psychologist, social worker, and bereaved sibling. She is Executive Director for the Open to Hope Foundation, and co-hosts the award-winning cable television and radio show, *Open to Hope*. She is Adjunct Professor at Columbia University and in private practice in Manhattan. Dr. Heidi is an award-winning author and has co-authored eight books. She serves on the board of directors for the Compassionate Friends, the Advisory Board for the Tragedy Assistance Program for Survivors of Military Loss, and the Elisabeth Kubler-Ross Foundation. She has worked on a Columbia University longitudinal study with firefighter families who lost someone in the 9/11 attacks, and wrote her doctoral dissertation on the sudden death of a sibling.

Nadine A. Kasparian, PhD is Associate Professor in Medical Psychology at the University of New South Wales, Sydney, Australia. She is also Head of Psychology at the Heart Centre for Children, The Sydney Children's Hospitals Network (Westmead and Randwick). In 2010 Nadine established the Asia Pacific region's first integrated psychology research program and clinical service dedicated to childhood heart disease. As program director, she leads a number of national and international collaborations, including research to identify and address the factors that contribute to psychological risk, resilience, and compassion in medical settings. Nadine's work has been acknowledged by numerous awards, including the International Psycho-Oncology Society Hiroomi Kawano New Investigator Award for outstanding contributions to research. She is also an active contributor on Twitter (@NKasparian).

H.D. ("De") Kirkpatrick, PhD is a board-certified specialist in forensic psychology and holds a diploma in forensic psychology from the American Board of Professional Psychology. He was born in Charlotte, NC, the youngest of three children. He graduated in 1970 from Harvard College (BA *cum laude* in Fine Arts), in 1973 from UNC-Charlotte (MEd in Guidance and Counseling), and in 1978 from Saybrook University in San Francisco (PhD in Psychology). De is married to Katie Holliday, a family law attorney, and is the proud stepfather to three stepdaughters and proud stepgrandfather to 3-year-old Alice.

David W. Kissane, MD is an academic psychiatrist, psycho-oncology researcher, and palliative care physician. He is currently Head of the Department of Psychiatry for Monash University in Australia, previously chairman of the Department of Psychiatry and Behavioral Sciences at Memorial Sloan-Kettering Cancer Center in New York, and, before that, foundation chair of Palliative Medicine at the University of Melbourne. His academic interests include group, couples, and family psychotherapy trials, communication-skills training, studies of existential distress, bereavement, and the ethics of end-of-life care. His most recent book with Routledge was *Bereavement Care for Families* (2014).

Ann Laverty, PhD is a psychologist at the University of Calgary, SU Wellness Centre, in Alberta, Canada. Her primary focus is providing individual and group counseling to students and supervision of graduate practicum students and interns within the center. Her doctoral research focused on Women's Experience of Adult Sibling Bereavement and she continues to pursue research and resource development related to grief and bereavement. She co-authored a monograph for the Canadian Association of College and University Student Services about Bereavement and Grief within a Post-Secondary Context and has particular interest in working with emerging adults.

Christopher Lourenco holds a BS in Industrial Engineering and is currently pursuing his PhD at Texas A&M University. In 2003, Chris Lourenco was only 9 when a day out with his dad, Manny, and two brothers, Zach and Alex, turned joy into horror. The sailboat they were on struck low-lying power lines, taking the lives of his brothers and turned his whole world upside down. Since 2005, Chris has been an active participant in the Compassionate Friends' Sibling Program. The relationships he has forged have helped him learn to live with his grief, not be defined by it.

Molly Murphy, MA, LCPC, a licensed counselor, serves as Assistant Director at Tamarack Grief Resource Center in Montana, providing support for youth and adults following loss. Since her father's death by suicide in 1999, Molly has immersed herself in healing settings with a special focus on growth after trauma. She completed her graduate degree in Counselor Education at the University of Montana. Pulling from her experience in group homes, university clinical settings, classrooms, and bereavement camps, Molly weaves together her personal and professional experience to support kids, teens, adults, and families.

Rose Planer, MSW, LCSW is a licensed therapist who has worked for the last five years in hospice and palliative care helping people navigate grief, illness, and loss and is currently seeing clients in a private practice setting. She graduated from the University of North Carolina at Chapel Hill with a degree in Journalism. However, after experiencing a personal traumatic loss, she decided to pursue a career in counseling, hoping to help others cope with loss and challenging life transitions. Rose graduated with a Master's in Social Work from Winthrop University in 2005.

Lyn Prashant, PhD, FT is a pioneer in the field and developed a unique approach to grief counseling called "Degriefing" or "Integrative Grief Therapy"; the main premise being "grief is the most available, untapped, emotional resource for personal transformation." She authored *Transforming Somatic Grief* (IGT Training Manual), contributed a chapter to *Techniques of Grief Therapy: Creative Practices for Counseling the Bereaved*, and can be seen on YouTube. Lyn's work is in honor of her late husband Mark Greenberg and beloved sister Donna Brown.

Vincent Rozalski, MA is a doctoral student at the University of Nevada, Las Vegas. His research and clinical interests include loss, trauma, complicated grief, post-traumatic stress disorder (PTSD), and their etiology and treatment in a variety of populations. He hopes to continue working with veterans at the Department of Veteran Affairs to study the unique impact of bereavement on PTSD, coping, and treatment trajectory.

Simon Shimshon Rubin, PhD is Professor of Psychology at the University of Haifa in Israel. He is Director of the International Center for the Study of Loss, Bereavement, and Human Resilience and Chairman of the Postgraduate Psychotherapy Program at his university. Dr. Rubin, an active clinician, has lectured and published extensively on bereavement, ethics, and psychotherapy. His book, *Working with the Bereaved: Multiple Lenses on Loss and Mourning*, written with Ruth Malkinson and Eliezer Witztum, was published by Routledge in 2012. A graduate of Boston University, he has held visiting appointments as Professor at Northwestern and Harvard University Medical Schools.

Michelle L. Rusk, PhD is best known as Michelle Linn-Gust and for her work around suicide, particularly suicide grief. She is a former past president of the American Association of Suicidology and her most recent book, her tenth, is *Flowers by Day, Stars by Night: Finding Happiness after Loss and Change* (2015).

Carol L. Sachs, EdD, LMFT is a bereaved sibling and a retired family therapist and bereavement counselor. She received additional training in group facilitation. The majority of her clinical work was based in the Department of Pediatric Hematology/Oncology at Baystate Medical Center in Springfield, MA where she worked with families whose children had life-threatening illnesses. She did grief work with those families whose children died. In addition, she facilitated bereaved parent support groups and for a number of years facilitated support groups for residents in pediatrics and medical pediatrics. She also has been a long-term member of the Association for Death Education and Counseling.

Diana C. Sands, PhD is Director, Bereaved by Suicide Centre for Intense Grief and a postvention, prevention clinician and educator. She is a clinical member of the Psychotherapy and Counselling Federation of Australia and CAPA, Deputy Chair of Postvention Australia, and Honorary Advisor to the Wings of Hope Charity. Diana has served on the New South Wales (NSW) Executive Committee, National Association for Loss and Grief, and as NSW representative with Suicide Prevention Australia. She is a member of the International Work Group on Death, Dying, and Bereavement, and recipient of the Vice Chancellor Post Graduate Research Grant, Australian Government Research Scholarship and has published peer-reviewed academic articles, chapters, and book and DVD resources for children bereaved by suicide.

Jennifer Kaplan Schreiber, LICSW, FT is Doctoral Candidate and Adjunct Faculty Member at Simmons College School of Social Work in Boston, MA. Her dissertation is testing the psychometric properties of the Inventory of Youth Adaptation to Loss, an outcome measure she developed collaboratively with bereavement programs. Kaplan Schreiber is Founder of Jeff's Place Children's Bereavement Center in Massachusetts and FRIENDS WAY in Rhode Island. She is the clinical director of Experience Camps, week-long overnight camps for grieving youths in California, Maine, and New York, and is the author of *You Are Not Alone: Young Adults Coping with Death* (2010), book chapters, and journal articles.

Anne M. Smith, MA graduated in Community Health with a concentration in Thanatology from Brooklyn College of the City University of New York. Her thesis is titled *A Study of Veterinarian Competency Managing Grief and Bereavement in Veterinary Practice*. She has been working in the field of hospice and bereavement for the past 15 years. In addition to her work as a bereavement counselor, she currently teaches thanatology courses at Ramapo College, New Jersey. She also works with her husband, a veterinarian, to support and educate clients regarding end-of-life issues for pets and pet bereavement.

Patty Wetterling is the mother of Jacob Wetterling, who was abducted in St. Joseph, Minnesota, at the age of 11, by a masked gunman. Jacob is still missing. She has become a nationally recognized educator on child abduction and sexual exploitation of children. Wetterling co-founded the Jacob Wetterling Resource Center and Team H.O.P.E., a national support group for families of missing children. She co-authored the books, *When Your Child Is Missing: A Family Survival Guide* (Fourth Edition, 2010) and *Perspectives on Missing Persons Cases* (2015). Wetterling remains actively engaged with the National Center for Missing and Exploited Children after chairing the Board from 2012 to 2015. In 2016, because of her expertise, she was appointed to the Ministerial Review Board for the Archdiocese of St. Paul and Minneapolis.

Theoretical Models Guiding Our Understanding of Sibling Bereavement

David W. Kissane and Nadine A. Kasparian

The sibling relationship can be a special bond between brothers and sisters that persists across a lifespan. Almost 80 percent of children grow up with a sibling in the home (Kreider, 2007). As one illustration, in North America, where some 60,000 children under the age of 20 die each year, sibling bereavement occurs for the young within society. Sibling deaths also occur across every phase of the life cycle, and so myriad others will eventually experience this form of life event.

Sibling relationships fundamentally influence our experiences of self and world. The death of a brother or sister poses particular developmental challenges and may create a distinctive form of grief, one undoubtedly shaped by the character of this relationship within the family. How close were they? How much did they see of one another? What joys had they shared and what adversities had they faced together? How might we understand the nature of this bereavement experience? What theoretical models can inform this understanding?

In this chapter, we aim to provide an orientation to the theories that guide our understanding of sibling bereavement across the lifespan. We will consider five dominant models: 1) Attachment Theory; 2) Family Systems Theory; 3) risk factors for complicated grief; 4) life-cycle perspectives; and 5) cultural influences. We will go on to illustrate from a small number of empirical studies some of the broad impacts of sibling bereavement. We trust that this will lay a conceptual foundation upon which to better understand later chapters in this book that embark on a review of sibling loss across the lifespan.

Theoretical Models Informing Sibling Loss

Attachment Theory

The British psychoanalyst, John Bowlby, first proposed that the quality of the relationship between child and caregiver was responsible for establishing the emotional security of the child, and that this security became a pre-requisite for the child being able to explore his or her surrounding environment, engage in imaginative play, and develop a capacity to manage stress and form affectionate bonds with others so that he or she could begin to fulfil their potential. In his seminal paper on the "Processes of Mourning" (Bowlby, 1961) and later three volumes on "Attachment and Loss" (Bowlby, 1969), Bowlby described key patterns of attachment based on the quality of the relational bond with one's primary caregiver. These were subsequently elaborated on in pioneering work by colleagues like Mary Ainsworth (Ainsworth, Blehar, Waters, & Wall, 1978) and Mary Main (Main, Hess, & Kaplan, 2005). Ainsworth, for example, used the Strange Situation paradigm to better understand children's responses to separation from their primary caregiver. Today, these patterns of attachment are well recognized and, in their simplest form, can be described as 1) secure, 2) ambivalent, 3) avoidant, and 4) disorganized in nature. Let us consider each in turn.

Through detailed observational research, secure attachment came to be understood as a pattern of behavior derived from a safe, predictable, and trusting relationship between infant and caregiver, whereby the infant learns that he or she is able to rely on caregivers to be available and sensitively attuned to emotions, and to organize, integrate, and make meaning of his or her experience. With this, the infant develops confidence in the safety provided by their caregiver and is empowered to be curious and to venture into the broader surrounds. This contrasts with ambivalent attachment, wherein the child does not feel safe to explore and clings to the parent, overtly anxious, lest he or she be abandoned. When such a pattern persists into adult life, an anxious insecurity may cause heavy dependence upon another, which can skew the nature of the relationship and the experience of grief if the relationship ends. For children who have developed an avoidant attachment pattern, separation is similarly painful; however, the child has learned to cope with his or her anxiety by predominantly responding to their caregiver with indifference, distancing him or herself and using toys or other objects as a form of distraction. The final pattern, disorganized attachment, has been linked to trauma in general, and unresolved maternal loss more specifically (Fonagy, Gergely, Jurist, & Target, 2002). It is best recognized as odd or unpredictable behavioral reactions in the child, most often in response to experiencing his or her primary caregiver as frightened or frightening.

The sensitivity of the adult caregiver of the infant, particularly in regards to responding to the child's distress, is formative in establishing security and a "state of mind" in regards to attachment, even in the presence of a difficult temperament within the child (Fonagy, 2001). Parental caregiving may be optimal when there is authentic sensitivity and responsiveness to the infant's emotional states, appropriate interest, and stimulation of the infant, and the development of a warm interactional synchrony as the basis for genuine engagement in the relationship (Belsky, 1999). If the caregiver is rejecting or dismissive of the child's needs, the infant may develop an insecure-avoidant pattern of relating (De Wolff & Van Ijzendoorn, 1997). If the caregiver is unresponsive to the child's needs because he or she is preoccupied and focused primarily on their own attachment experiences, and at other times attempts to compensate for this preoccupation with excessive or inappropriate responses to the infant, this will predict the development of an insecure-ambivalent attachment pattern in the child (De Wolff & Van Ijzendoorn, 1997). One example could be the mother who is grieving or depressed, with some resultant unavailability predicting an ambivalent or even disorganizing pattern of attachment.

As Attachment Theory has matured, its contribution to emotion regulation has become steadily apparent. When securely contained, the child may develop strategies for the regulation of aversive states of arousal through the experience of the parent accurately perceiving the child's distress, yet communicating a soothing reassurance at the same time (Fonagy, 2001). The development of a reflective capacity by the child is understood as the ability to think about one's own mind, as well as the minds of others, in large part due to the opportunity in early life to experience and come to understand the mind of the primary caregiver (Fonagy, 2001; Bretherton, 2005). Where that primary caregiver is secure, autonomous, loving, and caring, these relational capacities can grow, as can the capacity of the child to perceive others as trusting and supportive. In contrast, when the caregiver is dismissive or rejecting, he or she fails to mirror the child's distress accurately, while the preoccupied caregiver may paint an image of the distress with excessive clarity, but provide no balancing information or support to assuage this distress.

Attachment Theory provides an evidence-based, biologically driven, developmental framework for explaining individual differences in sibling vulnerability to bereavement. According to Attachment Theory, a person's internal working model of relationships (or attachment pattern) has unique effects on mental health and the process of coping with stress. For example, securely attached individuals generally appraise stressful events in more benign terms – they tend to regard themselves as capable of effectively coping with these events and rely on support-seeking coping strategies to maintain psychological well-being during stressful periods. In contrast, individuals who display characteristics of insecure attachment tend to appraise events in threatening terms, to report doubts about their coping abilities, and to exhibit high levels of distress.

Developmental researchers have postulated a psychoneurobiological model of development, where the emotion-regulation capacity of secure attachment corresponds with the protection of immune mechanisms on the one hand, and the stress and emotion regulation of the limbic circuits in the brain and the hypothalamic-pituitary-adrenal hormonal axis on the other hand (Schore, 2001; Holmes, 1997). A complex integration is achieved between reflective and mentalizing properties of the mind developed in an empathic family setting and other adaptive functions of the body. Moreover, where the child is exposed to unbalanced relational processes and contradictory behavioral strategies, a disorganized internal model of relationships may be incorporated (Lyons & Jacobovitz, 1999), establishing insecure relational processes, with difficult relationships potentially persisting throughout adult life.

From the very beginning, Bowlby's conceptualization of attachment demonstrated his deep appreciation of how these bonds of relationship were pivotal to understanding the adaptation made to bereavement. While separation and loss are an inherent part of normal development, the death of a sibling in childhood poses particular difficulties for the developing child, as the safety of the world and the efficacy of adults are called into question. Relatively secure attachments may be disrupted when a sibling dies; however, the secure aspects of the relationship endure as a foundational base that grounds the young person and helps him or her to survive more adaptively than might be the case without this grounding (Charles & Charles, 2006). Any form of insecure attachment predisposes the bereaved to the potential for unresolved grief. Recent studies exploring attachment processes across the lifespan point to attachment as a critical factor moderating the child's experience of stressful life events, suggesting that attachment style has profound implications for grief and mourning. However, the extent to which a person's attachment pattern may shift as a function of catastrophic life events, such as the loss of a sibling, remains unclear. Observational studies do, however, affirm that siblings are important objects of attachment and that the death of a sibling can put the child at risk of later difficulties in much the same way as does the death of a parent (Worden, Davies, & McCown, 1999). Moreover, sibling loss is compounded by the parents' concomitant loss, which may make a parent less accessible to the child as a resource (Schwab, 1997). Two classic forms of relational bond for siblings are found in highly ambivalent and overly dependent relationships. In the former pattern, conflict may prevail and yet the sibling remains important as well, such that mixed feelings of both love and hate make resolution more challenging when death occurs. In the latter pattern, a deep neediness for the sibling develops and the sibling becomes a vital source of security, such that death poses grave risk for the surviving brother or sister.

With appropriate allowance for cultural variation, the nature and intensity of the expression of grief is best predicted by the strength of bond with the deceased. For siblings, as with any relationship, these bonds are subject to many and complex influences. These include gender, birth order, closeness in age, time spent together, the quality of the relationship and perception of its importance, as well as the stage within the life cycle when the death occurs. Contrast the loss of one's identical twin with that of a fraternal twin, the death of a same-gender sibling (e.g. sisters who speak together daily), or the death of opposite-gender siblings who see very little of one another. Grief is the price paid for the closeness of whatever love has been shared between siblings. The clinician must understand the nature and depth of attachment to make sense of the grief response.

Attachment Theory provides a good framework or lens through which to explore the nature of any sibling relationship, so as to begin to understand the impact that the absence of that relationship will have on mourning, grief, and adaptation when death occurs.

Family Systems Theory

The family is generally the major source of support available to the bereaved. How the family as a whole responds is influential upon the coping and adaptation of its members. Family Systems Theory recognizes a spectrum of family responses, ranging from a highly supportive environment found in the resilient family through to unavailability, low communication, and conflictual relationships in dysfunctional families. Bereaved siblings will often follow the dominant response pattern of their family of origin, receiving both comfort and consolation in their grief from a supportive family, or alternatively, isolation, avoidance, blame, or conflict from a family that struggles to optimally support its own.

Considerable empirical work has focused on the relational functioning of the family, with attention to their communication style, sense of coherence as a team, and capacity for conflict resolution (Kissane et al., 1996a; Schuler, Zaider, & Kissane, 2012). Two adaptive patterns of family relating have been termed *supportive* and *conflict-resolving*. Supportive families communicate openly and display strong teamwork, mutual support, and availability, such that the grief of a bereaved sibling is recognized, accepted, normalized, and supported in a manner that favors its resolution over time. In like manner, the conflict-resolving family has some members who may fight, but their sense of loyalty and commitment to the family prevails, so that their effective communication and genuine closeness empowers them to tolerate differences of opinion without these harming the containing and nurturing processes within the family. People residing within supportive and conflict-resolving families, who have been studied longitudinally in bereavement, have been shown to develop little (if any) psychosocial disturbance or psychiatric disorder in bereavement (Kissane et al., 1996b, 2003; Schuler et al., 2012). They have the wherewithal to cope and adapt.

In contrast, three patterns of family relationships are associated with high rates of psychiatric morbidity in bereavement: *low communicating*, *uninvolved*, and *conflictual* families (Kissane et al., 1996a; Schuler et al., 2014). The fractured nature of the latter type is readily recognized by clinical services: they report many years of conflict, estrangements, and family breakdown. Siblings may see each other very intermittently. Yet if conflictual families are willing to meet together, family therapy has been able to open up communication channels, foster improved support, and reduce rates of complicated grief (Kissane et al., 2006, 2016). While conflictual families can thus be helped, uninvolved families won't naturally come together when serious illness afflicts one of its members, and siblings may thus remain isolated or alienated, with resultant bereavement risks. Uninvolved families have been described as having a more sullen relational style, where the anger is turned in upon the self with risk of depression, yet siblings may not support one another in bereavement. A family model of care provision is thus less effective when families will not meet together, and individual or group models of therapeutic support are conventional as interventions.

The final type of family relational pattern has been termed intermediate in nature (Kissane et al., 1996b, 2003), where a pattern of low communication is the dominant style (Schuler et al., 2012). Sometimes a single family meeting is sufficient to open up communication about the illness and its demands (Kissane et al., 2006). However, without intervention and when communication remains poor, the relational style of these families can deteriorate in bereavement, with consequent morbidity developing among family members, including siblings. The willingness of a family to meet and talk together serves as a marker of the probability that, by harnessing the mutual support mechanisms of the family, siblings can be supported and assisted to adapt in bereavement.

Thus we see from Family Systems Theory that the relational quality found within families is both influential and predictive of the development of morbidity among the bereaved. Hooghe has been one advocate of inviting other relatives to accompany a new client referred for grief counseling, thus seeking to open up a dialogue between different voices and harness the natural support resources that exist within the family (Kissane & Hooghe, 2011). In the Family Focused Grief Therapy model of intervention, relational patterns of communication, cohesion, and conflict resolution are examined as potential targets to enhance the family's resilience (Zaider, 2014). There are strong parallels between Attachment Theory at a dyadic level and these family relational processes at a triadic level to inform us about the quality of sibling relational bonds.

Developmental Life Cycle

Another framework which increases our understanding of adaptation to loss is the life cycle – just when, within the potential decades of family life, does any death occur: during childhood, adolescence, young adulthood, the middle years, or old age? For pragmatic reasons, the chapters in this book have been arranged into a life-cycle sequence. Each phase brings key developmental agendas that need to be addressed, but can be readily derailed by bereavement (Walsh & McGoldrick, 2013).

For children, does the illness or death of a sibling dominate family life and its activities to such an extent that it inadvertently causes neglect of the healthy children (Hutton & Bradley, 1994; McGoldrick & Walsh, 2004, 2011)? How does this impact upon their coping and maturation (Burns, House, & Ankerbauer, 1986)? For the adolescent, sibling loss could interfere with the normal movement to independence that ought to occur. Alternatively, the adolescent who has already formed new bonds with peers may have grown away from a younger sibling and thus be less affected by their death. For the young adult, does the death of a sibling disrupt the identity development of this new adult, or might it serve as a stimulus for growth and greater resilience? For the older adult, does the death of a sibling bring the family of origin back into renewed friendship and engagement after periods of preoccupation with each person's nuclear family?

The life-cycle perspective is also accompanied by social assumptions and sometimes myths that prevail within the community. Assumptive beliefs are those ideas and expectations that people and families carry automatically to define just how the world ought to be. Parkes (1972) recognized how these assumptions change naturally across the life cycle and are subject to influences from the local culture which, in turn, will influence the choice of various rituals adopted to assist the negotiation of transitions as the life cycle unfolds. As social customs, rituals provide a language and method to grieve collectively and aid one another.

A further dimension of both family system and life-cycle perspectives is the role occupied by the bereaved and how this impacts on the siblings (Walsh, 2014). Age and gender can influence considerably many of these family roles. Is the bereaved a child who played and shared much with siblings? Is the bereaved an adult who had grown apart from his or her siblings as a new nuclear family was formed by marriage? For many within society, there will be phases of the life cycle when the importance of siblings fades, and other periods like widowhood, when individuals turn back again to sibling relationships for succor and support.

Risk Factors for Complicated Grief

Bereavement research has developed an empirical framework that informs about a series of factors likely to impact upon outcomes of the mourning process. Listed succinctly, these include the nature of the death, the vulnerability of any individual, the quality of the shared relationship, and the support base within the broader environment. Collectively, these factors have been studied as predictors of morbid bereavement outcome; their recognition forms an important clinical approach to preventive bereavement care and will have applicability to sibling loss.

Whether a death occurs suddenly or develops gradually after a long illness, whether it is violent and traumatic, whether the loss is ambiguous because the person remains missing, disenfranchised because a miscarriage goes unacknowledged, or stigmatized because of suicide or death from AIDS, the nature and circumstances of the death have always had the power to impact upon the mourning of the bereaved. Trauma warrants specific attention as violence lies outside the range of most people's normal experience. The death might have been horrific, involving suicide, homicide, mutilation, or destruction. Under these circumstances, the risk for the development of traumatic memories, images, and post-traumatic stress symptoms is elevated (Walsh, 2006; Rynearson & Salloum, 2011). The need to understand and make sense of what happened can be compelling and has been termed "compulsive inquiry," and explains the need for relatives to attend coroner's inquests and related legal trials. Siblings are often seen to support bereaved parents through such proceedings. Traumatic death can therefore involve very complex emotional and adaptive processes, so much so that special expertise has developed to assist these families therapeutically (Harris & Rabenstein, 2014; Sands & North, 2014).

Irrespective of the sibling relationship, the robustness or vulnerability of any bereaved person is impacted upon by any history of mental illness, whether schizophrenia, bipolar disorder, recurrent affective disturbance, anxiety, or substance dependence. Whether through dint of genetics or resultant from the potential traumas of life, the bereaved sibling may carry an inherent vulnerability that places him or her at risk of morbid consequences from the loss of a loved one. Their personality may be pivotal, contributing to relational instability, turning them in upon the self and contributing to complex grieving of the loss.

When the sibling relationship was difficult, abusive, or harmful in some way to the survivor, complicated grief may be anticipated. Envy and jealousy can have powerful impacts on siblings, who may not have succeeded in sufficient reality testing of each other to achieve some balance and acceptance of the limits of selfhood. The ambitious and competitive temperament of one child or the easy-going and at times docile nature of another are examples of the mix that can exist within a kin relationship. While parents set limits, families uphold rules, and social values are laid down to guide the development of each person, the intricate web of interaction needs to be understood as each person's and each family's unique story. Sibling relationships are subject to all of these forces.

The support network is the fourth pillar of influences that should always be assessed in the bereaved. While the family has been considered earlier, there are many ways that people become orphans, alienated and desolate, seemingly cast alone in the world. Appraisal of the networks of friends, neighbors, or workers, whatever the nature of community, is again a basic component of any bereavement assessment. The widow might have lost her spouse and depended for a time on her sister; cumulative losses can lead to deepening isolation when this sister dies. The loneliness of the bereaved can be a source of deep existential angst, with sibling loss being one risk factor along this journey of life.

Cultural Influences on Sibling Bereavement

Culture can exert major influence on the traditions of families. In large Asian families, for instance, parents might delegate child-caring functions to older siblings, promoting emotional ties through this process. Sexism may predominate in some cultures, the son being favored over the daughter. The closeness of families within several Mediterranean cultures may see sisters sharing very close lives. Alternatively, the movement of young adults to interstate colleges remote from home in the USA may spread families across several states, weakening sibling links as a result of reduced contact. What do duty, honor, and respect command of one ethnic group? What do race, religion, or class expect of another? Migration, social deprivation, privilege, and education – many cultural factors and influences can have a profound impact upon the depth of relationships and how any group negotiates life-cycle transitions. The cultural lens is thus another very important framework through which the clinician is challenged to understand what might be going on with sibling attachments.

Traditional customs that operate within cultures might prescribe roles for certain children within the family. Thus the eldest son might be expected to assume patriarchal functions upon the death of his father. Or the youngest daughter might have been groomed to function as the caregiver of aged parents. The unexpected deaths of those designated to fulfill such roles in the family will portend major shifts in the role expectations of surviving siblings.

As we look back across this orientation to the conceptual models that underpin our understanding of sibling bereavement, and despite the universal nature of attachment to human relational life, it is quickly apparent that culture always exerts its contribution to attachment processes, family systems, predictors of complicated grief, and behaviors at varying phases of the life cycle. The impact of culture is extraordinary as it shapes the language and imagery of all mourning.

Illness and Death among Siblings

Let us finish by taking notice of some empirical studies of sibling loss. Do they confirm this overview of the theoretical models that guide our understanding of what might happen in sibling bereavement? A systematic review of the adjustment of siblings of children with cancer showed, on the one hand, that rates of psychiatric disorder are not elevated, but on the other hand, a significant subset experience post-traumatic stress symptoms, negative emotions, and poor quality of life (Alderfer et al., 2010). School difficulties are evident and distress is greater close to the time of diagnosis of cancer in a sibling. There should be no doubt that such illness brings a significant impact upon the whole family. While sibling maturity and capacity for empathy may grow, loss of attention and status may disrupt the developmental path of the siblings (Alderfer et al., 2010). Given that the medical model predominantly adopts an individual approach to care for the patient rather than family-centered care, it should not be surprising that bereavement consequences will follow when siblings are bereaved.

Most studies of bereaved siblings have focused on adolescents, where meta-analyses have revealed higher rates of both internalizing and externalizing scores on measures of behavioral function (Sharpe & Rossiter, 2002). Social functioning can be influenced, with lower social competence and higher social withdrawal found after sibling bereavement (Gerhardt et al., 2012). In elementary grades, males may be more vulnerable, while in middle and high school, some strengths and pro-social behaviors can begin to emerge (Gerhardt et al., 2012).

There is a narrative literature about the impact of sibling illness and loss upon the experience of family life. An illustrative account was the very public illness of the son of US oncologist and National Institutes of Health researcher, Vincent DeVita, whose son, Ted, developed aplastic anemia in 1972 (DeVita-Raeburn, 2007). Ted spent eight years in a laminar airflow room to protect him from infection. In adult life, his sister Elizabeth has written and lectured about the extraordinary impact of her brother's illness upon her growing up. Her chapter in this book will offer further evidence as to how the story is much larger than the actual death, for family life and its regular rhythms can be disrupted for very extended periods by the impact of sibling illness.

What does become apparent as one spans the literature about sibling bereavement is the relative dearth of studies exploring this field. Some issues, however, are strongly represented. Both disenfranchised grief – where there is stigma associated with the death or illness and sorrow may be kept hidden – and ambiguous grief – where the nature of the loss may be masked – are clearly evident in the literature on sibling loss. These are recognized risk factors for pathological outcomes. It is not, however, all discouraging, as evidence also emerges about post-traumatic growth and the building of resilience in those affected by sibling loss. The value of this book is its dedicated focus on sibling bereavement, building further evidence on what has hitherto been a neglected domain of scholarship.

Conclusion

The death of a sibling is an existential reality for the majority of people. More than 100 years ago, when family size was large and infectious disease the leading cause of mortality, the death of a sibling was a very familiar life event. Today, with the growth of science and improvement in medical care, death has become less expected by comparison. The potential for it to be impactful and detrimental may have increased as a result. Alongside this, the nature of family life in a global world is rapidly changing, altering the nature of our attachments and the depth of relational bonds found among siblings. The theoretical models that guide our understanding of sibling bereavement – Attachment Theory, Family Systems Theory, Complicated Grief Theory, life-cycle perspectives, and culture – form a series of lenses through which the experience of sibling loss can be viewed. The clinician must weave many of these dimensions into their formulation of any individual's grief, for it is only through such a rich understanding that the nature of the experience can be truly understood.

References

Ainsworth, M.D., Blehar, M.C., Waters, E., & Wall, S. (1978). *Patterns of attachment: A psychological study of the strange situation.* Hillsdale, NJ: Erlbaum.
Alderfer, M., Long, K., Lown, E., Marsland, A., Ostrowski, N., Hock, J., & Ewing, L. (2010). Psychosocial adjustment of siblings of children with cancer. *Psycho-Oncology*, 19, 789–805.
Belsky, J. (1999). Interactional and contextual determinants of attachment security. In J. Cassidy & P.R. Shaver (Eds.), *Handbook of attachments: Theory, research and clinical applications* (pp. 249–64). New York: Guilford Press.
Bowlby, J. (1961). Processes of mourning. *International Journal of Psychoanalysis*, 17, 317–40.
Bowlby, J. (1969). *Attachment and loss. Vol 1. Attachment.* New York: Basic Books.
Bretherton, I. (2005). In pursuit of the internal working model construct and its relevance to attachment relationships. In K.E. Grossman, K. Grossman, & E. Waters (Eds.), *Infancy to adulthood: The major longitudinal studies* (pp. 13–47). New York: Guilford Press.
Burns, E.A., House, J.D., & Ankerbauer, M.R. (1986). Sibling grief in reaction to sudden infant death syndrome. *Pediatrics*, 78, 485–7.
Charles, D.R. & Charles, M. (2006). Sibling loss and attachment style: An exploratory study. *Psychoanalytic Psychology*, 23, 1, 72–90.
DeVita-Raeburn, E. (2007). *The empty room: Surviving the loss of a brother or sister at any age.* New York: Scribner.
De Wolff, M. & Van Ijzendoorn, M. (1997). Sensitivity and attachment: A meta-analysis on parental antecedents of infant attachment. *Child Development*, 68, 571–91.
Fonagy, P. (2001). *Attachment theory and psychoanalysis.* New York: Other Press.
Fonagy, P., Gergely, G., Jurist, L., & Target, M. (2002). *Affect regulation, mentalization, and the development of the self.* New York: Other Press.
Gerhardt, C., Fairclough, D., Grossenbacher, J., Barrera, M., Gilmer, M., Foster, T., & Vannatta, K. (2012). Peer relationships of bereaved siblings and comparison classmates after a child's death from cancer. *Journal of Pediatric Psychology*, 37, 209–19.
Harris, D. & Rabenstein, S. (2014). Family therapy in the context of traumatic losses. In D.W. Kissane & F. Parnes (Eds.), *Bereavement care for families* (pp. 137–53). New York: Routledge.
Holmes, J. (1997). Attachments, autonomy, intimacy: Some clinical implications of attachment theory. *British Journal of Medical Psychology*, 70, 231–48.

Hutton, C.J. & Bradley, B.S. (1994). Effects of sudden infant death on bereaved siblings: A comparative study. *Journal of Child Psychology and Psychiatry*, 35: 723–32.

Kissane, D.W. & Hooghe, A. (2011). Family therapy for the bereaved. In R.A. Neimeyer, D.L. Harris, H.R. Winokuer, & G.F. Thornton (Eds.), *Grief and bereavement in contemporary society: Bridging research and practice* (pp. 287–302). New York: Routledge.

Kissane, D.W., Bloch, S., Dowe, D., Snyder, R., Onghena, P., McKenzie, D., & Wallace, C. (1996a). The Melbourne Family Grief Study, I: Perceptions of family functioning in bereavement. *American Journal of Psychiatry*, 153, 650–8.

Kissane, D.W., Bloch, S., Onghena, P., McKenzie, D., Snyder, R., & Dowe, D. (1996b). The Melbourne Family Grief Study, II: Psychosocial morbidity and grief in bereaved families. *American Journal of Psychiatry*, 153, 659–66.

Kissane, D.W., McKenzie, M., McKenzie, D., Forbes, A., O'Neill, I., & Bloch, S. (2003). Psychosocial morbidity associated with patterns of family functioning in palliative care: Baseline data from the Family Focused Grief Therapy controlled trial. *Palliative Medicine*, 17, 527–37.

Kissane, D.W., McKenzie, M., Bloch, S., Moskowitz, C., Mckenzie, D., & O'Neill, I. (2006). Family focused grief therapy: A randomized, controlled trial in palliative care and bereavement. *American Journal of Psychiatry*, 163, 1208–18.

Kissane, D.W., Zaider, T. I., Li Y., Hichenberg, S., Schuler, T., Lederberg, M., Lavelle, L., Loeb, R., & Del Gaudio, F. (2016). Randomized controlled trial of family therapy in advanced cancer continued into bereavement. *Journal of Clinical Oncology*. doi: 10.1200/JCO.2015.63.0582.

Kreider, R. (2007). *Living arrangements of children: 2004. Current population reports.* Washington, DC: US Census Bureau.

Lyons, R. and Jacobovitz, D. (1999). Attachment disorganisation: Unresolved loss, relational violence and lapses in behavioral and attentional strategies. In J. Cassidy & P.R. Shaver (Eds.), *Handbook of attachment theory and research* (pp. 520–54). New York: Guilford Press.

Main, M., Hesse, E., & Kaplan, N. (2005). Predictability of attachment behaviour and representational processes at 1, 6 and 19 years of age. In K.E. Grossman, K. Grossman, & E. Waters (Eds.), *Attachment from infancy to adulthood: The major longitudinal studies* (pp. 245–304). New York: Guilford Press.

McGoldrick, M. & Walsh, F. (2004). A time to mourn: Death and the family life cycle. In F. Walsh & M. McGoldrick (Eds.), *Living beyond loss: Death in the family* (pp. 27–46). New York: W.W. Norton.

McGoldrick, M. & Walsh, F. (2011). Death, loss, and the family life cycle. In M. McGoldrick, B. Carter, & N. Garcia Preto (Eds.), *The expanding family life cycle* (4th ed., pp. 278–91). Boston, MA: Allyn & Bacon.

Parkes, C. (1972). *Bereavement: Studies of grief in adult life.* New York: International Universities Press.

Rynearson, E. & Salloum, A. (2011). Restorative retelling: Revisiting the narrative of violent death. In R.A. Neimeyer, D.L. Harris, H.R. Winokuer, & G.F. Thornton (Eds.), *Grief and bereavement in contemporary society: Bridging research and practice* (pp. 177–88). New York: Routledge.

Sands, D. & North, J. (2014). Family therapy following suicide. In D.W. Kissane & F. Parnes (Eds.), *Bereavement care for families* (pp. 154–70). New York: Routledge.

Schore, A. (2001). Effects of a secure attachment relationship on right brain development, affect regulation, and infant mental health. *Infant Mental Health Journal,* 22, 7–66.

Schuler, T.A., Zaider, T.I., & Kissane, D.W. (2012). Family grief therapy: A vital model in oncology, palliative care and bereavement. *Family Matters,* 90, 77–86.

Schuler, T.A., Zaider, T.I., Li, Y., Hichenberg, S., Masterson, M., & Kissane, D.W. (2014). Typology of perceived family functioning in an American sample of advanced cancer patients. *Journal of Pain and Symptom Management,* 48, 281–288.

Schwab, R. (1997). Parental mourning and children's development. *Journal of Counseling and Development,* 75, 258–65.

Sharpe, D. & Rossiter, L. (2002). Siblings of children with a chronic illness: A meta-analysis. *Journal of Pediatric Psychology,* 27, 699–710.

Walsh, F. (2006). *Strengthening family resilience.* New York: Guilford Press.

Walsh, F. (2014). Conceptual framework for family bereavement care. In D.W. Kissane & F. Parnes (Eds.), *Bereavement care for families* (pp. 17–29). New York: Routledge.

Walsh, F. & McGoldrick, M. (2013). Bereavement: A family life cycle perspective (Special issue. Bereavement: Family perspectives). *Family Science,* 4, 20–7.

Worden, J.W., Davies, B., & McCown, D. (1999). Comparing parent loss with sibling loss. *Death Studies,* 23, 1–15.

Zaider, T.I. (2014). Assessing bereaved families. In D.W. Kissane & F. Parnes (Eds.), *Bereavement care for families* (pp. 79–91). New York: Routledge.

Childhood (Birth–11)

chapter 1

Shadows in the Sun
Towards Understanding the Grief of Young Siblings

Betty Davies

Development of Shadows in the Sun: A Model of Sibling Bereavement

For a long time, causal models have permeated the exploration of relationships among data, particularly in clinical fields where the goal is to seek solutions for relieving problems, such as in the study of sibling bereavement. Variables such as age, gender, suddenness of death, self-esteem, attendance at funerals, and family environment have been studied to determine those factors that most affect siblings' grief, with the underlying purpose of reducing as much as possible the potentially deleterious effects of the loss experience. Outcome has been measured primarily in terms of behavior and emotional problems, although some studies refer to competencies and personal growth (Hogan & DeSantis, 1996). Each study has contributed to understanding sibling bereavement, but findings have often been contradictory or inconclusive in identifying which variable is the most influential in predicting bereavement outcome among siblings. This is not surprising, however, because how siblings respond to the death of a brother or sister depends upon many factors, including the child's social context, and all interact in unique ways for each bereaved child. If the social or contextual factors are overlooked, a process of pathologizing is reinforced, reductively locating a behavior within the individual child, rather than understanding it more holistically in terms of the interplay of a wide range of individual and sociological factors (Thompson et al., 2016).

Thus, exploring sibling bereavement from a grounded theory approach (Strauss & Corbin, 1994) allowed for systematic examination of a wide range of data (from both research and clinical work) and to relate them in meaningful ways. The model uses the metaphor of "Shadows in the Sun" to guide the understanding of and interventions with bereaved siblings. The death of a brother or sister, like any significant life-altering event in a young child's life, has a lifelong impact – like shadows in the sun – perpetually influencing their ways of being in the world (Davies, 1999). Children have a natural propensity to grow and develop; they often struggle to find the sun even in the darkest of circumstances. Attempting to prevent the pain and suffering of bereavement is like trying to stop the sun from casting shadows during the course of a day. Instead, significant adults in the child's life, when equipped with knowledge and compassion, journey with the child through the shadows. Through their interactions with one another, the shadows lengthen and shorten, darken and fade, come and go, and the child learns to travel with the shadows.

Components of the Model

Sibling Responses

The model emphasizes that siblings exhibit four major interrelated and intertwined responses to the death of a brother or sister, best described in the words of siblings themselves: "I hurt inside," "I don't understand," "I don't belong," and "I'm not enough."

"*I hurt inside.*" Reactions typically associated with grief that arise from the vulnerability of being human, from loving others, and missing them when they are no longer with us, include sadness, anger, frustration, loneliness, and fear. Children, often unable or inexperienced at identifying what they are feeling, typically express emotions through behavior. Some may be hesitant to return to the familiar activities of playing, of wanting to be with friends, of walking to school, or of wanting to do new things. Others act out by not listening to their parents or becoming irritable and belligerent. Some may complain of headaches, general aches and pains, stomach cramps, or disruptions in eating or sleeping patterns, or in school performance. Bereaved siblings frequently complain of loneliness. Some bereaved children also feel guilty for the death of their sibling even when they held no responsibility for the death.

"I don't understand." Children's level of cognitive development and their understanding of death contributes to their confusion and bewilderment by all that is happening. Younger children may not comprehend that their brother or sister is never coming back; they may not understand that death is forever. Children of all ages may be confused by the array of powerful feelings that surge within them, and that they see in others. They may be mystified and anxious by the activity going on around them.

"I do not belong." Younger siblings may feel left out of what is happening. In the aftermath of a child's death, siblings often want to help, but do not know how; or if they try to help, their efforts are not acknowledged or are even criticized. If their questions go unanswered, they sense they do not belong. Reorganization of roles and responsibilities within the family may leave siblings feeling as if they have lost their place in the family. Bereaved siblings also often feel different from their non-bereaved friends which contributes to feeling that they no longer fit with their peers.

"I am not enough." Siblings' perceptions of "not being enough" arise from perceptions that they should have been the one to die since, in their view, the deceased child was the parents' favorite, the smartest, or the best in some way. Typically, children want to alleviate distress in their parents, but regardless of what siblings do, it seems they are "not enough" to make their parents happy ever again. Feelings of "not enough" may be enhanced for siblings who feel responsible for the death or who feel displaced by the addition through adoption or birth of other children to the family.

Responses in Context

No one category of factors, nor any one isolated factor, accounts for the total experience of any one sibling. Three categories of factors come into play: individual, situational, and environmental. Individual factors include age, gender, health status, temperament, and past experience with loss. Problematic behavior seems to be most common in pre-school and elementary school-age children.

Situational factors include characteristics of the situation itself, such as duration of illness, cause of death, location of death, and the degree to which children were involved in the events pertaining to their brother or sister's illness, death, and related events such as the funeral or memorial service. For example, siblings who choose to be actively involved in the care of an ill child or who have a role to play in the funeral or other commemorative rituals demonstrate fewer behavioral problems than children who are excluded from such activities (Davies, 1999, pp. 106–22).

Also contributing to the context are environmental variables, such as the pre-death relationship between the siblings. When children have shared a close relationship, the loss of one child leaves an empty space in the surviving sibling, often resulting in more internalizing behaviors than are related to closeness in age, length of illness, or number of surviving children in the family. The family environment, including the social climate and level of functioning, also plays a central role. For example, in families where communication is more open than closed, feelings, thoughts, and ideas are more freely expressed, and a sense of cohesion or closeness exists, bereaved siblings exhibit fewer behavioral problems. Since families do not live in social vacuums, their culture and community values and priorities also impact sibling bereavement. But the central critical factor influencing sibling bereavement is the nature of the interactions between the siblings and the significant adults in their lives.

Adult–Sibling Interactions

Children seldom verbalize their thoughts and feelings so adults must understand that grief may take many forms, be tolerant of children's various reactions, and allow them to express their thoughts and feelings in their own time. Children may still feel sad or irritable, but they learn that such feelings are acceptable and normal. They do not need lectures, judgments, or pressure to get on with things before they are ready – all of which make children feel as if their feelings, thoughts, and fears are wrong. Rather, children who "hurt inside" need adults who comfort and console, are consistent, honest, and willing to engage in a two-way process of sharing thoughts and feelings with the child.

To help children who "don't understand," adults must remember that confusion and ignorance are additional forms of hurting which require ongoing comforting and consoling. Adults have a responsibility to be aware of what children understand, and to offer honest explanations that fit with the children's developmental capabilities. They must be open to children's questions, giving them freedom to ask whatever they want without fear of ridicule. Helping children understand is not just providing information about facts and events; it is also giving information about feelings, about what to expect, and about what not to expect. Teaching them about the reality of death and responding to their feelings and questions is paramount. Interacting with children in these ways helps them learn that it is okay to ask questions and they begin to understand death even though they learn that some questions have no answers. If, instead, adults dismiss children's questions or comments; provide misleading, inaccurate, or platitude-filled "explanations"; or do not provide information in a timely way, their feelings of "I do not understand" are reinforced. Moreover, children's confusion may lead them to devise their own explanations such as assuming that they are stupid or responsible for what has happened.

Adults' behavior also influences siblings feeling as if they "don't belong." When adults include children in planning for and participating in events, such as funerals, and when they prepare children for what to expect and what their roles and responsibilities might be, siblings feel as if they have something worthwhile or unique to contribute; they feel part of what's happening. When adults do not interact with siblings in these ways, then their feelings of not belonging are validated. Such children may take risks, act out, or escape into their own world of silence.

When bereaved children hurt inside, feel as if they are stupid because they do not or cannot understand what has happened, or perceive that they do not belong, feelings of "I'm not enough" are heightened. Adults, particularly parents, can prevent or alleviate this response when they reassure children, both verbally and non-verbally, of their love for them. Feelings of "I'm not enough" occur when adults compare siblings unfavorably to the child who died, when siblings feel displaced by the addition of new children to the family, when they do not feel special in their parents' eyes, or when they are given responsibilities beyond their years. Such children may deal with their feelings of inadequacy and inferiority by overachieving, taking on various characteristics of the deceased child, excelling at meeting the needs of others, or becoming unrealistically good.

Consequences for Siblings

When adults comfort siblings who are hurting, teach those who do not understand, include siblings so they feel as if they belong, and validate siblings' sense of worth, siblings are likely to have increased self-esteem and maturity, be more sensitive and empathetic, and be better prepared to handle death. In contrast, when adults belittle children's expressions of hurt, disregard their questions and level of cognitive development, exclude them from day-to-day events and activities, and shame them for not responding as the adults expect, then those siblings are more likely to feel invisible, insecure, insignificant, and incomplete (Davies, 1999, pp. 196–204).

Siblings' perceptions, whether affirming or diminishing of their capabilities, like shadows stretching across the land at day's end, may extend far into the future. In fact, the consequences of shadows in the sun set the stage for when bereaved siblings themselves become parents; their shadows become contextual variables for the next generation. If bereaved siblings experience the death of one of their own children, a dark shadow may become even darker. Thus, with the help of wise and loving adults who are willing to share the shadows, who are willing to share the journey, bereaved siblings learn that shadows, although ever present, can become comforting companions.

Implications of the Model for Helping Grieving Siblings

Experiencing the death of a brother or sister in childhood means that surviving siblings live forever with shadows in the sun. For some, the shadow is shorter and lighter; for others, the shadows are darker and longer. Thus, the first implication of the model is that the goal of helping bereaved siblings is not to prevent the shadows, to "fix" them or to make them disappear. Rather, the goal is to soften and shorten the shadows – to help bereaved siblings integrate their losses in ways that are regenerative rather than degenerative in the continual unfolding of their lives.

Second, since adult interactions with children are so influential, efforts to help siblings must be directed toward the interpersonal level. However, most interventions for bereaved siblings focus primarily on the individual child. The foundation for this approach was clearly established by the well-known and respected psychiatrists and psychologists who pioneered the study of grief, such as Freud and Lindeman. This focus carried over into the study of child bereavement resulting in interventions that emphasize psychoanalytic approaches to loss (for example, Furman, 1974; Bowlby, 1980; Baker, Sedney, & Gross, 1992). Developmentally specific attributes, such as cognitive status, have also provided interventions for bereaved children (Piaget, 1959; Speece & Bent, 1984). Although intrapsychic responses and cognitive understanding are included in the model as individual variables, adult–child interactions are key. Just as siblings' processes of dealing with grief are active ones (Attig, 1996), so too are those of the adults who must let siblings know that they understand the journey may be a long one, requiring physical and emotional energy. Adults must offer their own presence, concern, and empathy, and with consistency and constancy.

To be effective in their interactions with bereaved siblings, adults must reflect on their beliefs about the effect of death on children, such as having the capacity to grow and flourish or as a "problem" to be "fixed." Although well intentioned, adults may have to alter their perceptions and their actions so that they deal with the uniqueness of every child and the child's needs within the context of a particular time. Effective caregiving adults must cultivate sufficient self-awareness to recognize honestly when they have difficulty meeting the challenges inherent in helping bereaved children and to gain insight into how their own fears, frustrations, histories, expectations, and beliefs influence how they relate to grieving children. Finally, adults must recognize that their own comfort level in dealing with death affects their interactions with bereaved children.

The third implication of the model arises from parent–child interactions being the most significant contributor to sibling bereavement (Davies, 1999, pp. 160–70, 202–4). But because parents too are greatly affected by the death of one of their children, they cannot be expected to be responsible, understanding, and patient at all times. Thus, it is important for parents to explore how they would like to fulfill their own expectations and desires in helping their children. Some parents need guidance and encouragement in how they interact with their children who hurt, do not understand, feel they do not belong, or as if they are not enough. Such parents may find parent support groups to be particularly helpful.

The model indicates that family environment is a critical contextual variable in sibling bereavement. Therefore, a fourth implication of the model is that professional interventions at the family-systems level may also benefit grieving siblings. Family-level interventions must focus on getting to know the family, discovering members' beliefs, family characteristics such as openness, and family involvement in religious or other communities, and exploring relationships within the family (Davies, 1999, pp. 134–59). Also important, especially when encountering families with diminished levels of family functioning, the goal is not to judge or impose expectations on the family but to assist the family in a manner that supports the integrity of the family.

Finally, a fifth implication derives from the fact that families exist within the larger context of culture, community, and society. Thus, also important to helping bereaved siblings is attending to the larger context, such as striving to better understand cultural variations, rituals, beliefs, and practices. Helping bereaved children may be accomplished indirectly by advocating for discussions of death, dying, and bereavement in schools, churches, children's organizations, and community groups.

Conclusion

Following a brother's or sister's death, siblings experience shadows in the sun that vary in intensity and length and are influenced by a variety of factors, particularly interactions with their parents. Because bereaved siblings and their parents are thinking, feeling, behaving, socially interacting, and experiencing beings with histories and stories of their own, we cannot predict the exact nature of the shadows with certainty. What we do know is that comforting, explaining, including, and validating siblings' worth will go far to softening the shadows.

References

Attig, T. (1996). *Relearning the world*. New York: Oxford University Press.

Baker, J.E., Sedney, M.A., & Gross, E. (1992). Psychological tasks for bereaved children. *American Journal of Orthopsychiatry*, 62, 105–16.

Bowlby, J. (1980). *Attachment and loss. Vol. III: Loss*. New York: Basic Books.

Davies, B. (1999). *Shadows in the sun: The experiences of sibling bereavement in childhood*. Philadelphia, PA: Taylor & Francis.

Furman, E. (1974). *A child's parent dies: Studies in childhood bereavement*. New Haven, CT: Yale University Press.

Hogan, N.S. & De Santis, L. (1996). Adolescent sibling bereavement: Toward a new theory. In Charles A. Corr & David E. Balk (Eds.), *Handbook of adolescent death and bereavement* (pp. 173–95). New York: Springer.

Piaget, J. (1959). *The language and thought of the child* (trans. M. Gabain). London: Routledge & Kegan Paul.

Speece, M.W. & Bent, S.B. (1984). Children's understanding of death: Three components of a death concept. *Child Development*, 55, 1671–85.

Strauss, A. & Corbin, J. (1994). Grounded theory methodology: An overview. In N.K. Denzin & Y.S. Lincoln (Eds.), *Handbook of qualitative research* (pp. 273–85), Thousand Oaks, CA: Sage Publications.

Thompson, N., Allan, J., Carverhill, P.A., Cox, G., Davies, B., Doka, K., Granek, L., Harris, D., Ho, A., Small, N., & Wittkowski. J. (2016). The case for a sociology of dying, death, and bereavement. *Death Studies*, 40(6), 172–80.

chapter 2

Why Did My Sister Have to Die?
Helping Children with Sibling Death

Linda Goldman

In the previous chapter, Davies describes four responses of bereaved siblings that can serve as a conceptual map for caregivers: "I hurt inside, I don't understand, I don't belong, and I'm not enough." In this chapter, aided by children's art work and writing, I present a typical clinical case study to illustrate how these responses are interrelated and how parents and educators can support bereaved children when a sibling dies by responding to their hurt, engaging in age-appropriate dialogue with them, and involving them in memorializing and acknowledging them as honored and recognized mourners. Resources are suggested and peer grief support groups are highlighted, with an awareness of their benefits in helping the bereaved sibling not feel alone and promoting friendships.

Case Study

> Sometimes my friends ask me questions about my sister...and sometimes I don't know what to say.
>
> (Isabella, age 7)

Isabella was referred to grief therapy after the recent death of her sister Sophie, age 5, following several years of living with a rare form of leukemia. Sophie's death changed Isabella's life forever, starting with her shock on the day of Sophie's death. Isabella ran home from school, opened the door to say "hi" to her mom, and realized her house was filled with people, talking and crying. Her father was sitting in the corner, his head in his hands, rocking back and forth. "What did you think was going on?" I wondered. She shook her head and looked down. "I didn't know." Aunt Diane appeared, put her arm around her, and whispered. "I have some bad news for you. Your sister has died." Isabella sobbed. "Aunt Diane said Sophie died. When I heard the words...I didn't believe her. I was crying so much I couldn't see through my tears. How could Sophie have died? We had just eaten breakfast together this morning. Why did she have to die?" She burst into tears again.

Isabella was overwhelmed with emotion and frustrated when people asked questions about Sophie's death. It was difficult for her to find words to use. When working with bereaved siblings, an initial focus is providing age-appropriate language to dialogue about death, such as: "Death is when the body stops working. Usually people die when they are very, very old, or very, very sick, or so injured that their body doesn't work anymore." Isabella responded immediately to this discussion. "That's what happened to Sophie. Her body stopped working." "What couldn't she do?" I asked. She replied, "She couldn't eat, she couldn't play soccer, and she couldn't hug me anymore."

Developmental Understandings of Death and the Young Grieving Sibling

A child's understanding of death changes as she or he develops. Knowing how children perceive death at different developmental stages of childhood is important so that we can then work with predictable and appropriate responses.

Piaget's cognitive theory of development provides an overview of a child's thought process at different ages (Gindsberg & Opper, 1969). These processes impact a child's perceptions about death. Piaget's sensorimotor stage is approximately ages 0–2. Infants and toddlers' concept of death may be related to their perceiving "all gone" or "out of sight, out of mind." If they can't see it, it does not exist. Yet, even the youngest of children can sense living in a grief environment.

Piaget's preoperational stage of development is approximately ages 2–7, characterized by magical thinking, egocentricity, causality, and reversibility. Youngsters may view death as a journey with no return, conceive the possibility of reviving the dead person, believe some functions continue such as feeling and thinking, and see dead people as living in a box underground, a cloud or heaven, or both. Children often believe their thoughts and actions might have caused the death, and feel guilt or fear of retribution for perceived bad things done or angry thoughts. Isabella's placement of Sophie after death and her magical thinking are typical of this age group.

Isabella wondered out loud in a therapy session. "Linda, it's Sophie's birthday and no one has said her name. Where do you think she is?" Knowing children's questions can be a reflection of what they are thinking; I asked her, "Where do you think she is?" She thought for a moment, and then wrote the following note to Sophie.

> Dear Sophie,
>
> I really miss you. I am doing fine in school. I am really sorry you had to go down there. I wouldn't like it there myself. I don't know yet what to give you for your birthday.
>
> Love,
>
> Isabella
>
> (Adapted from Goldman, 2014a, p. 60)

We walked to the nearby drugstore and bought a balloon for Sophie. Isabella attached an "I Love You!" note, sent the balloon off, and said she felt much better.

Isabella continued to explore her magical thinking and grief surrounding Sophie's death. Even though she thought Sophie was in the ground, she also thought she was in heaven. In locating a loved one, many children place them in a place called "heaven" (Silverman, Nickman, & Worden, 1992, p. 497). "What would heaven look like to you, Isabella?" I asked. She drew a picture and described heaven.

> It's a magical place where everything comes true. There's a rainbow there every day. The rainbow would have a cloud and a pot of gold. There would be flowers and lots of animals, and a mansion bigger than any kingdom.
> P.S. If I lived in a magical place, I'd make nice people never die and bring a few people back from the dead. I'd like to meet God.
>
> (Goldman, 2002, p. 118)

Magical thinking predominated Isabella's perceptions. "It's my fault Sophie died," she insisted. "Why do *you* think it's your fault?" I asked. Responding to her question with a question instead of an answer allowed

Isabella to reflect on her own thoughts and feelings. "I think Sophie died because I was a bad girl and now God is mad at me." Isabella shared her age-appropriate magical thinking that she was the cause of her sister's death. By expressing her fears openly, we could begin to dispel them by discussing the facts about Sophie's illness and death. "Sophie died from having a very, very bad disease. She had been sick for many years. The doctors couldn't help her anymore. It was not your fault," I explained. "I'm happy Sophie is with God. He can give her all the medicine she needs to make her well," responded Isabella. These ideas and images were comforting to her.

Piaget's concrete operations stage applies to children approximately ages 7–11. Children's concepts of death appear curious and realistic. Girls and boys are interested in details about the death, and begin to internalize the universality and permanence of death. They can conceptualize that all body functions stop, comprehend thoughts about an afterlife, and think of death's occurrence in specific observable concrete terms. They may ask, "What are the reasons people die?" or "Why didn't the chemotherapy work?" Isabella asked, "What did the doctors do for Sophie when she was dying?" and "Did she suffer?" To help her find out the facts, I arranged a meeting with her parents and Dr. Adams, Sophie's doctor, who was with her when she died. He explained Sophie was given a drug that took away any pain, and that he was holding her hand when she died. These details comforted Isabella. She hugged Dr. Adams, saying, "I'm glad you were with Sophie when she died."

Clichés that Inhibit Sibling Grief

Clichés often block a bereaved child's understanding of death because they are taken literally. Many grieving siblings are given the message that their grief is less important than their parents' grief. They can become a forgotten or neglected griever. A few examples are:

> "You have to take care of your mom and dad now."
> "Don't cry, it will make your parents sad."
> "It's so difficult on your parents."
> "You need to be strong for your parents."
> "God loved your sister so much, he wanted to be with her."
> "God took your sister because she was so good."
> "It was God's will."

Many of these clichés relate to God. Isabella repeatedly heard it was *God's will* that Sophie died. She misinterpreted explanations, creating unnecessary anxiety and worry: "My daddy said Sophie was so good God took her away. Aren't I good too? Why doesn't God want me?"

Figure 2.1 Safe box. From Goldman (2014a). Reproduced by permission of Routledge.

I invited Isabella to make a "safe or peaceful box" to put in her bedroom. She could go to it whenever she felt worried or anxious to help reduce her stress: "Comforting objects and pictures can be placed inside the box, and the box can be put in a convenient place with easy access for the girls and boys" (Goldman, 2014a, p. 81; see Figure 2.1).

Memorialization

I invited Sophie to list her top five worries. To my surprise, her top worry was that she would forget Sophie: "Now Sophie isn't at dinner, or story time, or soccer. Do you think I will forget her?" We began to use memory work to reassure her of holding memories of Sophie.

Memory work is a useful technique for bereaved siblings. Memory books are valuable tools to allow children to express their feelings through writing and drawing. Isabella made a memory book about Sophie. One

Figure 2.2 Memory book. From Goldman (2014a, p. 76). Reproduced by permission of Routledge.

question asked "What worries you?" Isabella wrote, "I'm worried about my family being sad" and drew a picture (Figure 2.2). She questioned, "Will mommy and daddy ever be happy again? Before Sophie died, Mom read us a story every night. Now when Mom reads me a story, Sophie isn't there. It makes me feel so alone."

In my experience grieving siblings may feel lonely. Isabella and Sophie shared a bedroom. At night, she confided, she gets very sad. Sophie isn't there to talk to, and she missed her. Isabella thought of an idea. "I'll ask Mom if I can have Sophie's favorite bear, Snuggly. Then I can sleep with Snuggly and feel Sophie is with me." Linking objects can be special items or pictures that are reminders of the person that died, and help children maintain a connection or link to their loved one (Silverman et al., 1992). Using Snuggly to form a link with Sophie was helpful in creating a loving, nurturing ongoing bond.

Figure 2.3 Memory project. From Goldman (2014a, p. 74). Reproduced by permission of Routledge.

Even the youngest of children can create a memory box, a memory table, a memory picture album, or memory project. Isabella made a simple heart, a picture frame, and a holiday ornament. She put Sophie's picture in the frame and placed it next to her bed. That helped her remember Sophie. Sometimes she would say a prayer or light a candle for Sophie with her Mom and Dad (Figure 2.3).

Projective Play

Because children have a limited verbal ability for describing their feelings and a limited emotional capacity to tolerate the pain of loss, they communicate their feelings, wishes, fears, and attempted resolution to their problems through play (Webb, 2011). Projective play, through imagination and the creation of dialogue, often empowers young kids to work through difficult challenges. Playing with puppets, costumes, and other projective

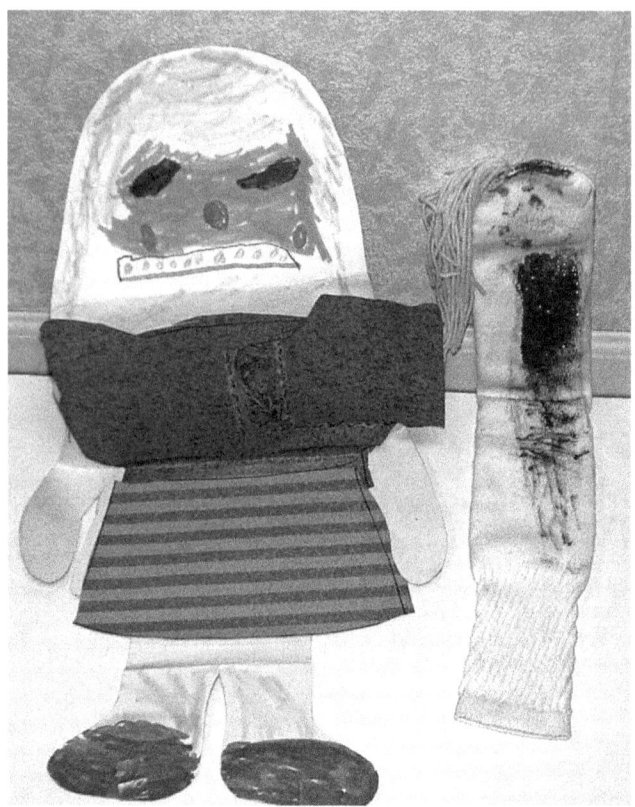

Figure 2.4 Projective drawing. From Goldman (2014a, p. 83). Reproduced by permission of Routledge.

props allows bereaved siblings to recreate their experience and role play thoughts and feelings.

Isabella's favorite stuffed animal to play with in therapy was Muncie. She chatted with Muncie about her life and would dialogue, "I miss Isabella so much. Do you?" Pretending to answer for Muncie, she would say, "Me too. I want to play with her again." Isabella asked to take Muncie home to keep her company at night. She put Muncie in Sophie's bed, and tucked him in tight with Sophie's favorite blanket. "It just made me feel better." This symbolic nurturing accomplished through projective props enabled Isabella to give and receive the love and affection for Sophie she was missing.

Another projective technique, a life-size drawing of herself, also helped Isabella express angry feelings: "I'm angry that Sophie died. It's not fair!" she shouted. Then she made a sock puppet of Sophie and told her how much she missed her (Figure 2.4). It is normal for children "to maintain a presence and connection with the deceased and that this presence is not static" (Silverman et al., 1992, p. 495). Isabella's play enabled her to maintain that ongoing, ever present relationship with her sister.

Common Characteristics of Bereaved Siblings

Packman, Horsley, Davies, and Kramer (2006) cited Elizabeth Devita-Raeburn (2004) referring to continuing bonds as the phenomenon of "carrying" (2006, p. 822). These authors noted that "surviving siblings carry, or bring forward, their deceased sibling into their current lives without attempting to replace them...carrying their deceased sibling with them and continuing the very bonds that had always defined the relationship" (p. 822). This ongoing relationship is common among grieving children. Isabella's parents were concerned that she spoke to Sophie in the present and were comforted to know this was normal for bereaved siblings. In turn, their reduced anxiety lessened Isabella's anxiety; an example of how educating and reassuring parents about grieving children aids a child's healing.

Isabella often said she felt Sophie was with her, especially when she saw a butterfly. "Sophie loved butterflies. I think she is sending them to me!" she declared to her dad. Listening to her and honoring her belief system, he gave Isabella a butterfly necklace. Isabella wore it every day, a tangible link to Sophie.

Taking on a caretaker role is another common behavior among grieving siblings. Isabella explained, "Now it's just me. I'm the only child. I have to take care of Mommy because she cries a lot." Compounding feeling responsible for their parents, many bereaved siblings feel diminished or ignored because a seemingly strong grief hierarchy places parents first as grievers. "Most people ask about how Mommy and Daddy are, but don't ask about me. They got so many letters after Sophie's death. I got two." She wondered why nobody seemed to notice her and not many friends or relatives asked how she was doing. "I guess it's my job to make sure they are OK and give everybody a report on how they are doing." Davies explains in Chapter 1 that bereaved siblings' feeling of "I'm not enough" is emphasized when they "fail" at changing their parents' sadness: "I kiss and hug mommy, bring her drinks to help her feel better, but it doesn't seem to work. She still cries and cries and I can't make her stop. Even if I pretend to be happy all of the time and never do anything wrong."

Davies adds in her chapter that for some bereaved siblings, additional losses may be associated with birth order ("now I am the only child"), increased responsibility, no longer having a shared history and shared future, parental grief, and parental idealization of the deceased sibling. Isabella confided, "Now I have to clean my whole room. Before, Sophie and I did this together. Mom always says, 'Why can't you be more like Sophie.

She kept the room neat all of the time.' I wish I could be more like Sophie, but I can't."

Again, teaching parents about the possibility of such responses is invaluable in helping them support their grieving children. The following common manifestations of grief in children are instructive for parents.

Grieving kids can...

- become the class clown or bully
- seem withdrawn and unsociable
- have bed-wetting or nightmares
- appear unable to concentrate
- act impulsively
- not complete schoolwork
- show difficulty listening and being focused
- appear overly talkative, disorganized, and unable to follow directions
- complain of stomachaches or headaches
- feel overly responsible.

They may...

- talk to their sibling in the present
- imitate gestures or idolize the sibling that died
- create their unique spiritual beliefs
- worry excessively about health and death
- show regressive behaviors (clingy, babyish, etc.).

(Adapted from Goldman, 2009, pp. 104–5)

Supporting Bereaved Siblings

Davies' model suggests we support bereaved children by advocating within schools. Isabella's teacher did not respond to Isabella when she told her Sophie had died. Isabella was devastated. Educating school personnel about common behaviors among bereaved children and helpful strategies is crucial. Suggestions include giving the child: (a) permission to leave the room, if needed, without explanation, (b) letting them choose a designated adult or location in school as a safe place, or (c) calling home if needed. Isabella's teachers were encouraged to give her permission to visit the school nurse, appoint a class buddy, create private teacher time, modify work assignments, and inform faculty, parents, and children of the death (Goldman, 2012).

Age-appropriate resources are essential educational tools for facilitating discussion. Recommendations are Forrester, *Leo and the lesser lion* (2009), Goldman, *Lucy lets go* (2014b), Jackson, *Can you hear me smiling?* (2004), and Reagan, *Always my brother* (2009).

"I can't talk to any of my friends about how I feel about Sophie," confided Isabella. "They just don't understand. They ask me how many brothers or sisters I have, and I don't know what to say." Providing peer support groups for children can be effective for establishing community support, a safe haven with grieving peers, an environment for sharing common experiences, and a foundation for new friendships. Isabella joined a group of bereaved siblings, ages 5–8. Her favorite part was family night when she and her parents shared a memory montage about Sophie with other children and their families.

Summary

The unique bond shared by siblings begins at birth and continues through life, acting as friends and mentors. Thus, a sibling's death may profoundly impact the surviving children. The degree of impact is influenced by the uniqueness of the sibling relationship, the developmental understandings of the young child, and by adult interactions with the bereaved child. "The importance of parental support cannot be underestimated in mediating surviving children's experiences of a sibling's death" (Packman et al., 2006, p. 826). To facilitate an open and safe journey for siblings through the shadow of grief, adult support and education are vital. Providing parents and educators with information about grieving children and applying techniques to encourage expression of children's grief proved central in forming dialogue and identifying unresolved aspects of Isabella's grief. Participating in a peer grief support group helped Isabella feel less alone.

Therapeutic techniques tailored to a child's developmental understanding helped facilitate Isabella's grief journey as well. "Play and expressive therapies help to bridge the verbal chasm that is so daunting for bereaved children who do not have the words nor the life experience to verbalize their feelings about death" (Webb, 2011, p. 19). Age-appropriate language, projective techniques, memory work, and inclusion in rituals underscored Isabella's significance as a bereaved sibling, a grieving family member, and a valued recognized mourner.

"We are *powerless* to control the losses and catastrophic events our children may need to experience, but by honoring their inner wisdom, providing mentorship, and creating safe spaces for expression, we can *empower* them to become more capable, more caring human beings" (Goldman, 2005, p. 72).

References

Devita-Raeburn, E. (2004). *The empty room: Surviving the loss of a brother or sister at any age.* New York: Scribner.

Forrester, S. (2009). *Leo and the lesser lion.* New York: Knoph.

Ginsberg, H. and Opper, S. (1969). *Piaget's theory of intellectual development.* Englewood, NJ: Prentice Hall.

Goldman, L. (2002). *Breaking the silence: A guide to help children with complicated grief* (2nd ed.). New York: Taylor & Francis.

Goldman, L. (2005). *Children also grieve.* London: Jessica Kingsley.

Goldman, L. (2009). *Great answers to difficult questions about death: What children need to know.* London: Jessica Kingsley.

Goldman, L. (2012). Helping the grieving child in school. *Healing Magazine. KidsPeace,* 26–31.

Goldman, L. (2014a). *Life and loss: A guide to help grieving children* (3rd ed.). New York: Routledge.

Goldman, L. (2014b). *Lucy lets go.* Omaha, NE: Centering Corporation.

Jackson, A. (2004). *Can you hear me smiling?* Washington, DC: Child and Family Pr.

Packman, W., Horsley, H., Davies, B., & Kramer, R. (2006). Sibling bereavement and continuing bonds. *Death Studies,* 30, 817–41.

Reagan, J. (2009). *Always my brother.* Gardiner, ME: Tilbury House.

Silverman, P., Nickman, S., & Worden, J.W. (1992). Detachment revisited: The child's reconstruction of a dead parent. *American Journal of Orthopsychiatry,* 62, 494–503.

Webb, N.B. (Ed.) (2011). *Helping bereaved children: A handbook for practitioners* (3rd ed.). New York: Guilford.

chapter 3

Growing Up Grieving

Alicia Sims Franklin

    Silently, while the world slept, you changed my life forever.

                                                                                            (Age 11)

These are the words of a grieving child, me. Thirty-nine years ago, my little brother, Austin, died of brain cancer. He was my only sibling and I loved him more than anything. His death sent shock waves through our family, as we each attempted to cope with the loss in our own ways. Over the years, I have learned that my experiences of being a young child when this significant loss occurred are different than the experiences of my friends who were adults when their siblings died. This is not to say that one is "better" or "worse" than the other, simply different.

    I work in the field of grief. Many times I have been asked if I would have chosen this field if my brother hadn't died. The truth is that I don't know. That question cuts right to the heart of the matter for me. I was so young when my brother died that I don't know who I was or who I was going to be before. For me, my life is marked by BEFORE and AFTER. He was sick for almost a year before he died, so my memories are colored by an urgency to cram in a whole lifetime of experiences into a very short time. I remember hearing my mom tell a friend of hers while my brother was alive that she felt bad paying so little attention to me but she knew there would be a lot more time for me after…

After he died, I saw adults in my life struggling to redefine who they were. My mom struggled with the questions about how many children she had. But, as a child who was still trying to figure out who I was, as a person, I asked, "Who Am I?" I was attempting to *create* my identity in the midst of uncertainty. This created a sense that the world was a dangerous place. If my brother could die, then what would protect me from dying, too?

> Do they have Twinkies in Heaven, Mom? We should send some with him, just in case.
>
> (Age 4)

It felt to me that there was a myth that the death of a loved one wasn't as painful for a young child. A lot of people would come up to me and ask me how my parents were doing. Almost no one asked me how I was doing. I felt like a forgotten griever. Even though I didn't understand death in the same way as my parents, the pain was still very real. This played out for me when we moved after my brother's death. I was 5.

I had so many plans for our life together. I was going to teach him how to ride a bike, how to drive Mom and Dad crazy! And then, he was gone. I didn't understand where he went or why we couldn't see him. When we moved to a new town, I was terrified that when he was done being dead and came back from Heaven that he would go to the old house. How could he find us in a new state, with a new address? It felt as though not only had he died and left us but now, *we* were leaving *him*. After trying to explain the permanence of death to me multiple times, my mom tried something different. We crumbled cracker crumbs outside of the car, for miles. He liked crackers and I knew that he would follow the trail to find us. In that moment, even though I didn't have an adult's understanding of death, I felt the intense pain of grief.

As a child I could not understand reasons for adults' discomfort with my grief. Now I do – I hate to see my own child in pain. My mother always told me the hardest thing she did as a parent was see me hurt. Only now can I be thankful for that gift.

> Mom,
> I didn't know what to say.
> You didn't know what to hear.
> Nightmares made me afraid to close my eyes at night.
> Reality made you afraid to open yours.
> I was afraid to need you.
> You were afraid I would.

> I looked to you for answers.
> You had none to give.
> You wanted to protect me.
> While I protected you.
> I am afraid of silence.
> You are, too.
>
> (Age 14)

We dealt with isolation that came from trying to protect one another from the depths of our pain. My parents have told me that they thought they were doing the right thing when they shielded me from seeing the intensity of their grief. I thought they didn't grieve, or couldn't cope, so I didn't want to burden them with my painful feelings. Who wants to be the one that makes everybody cry? Only after we started talking more openly as a family did we learn that the protection went both ways. There was a lot of silence in our family. We were each suffering together, yet, totally alone. Separated by the barriers of protection, we denied each other the support of the family. We were able to find a way to work together to find hope, but there were a lot of hurt feelings before we were able to break the silence.

Another issue we faced was how to deal with special events such as birthdays and anniversaries. Because I was so young when my brother died, my grief experience included extra milestones, like the year I stopped sending the letters that I wrote to my brother because I realized that he couldn't come home. That day it felt as though he had died, again. Then, quite a few years later, we were all caught by surprise by how difficult it turned out when I moved to college. It had been 12 years since he died, but suddenly, it felt brand new. When we talked about it, my Mom pointed out that if he hadn't died, I wouldn't have been the last child to leave home.

> Must I fill the spaces that my brother won't be able to? Do I have to live for two, running races he'll never enter, dreaming dreams he'll never know? Or can I still be me? Don't forget me!
>
> (Age 16)

These words describe the struggle I had with trying to find the right balance between honoring my brother's life and maintaining my own identity. My parents' struggle with this contributed to the confusion, too. There were a lot of times when I felt like I was competing with a ghost. My family was military, so we moved every year. Without realizing it, my parents had developed a shrine to honor my brother. This ended the year my mother caught me giving shrine tours to the neighbor children for a quarter apiece. After she made me give everyone their quarters back, we sat down and really talked about how I felt that I was living with this "angel/ghost." I had to point out to her that angels don't make any new mistakes or get low grades in handwriting. It was really hard for me to admit to my parents that when the "shrine" was up and my pictures were nowhere to be seen, I sometimes wondered if they thought that the wrong child had died. We handled it by making sure that both of our pictures were placed side by side. As a child, I had to figure out how to answer the question of how many brothers and sisters did I have. Am I still a sister if there is no brother to tease? I decided to say yes that I had a brother but he died. When I was older I had to face the decisions about how to introduce the idea of my brother's legacy to a serious boyfriend. More than one guy was freaked out by the idea that we continue to hang all the stockings at Christmas. To my relief, the man I married was great. When he saw the stockings, he said, "So you have a living and a dead section." Shortly before we became engaged, I took him to my brother's grave and he took me to "meet" his dad at the cemetery. He admired the ongoing legacy of my brother.

Several years later, when it was time to start a family, the death of my brother played a much bigger role in our discussions than either of us had anticipated. I wanted more than one child so our child would have a sibling. He wanted only one because he had been thrust into raising his younger brother after the death of their father. I know so many siblings who were unprepared for how this "happy" conversation about family planning can become such a painful event for bereaved siblings.

This year my mother died and I felt his absence as a deafening silence when it fell to me to make all of the funeral arrangements and to support our father. I don't know if we would have handled this huge event as a team or not. But I would have liked to have had him there, with me. Every once in a while I talk to him and say that it is his turn to spend time with her, I got her all to myself for many years. And yet, he was there, not the way we had planned, but there. Austin was always a part of our lives, and is still a presence in our family.

Growing up grieving is a difficult task. It strained the very threads of our family fabric. As part of my journey, I wrote letters to my brother asking, "Am I still a sister?" You bet I am. Because of my experiences, I have learned not to take things for granted. Each new event brings memories of my brother. I see him in my daughter, his eyes, and his smile. We talk about him in our home and found a way to acknowledge him in our wedding without having him be the focus. His death brought me the knowledge that people die, and I know to spend quality time with the ones I love rather than build walls to keep my heart "safe" from being broken. Am I a better person, stronger? I don't know. If I had the choice, I'd choose to have my brother.

Thank you, little brother, for your short time on earth. You taught me to choose love over loneliness, hope over hatred. I can see that love shining through the eyes of my daughter. In her laughter, I hear you. When she runs and plays, I know you are free. You are the part of love that never goes away. You are my hope!

(Age 31)

chapter 4

A Brother's Loss

Christopher Lourenco

I started my life in a relatively "normal" situation, an American family of five with two older brothers. Growing up, we did the usual family things: weekend visits with my grandparents, occasional trips to Busch Gardens, and yearly trips to Disney World. My father was a big proponent of water activities; thus we frequently went on canoe and kayak trips on rivers in eastern North Carolina where we called home.

In 2003, my father purchased a sailboat that he planned to use to take my two brothers and me out on the water for small trips. Before he would take us, however, he enrolled in a boating safety course and completed it with perfect marks. We were to take our maiden voyage on July 4, 2003. This specific July 4 was a Friday in which my mother worked so she could take the following Monday off. We left from New Bern, NC with the plan to spend a few hours on the water then return home that night. The boat had two seating areas, one in the front near the mast and one in the rear by the tiller. I was 9 years old and sat with my father in the back while my brothers Zach (17) and Alex (14) sat in the front. The first voyage on the new sailboat was fun for a time; little did we know that tragedy would strike.

In the early afternoon we were sailing along and saw a train trestle above us. Though there was no chance for our small craft to hit it, my father decided to turn the boat slightly to avoid it. A routine maneuver suddenly led to the unthinkable. The mast of our sailboat struck low-lying power lines, electrocuting my two older brothers and snapping the mast of the boat in half. Little did I know, but in that brief moment everything in my life changed.

A rescue boat heard our cries for help and towed us to shore. I recall being taken to the hospital in the back seat of a police car, all the while horrible images flashing through my mind. When we arrived at the hospital we were ushered into a small room and after a short time told the worst news possible: my two older brothers had been electrocuted and died. We later learned that the power lines that our boat hit were much lower than laws allowed. In fact, larger boats had hit the lines before; however, the city of New Bern did not find reason to remove the power lines since no one had ever been harmed in the past. Instead, the city was content with the fact that there would be the occasional electrical outage when a boat hit the lines.

The funeral and first couple of years following the accident are largely a blur. The message conveyed to me was simple: "Be strong for your parents and continue to do well in school." I couldn't help but think if I was to be strong for my parents, then who would be strong for me? Despite the accident occurring on July 4, 2003, I was back in school in August to start fifth grade. I began to see a therapist and attended a different school for sixth grade, but for me the circumstances were still the same. I felt as if no one could relate to me and that even though I put on a strong face and acted as if everything was fine, in reality, I was in turmoil. Countless questions went through my mind. Why did this happen? Why hadn't this issue been corrected by the city? Why is no one asking me how I feel? Why does everyone tell me to stay strong for my parents? I am pretty sure if I had a dollar for every time someone asked me "How's your mother?" I would be a rich man and never have to work again at this point.

In the summer of 2005, my parents dropped a bombshell on me. We were going to the Compassionate Friends (TCF) national conference in Boston, MA and I was to attend the sibling events. I thought "Great, they go to these meetings every month, come home in tears and now they want me to go to this dumb conference and cry with people." I was completely opposed to it. Since I was only 11, I really didn't have much say in the matter; so, despite all of my objections we drove to Boston for the TCF national conference. If you had told that bratty kid that ten years later he would be extolling the virtues of this organization, you would have met with a lot of disbelief. What I found was that TCF is not a place for you to cry it out or be told how you should feel. Instead it is a place where grieving siblings from all over the country can gather, talk about school, complain about parents or just how much life sucks, and how we miss our deceased siblings. In addition, at my first TCF conference I met numerous siblings that have spent countless hours throughout the years helping me deal with the loss

I experienced and have become part of my family. Family summarizes TCF very well; for these people that I see once a year end up being a family as they are the only ones who truly understand how I feel.

The next few years unfolded relatively in the same way. I went to school during the school year and to the TCF conference each summer. In 2008, we moved to Myrtle Beach, SC. At first I was not happy about the move; however, after it happened I was glad to be away from the town I had spent my entire life in. In Myrtle Beach everything was new, and memories of what once was did not linger at every corner. In 2011, I graduated from high school as the valedictorian and decided to attend college at Clemson University, the premier institution of higher education in South Carolina, to pursue a degree in engineering. Clemson was about five hours away from home, and I could tell that my parents were not delighted about the distance. I was their last surviving child, and for the first time in their 26 years of marriage there would not be any children at home. However, I relished the change. I wanted to be somewhere new where I could make my own identity without having to tell people about my brothers if I didn't want to. One thing I never liked about living at home was that as soon as a friend came over they instantly were told my entire life history. I knew all of that would change once I went off to college.

In August 2011, I moved to Clemson, SC to begin my undergraduate education. After trying out a few different disciplines in my freshman engineering course, I decided that industrial engineering was the branch of engineering for me. I enjoyed my time in college and spent a lot of time in my own thoughts. I truly believe this time I spent alone with my thoughts really helped me grow as a person. I reflected on my own life as well as the countless stories I had heard through years of attending TCF conferences. I heard too often stories of people going through personal tragedy and destroying their own lives through bad decisions involving drugs, alcohol, or other things. I decided I wanted to be different. Not only did I want to be successful, but I also wanted to show people that it is possible to go through a life-altering tragedy and emerge happy while still carrying on the memory of your lost loved one. Thus, I volunteered as a workshop presenter for the first time at the TCF national conference in 2013. I focused on this very topic. My message was simple. Although we change a lot and are never the same person, we can still be happy and honor the memories of our lost siblings. Over the past few years, I have repeatedly thought that if somehow through my life I can help or inspire even one person, then I have succeeded. I have no therapy degrees or psychological training but I truly believe that the key to healing after a loss is finding someone to confide in who won't judge and to spend time with your own thoughts. I guess I believe that much of grief is a self-healing process.

I graduated college magna cum laude on May 8, 2015, and have enrolled in graduate school at Texas A&M University to pursue my doctorate degree in industrial engineering. I plan on helping educate the next generation of engineers by obtaining a job in academia after graduation. In addition, I will continue to volunteer with TCF and share my story in the hope that I can help one person heal following the death of their sibling.

PART II

Adolescence (12–17)

chapter 5

Adolescent Sibling Loss

David E. Balk, Corinne Cavuoti, and Anne M. Smith

The focus of our chapter is adolescent bereavement over sibling death in the 12–17-year-old age range. We begin with the back story central to appreciating adolescent responses to sibling death.

The Back Story Enveloping Adolescent Sibling Bereavement

Adolescence extends over several years, beginning with the onset of puberty and lasting into the mid-20s. A developmental systems framework identifies three phases to adolescent development: early adolescence (10–14), middle adolescence (15–17), and later adolescence (18–23) (Balk, 1995; Blos, 1979; Fleming & Adolph, 1986). This framework focuses on core issues, conflicts, and tasks during the three phases as central to the individual's resolution of the major challenge of the adolescent years, namely, to form a stable identity marked by personal autonomy, interpersonal fidelity, and career direction (Erikson, 1968; Hogan, 2014; Josselson, 1987). We look more closely at the core issues, conflicts, and tasks a bit later in this chapter. We also emphasize the salience of social media in the lives of adolescents.

Our position is that adolescent sibling loss occurs within overall cultural and societal expectations placed on young persons during their adolescent years. These expectations are understood as the core issues, conflicts, and tasks we expect adolescents to master. Social media has entered as the pervasive milieu within which (and at times by which) adolescents deal with these matters.

Core Issues, Conflicts, and Tasks during the Years 12–17

Five core issues endure across early, middle, and later adolescence. An individual's responses to these five core issues influence the formation of the person's assumptive world (Balk, 2014; Kauffman, 2002). The five issues encompass these matters: (a) deciding on the predictability of events, (b) gaining a sense of mastery and control, (c) developing a sense of belonging, (d) making decisions about fairness and justice, and (e) fostering a positive image of oneself.

During early adolescence (10–14) youth face the five core issues as they cope with the developmental task of separating psychologically from their parents. The tension of this developmental task leads youth to deal with the conflict of remaining safe versus the fear of being abandoned.

When a sibling dies during a young person's early adolescence, the impact not uncommonly plays out in this manner:

- Randomness intrudes on existence, shaping assumptions about the predictability of events.
- The early adolescent may begin to idealize the sibling who died.
- A feeling of being different from peers may invade consciousness and affect a sense of belonging and of being accepted.
- The sibling's death will almost assuredly challenge notions of fairness and justice.
- Early adolescents bereaved over a sibling's death not uncommonly emerge with a sense of being more mature than their peers.

For some middle adolescents, responses to a sibling's death began during their early adolescent years. Longitudinal studies are needed to determine what changes over time impact middle adolescents whose sibling died during the youth's early adolescent years.

During the middle adolescent phase (15–17) youth face the five core issues as they cope with securing a sense of self-efficacy, individual autonomy, and personal control. The chief developmental task for this phase of adolescence is "gaining a sense of mastery, and the conflict lies in the tension created over the press to be independent" while remaining dependent on parents (Balk, 2014, p. 3).

Sibling death during middle adolescence can manifest in terms of the five core issues in these ways:

- The unpredictability of life scares the adolescent: aggressive risk taking may be employed as defiance against life's randomness, or timidity may overwhelm natural spontaneity.
- Some adolescents identify and deepen commitment to long-term goals, whereas others decide there is no purpose in planning for the future.
- Grieving adolescents learn that peers have no appreciation or comprehension, emotionally or intellectually, about the challenges of bereavement.
- The utter indifference of the universe angers the adolescent.
- For many grieving adolescents, vulnerability, empathy, and interpersonal maturity emerge, particularly in contrast to the comparable development of unaffected peers.

Social Media and 12–17-Year-Old Adolescents

Eighty-one percent of online adolescents use social messaging sites such as Facebook and Twitter on a daily basis. As an increasing number of adults begin using these social networking platforms (71 percent of adults now use Facebook), many adolescents explore other means of online connectivity to create layers of privacy and connection outside the scrutiny of adults (Madden et al., 2013a). Adolescents continue to use the mainstream platforms for connectivity; however, they have also added newer applications such as Instagram (social networking via photos), Snapchat (temporary photo application), Tumblr (social messaging site), and Meerkat (temporary video networking). Adolescents continually try to stay ahead of the "adult usage curve" to maintain an online environment safe for sharing and expression among peers. Although there is discussion and controversy regarding adolescent online interaction, social media is inherent in all communication among adolescents with access to the internet. Therefore, it is imperative to consider and assess how adolescents are using this modality to cope with loss and/or life crises (Smith & Cavuoti, 2014).

Sibling Death as a Crisis Event

Examination of life crises has determined that these experiences share common structural properties: (a) they pose a threat to well-being, (b) they defy current coping skills, and (c) depending on how managed, they offer the possibility of harm or of growth (Moos, 1986).

Extensive examination of how people cope with a variety of life crises (divorce, alcoholism, terminal illness, and bereavement) disclosed that five adaptive tasks come into play (Moos, 1986). These five tasks are:

- Confront the requirements of the situation. For instance, when a family member dies, one adaptive task is to arrange the funeral, and another is to notify persons of the death.
- Determine the meaning of the event. For instance, when a sibling dies, the adolescent is faced with integrating this loss into his (her) understanding of human existence.
- Sustain interpersonal relationships. For instance, when a sibling dies, it is important for the adolescent to maintain communication with family members in order to deal with the distress and the confusion caused by the death.
- Regulate one's emotional responses. When a sibling dies, an adolescent commonly is faced with overwhelming dread, anger, and confusion. The intensity of grief may wax and wane, and the duration of the grief may leave the adolescent fearful of ever regaining emotional balance.
- Preserve a satisfactory self-image. For instance, the death of a sibling can undermine the adolescent's self-confidence and belief in her (his) ability to accomplish things that matter.

Empirical Evidence about Adolescents' Responses to Sibling Death

Empirical studies of adolescent sibling bereavement began in the early 1980s and continued with regular contributions into the decade of the 1990s, and then interest in the topic seemed to wane. Self-concept, academic performance, religion, emotions, and family dynamics and relationships were among the chief topics investigated. Due to space limitations we have limited ourselves to two topics: (a) self-concept and (b) family dynamics and relationships.

Self-Concept and Adolescent Sibling Bereavement

A widespread assumption still held by many persons is that adolescents are emotionally unstable. Anna Freud captured this viewpoint with her notion that the only thing normal about adolescents is that they are abnormal (Freud, 1971). Building on this assumption, people commonly believed the distress of a sibling's death would exacerbate an already volatile situation. Scholars from backgrounds as divergent as social learning theory and psychodynamic psychology, however, have presented evidence that indicated most adolescents are happy, well-adjusted, and calm (Bandura, 1964; Offer, 1969). The Offer Self-Image Questionnaire for Adolescents (OSIQ) has shown that most adolescents are normal, well-adjusted young persons and at most 20 percent are in serious psychological turmoil (Offer, Ostrov, Howard, & Atkinson, 1988).

Researchers (Balk, 1981, 2014; Hogan, 2014; Hogan & Greenfield, 1991) into adolescent sibling bereavement have gathered persuasive evidence that most adolescents (80–85 percent) respond resiliently to this life crisis; they get along with peers, respect their parents, have begun setting life goals, and have a sense of right and wrong. When using the OSIQ to examine the self-concepts of sibling-bereaved adolescents, researchers learned the great majority have self-concept scores no different than scores of non-bereaved peers: around 30 percent have self-concept scores significantly higher than the scores of most adolescents, over 50 percent have self-concept scores that match how most adolescents respond to the questionnaire, and 15–20 percent of bereaved adolescents have self-concept scores lower than how most adolescents respond (Balk, 1981, 1983). Hogan and Greenfield (1991) showed that grief intensity and duration correlated inversely with the self-concepts adolescents reported about themselves: that is, adolescents with high self-concept scores reported lower intensity and duration of grief, whereas low self-concept scores were associated with higher grief intensity and duration. In fact, "low self-concepts for bereaved adolescents were particularly associated with long-term vulnerability to problems in psychological development" (Balk, 2014, p. 154; see also Hogan, 2014).

Family Dynamics and Relationships

The death of a sibling has a marked impact on the family, its structure, obviously its membership, and the interactions within the family's milieu. Hogan (2014, p. 83) wrote, "Their family is different now; it is smaller and there is a pervasive sense of missing and longing for the sibling who died."

When coping with a sibling's death, an adolescent benefits greatly when in a family that engages in close, personal communication and expresses close emotional attachments to one another (Balk, 1981, 1983; Hogan, 2014). On the other hand, adolescents living in families that seldom if ever engage in personal conversations and seldom express close attachments to one another face difficulties. These two family environments (more coherent versus less coherent) are distinguished by significantly different emotional reactions over time to a sibling's death. For instance, in a more coherent family, adolescents report their initial responses to a sibling's death are marked by shock, numbness, loneliness, and fear that their painful feelings will never end; as time passes, these reactions do subside, to be replaced by an enduring sadness that permeates their lives but does not leave them incapacitated. Hogan (2014, p. 83) noted, "Adolescents who successfully work through their grief find no closure to their grief, but in time they realize their grief softens." However, in less coherent families, the adolescents report their initial responses were guilt and anger, but few report feeling shocked, numb, lonely, or afraid; over time these adolescents report that confusion is their most dominant response to the death of their sibling.

How do family dynamics and relationships produce such divergent reactions? While in-depth family research is needed to know the answer for certain, it strikes us as plausible that interpersonal expectations and bonds of attachment provide important clues. For instance, an adolescent raised in a family with ongoing personal conversations and expressions of emotional caring would experience a sibling's death as not only individually distressing but as a threat to the security her (his) family offers. Because the more coherent family has a history of intimate conversation and attachment, eventually persons gravitate toward one another, listening to each other's story and getting questions answered. However, an adolescent raised in a family with impersonal relationships and distancing as the norm, while the death of the sibling may well be distressing, the destruction of the family poses less of a threat, if any; there has not been a history of relying on the family. Over time there are no discussions about the death, how one feels, or how one understands what happened. Over time, questions remain unanswered (Balk, 1981).

The Place of Social Media in the Lives of 12–17-Year-Old Adolescents Bereaved over a Sibling's Death

Social media provides varied opportunities for an adolescent to work through the adaptive tasks of a life crisis by providing a means to target specific social communities for support. Each social platform and community provides distinctive connections, privacy, and unique means of support. For adolescents, Facebook and other widely used social platforms provide a means for memorialization, information posting, and connectivity in a general, public forum. In addition to using Facebook, adolescents will seek out new applications that promote anonymity and privacy from adults. For example, the application Whisper allows users to post "anonymous secrets" superimposed over an image, and Ask.fm is a social site that allows users to ask questions and post answers to other peers. Similarly, the advent of temporary applications such as Snapchat and Meerkat provide platforms for adolescents to send a photo or video with a set time limit for viewing before the message disappears, and Burn Note, a text-only application that deletes the message after a set time period (Watts, 2014). These different opportunities for interaction enhance the ability of an adolescent to retain a sense of self while working through the tasks of sibling bereavement by providing options for support. The support is portable and available 24 hours a day allowing self-determination of need.

Understanding the adaptive tasks of adolescent bereavement requires that technology, specifically social media, be superimposed over each task. Whether confronting the reality of the loss, sustaining interpersonal relationships, or attempting to regulate emotional response, an adolescent's primary means of connection and interaction is often through social media. In a 2013 Pew Internet study, teens (12–17) were more likely to report positive interaction rather than negative utilizing social media with 52 percent citing online experiences that left them "feeling better about themselves" (Madden, Lenhart, Duggan, Cartesi, & Gasser, 2013b, para. 2). For example, as an adolescent attempts to confront the reality of the loss, social media provides a platform to notify friends and peers, plan to memorialize in age-relevant ways, and start a process to integrate the loss. By using different media applications and social platforms, an adolescent is able to target specific connections. By identifying different levels of connection through different groups, adolescents may be able to customize emotional support as they cope with grief. Adolescents see Facebook as a public forum utilized by adults including their parents. When bereaved by sibling loss, adolescents will carefully select appropriate photos and language to share. Posting generic photos and emotion-regulated "status" entries in Facebook is consistent with an adolescent's need to protect parent and family members from further distress. However, this interaction still provides a level of connection, interaction, and support from family members and Facebook community members. Through Facebook, an adolescent may gain a superficial or casual level of support from members of their community of "friends." Instagram and Twitter provide a more peer-friendly support atmosphere. Adolescents view Instagram and Twitter as an emotional outlet safe from most adults, freeing them to post more open and honest expressions of grief. By posting more familiar, relevant photos and personal "tweets," an adolescent engages in more peer-focused support. In turn, peer response and support normalizes feelings of grief and promotes social acceptance. Interaction through these two platforms provides a higher level of support focused on connection with peers. Going further, Snapchat and Meerkat (temporary photo/video applications) provide a very intimate form of connection targeting core peer support group members. These "snaps" are often private and reflect emotions in real time, releasing hidden feelings of loss and grief to selected, trusted individuals. The "snaps" often initiate emotional responses from core friends allowing adolescents to share the loss and express emotions hidden from adults.

Concluding Remarks

We have reviewed some of the traditional topics scholars have studied when examining sibling death during adolescence. As the back story to any study of adolescence, we used the developmental systems framework of phases to adolescence and of core issues to be mastered during adolescent development. The ascendancy of social media is one phenomenon that must be examined more carefully by persons interested in adolescents dealing with sibling death. Understanding adolescent culture and use of social media is critical to assessing the status of an adolescent bereaved by the death of a sibling.

References

Balk, D.E. (1981). *Sibling death during adolescence: Self-concept and bereavement reactions.* Unpublished doctoral dissertation, University of Illinois at Urbana-Champaign.

Balk, D.E. (1983). Adolescents' grief reactions and self-concept perceptions following sibling death: A study of 33 teenagers. *Journal of Youth and Adolescence,* 12, 2, 137–61.

Balk, D.E. (1995). *Adolescent development: Early through late adolescence.* Pacific Grove, CA: Brooks/Cole.

Balk, D.E. (2014). *Dealing with dying, death, and grief during adolescence.* New York: Routledge.

Bandura, A. (1964). The stormy decade: Fact or fiction? *Psychology in the Schools,* 1, 3, 224–31.

Blos, P.A. (1979). *The adolescent passage: Developmental issues.* New York: International Universities Press.

Erikson, E.H. (1968). *Identity: Youth and crisis.* New York: Norton.

Fleming, S.J. & Adolph, R. (1986). Helping bereaved adolescents: Needs and responses. In C.A. Corr & J.N. McNeil (Eds.), *Adolescence and death* (pp. 97–118). New York: Springer Publishing.

Freud, A. (1971). Adolescence as a developmental disturbance. In *The writings of Anna Freud* (Vol. VII, pp. 39–47). New York: International Universities Press.

Hogan, N.S. (2014). When a sibling dies. In K.J. Doka & A.S. Tucci (Eds.), *Helping adolescents cope with loss* (pp. 79–94). Washington, DC: Hospice Foundation of America.

Hogan, N.S. & Greenfield, D.B. (1991). Adolescent bereavement symptomatology in a large community sample. *Journal of Adolescent Research*, 6, 1–32.

Josselson, R. (1987). *Finding herself: Pathways to identity development in women*. San Francisco, CA: Jossey-Bass.

Kauffman, J. (2002). *Loss of the assumptive world: A theory of traumatic loss*. New York: Brunner-Routledge.

Madden, M., Lenhart, A., Cortesi, S., Gasser, U., Duggan, M, Smith, A., & Beaton, M. (2013a). Teens, social media, and privacy. Retrieved from http://www.pewinternet.org/2013/05/21/teens-social-media-and-privacy/.

Madden, M., Lenhart, A., Duggan, M., Cortesi, S., & Gasser, U. (2013b). Teens and technology. *Pew Internet and American Life Project*. Retrieved from http://www.pewinternet.org/Reports/2013/Teens-and-Tech.aspx.

Moos, R.H. (1986). *Coping with life crises: An integrated approach*. New York: Plenum.

Offer, D. (1969). *The psychological world of the teenager*. New York: Basic Books.

Offer, D., Ostrov, E., Howard, K.I., & Atkinson, R. (1988). *The teenage world: Adolescents' self-image in ten countries*. New York: Plenum Medical.

Smith, A.M. & Cavuoti, C. (2014). Beyond websites: The relevance of the internet and technology for adolescents coping with illness and loss. In D.E. Balk (Ed.), *Dealing with dying, death, and grief during adolescence* (pp. 219–33). New York: Routledge.

Watts, A. (2014). A teenager's view on social media. *Backchannel*. Retrieved from https://medium.com/backchannel/a-teenagers-view-on-social-media-1df945c09ac6.

chapter 6

Bereaved Adolescent Siblings
The Forgotten Mourners

Jennifer Kaplan Schreiber

Adolescent Sibling Grief in the Literature

Adolescent bereavement must be viewed within the context of the period of adolescence. The normative life transitions encompassing adolescence both influence and are influenced by the non-normative experience of sibling bereavement. Literature regarding adolescent bereavement notes the impact of adolescence as a relevant factor in coping with a primary death loss (Corr & McNeil, 1986; Corr & Balk, 1996; Balk & Corr, 2009). Balk (1991) reviewed research conducted in the 1980s on death and bereavement and concluded that for adolescents, "bereavement presents an extremely serious life crisis at a time when development is marked by significant physical, cognitive, moral, interpersonal and psychosocial transitions" (p. 8).

Erikson (1963, 1994 [1968]) conceptualized a psychosocial theory of development where individuals move through a continuum of eight stages that reflect lifelong issues. Certain tasks within a given stage are brought to the forefront during specific life experiences. Erikson viewed each stage as representing a psychosocial normative crisis where the developing self or ego is able to gain and restore a sense of mastery within the frame of social factors. Adolescence, composed of biological, physical, behavioral, cognitive, and social transformations represents the shift from childhood to adulthood, and is considered one of the most complex transitions in the lifespan.

In Erikson's model (1963, 1994 [1968]), the period of adolescence includes two developmental tasks. The first, *Identity versus Identity Diffusion*, involves the determination of how adolescents see themselves compared with how others may view them, and how they begin to differentiate self from other. This is similar to Elkind's (1981) concept of *egocentrism*, the adolescent's belief that people around him or her are as preoccupied with his or her appearance and behavior as he or she is. Bereaved adolescents are developmentally challenged by their desire to "fit in" with peers, but having experienced the death of a sibling, they may find themselves feeling "different" than their non-bereaved peers, creating a sense of isolation and social withdrawal. Another concept of Elkind's is that of the *personal fable*. This is the story that an adolescent tells himself or herself about himself or herself, which tends to have egocentric overtones. The *personal fable* often contains themes of omnipotence and immortality. In other words, because adolescents often view themselves as omnipotent, they may participate in risk-taking behaviors such as driving recklessly or consuming large amounts of alcohol or mind-altering substances. Furthermore, Noppe and Noppe (1996) added that physical risk often earns social approval for adolescents.

The second task described by Erikson (1963, 1994 [1968]), *Intimacy versus Isolation*, refers to the adolescent's increased sense of self while creating and maintaining satisfying personal relationships. These developmental crises are similar to *the second individuation process* as described by Blos (1979). Combined with the complexities associated with the developmental stage of adolescence and the distinct nature of the parent or sibling bond, adolescents are constructing their own identities and now must address the fundamental question, "Who am I now that my sibling is dead?" Furthermore, Oltjenbruns (1991) noted that adolescents often use siblings as a mirror to help define either perceived positive or negative aspects of the self, which is problematic for those whose sibling has died. While recognizing another's shortcomings is a natural part of adolescent development, oftentimes adolescents idealize a sibling who has died. Some bereaved adolescents have difficulty separating from the deceased or reallocating their emotional investment from their parents to their peers due to the idealization.

As adolescents develop greater autonomy, their primary attachments move away from parents and siblings, and peers take on a significant role in their identity formation. Since adolescents are emotionally dependent upon peer relationships, adolescents may be significantly impacted by "concepts of loneliness and ultimate nonexistence" (Noppe & Noppe, 2004, p. 154) after a meaningful death. Lawrence, Jeglic, Matthews, and Pepper (2005) found no gender differences between bereaved college students on measures of psychological distress, though an avoidant coping style was related to symptoms of depression in females. Adams (2001) found that adolescent boys have been socialized to hide or deny their feelings of grief more so than girls, as well as to display more aggressive behavior. Doka and Martin (2010), pioneers of masculine models of grief, found that grieving men find comfort in physical activity and problem solving. No such evidence exists for bereaved adolescent boys, although many bereavement programs incorporate rigorous physical activity in their programs and anecdotally report positive response by participating boys. For example, the author and her colleagues intentionally plan grief activities with that notion in mind (e.g. having the boys mix cement as part of the activity of making memorial stones).

Open-ended groups are particularly helpful for individuals in crisis or transition. Groups enable individuals to recognize their sense of self through interactions with each other. The group process enables individuals to not only gain support, but also develop coping skills and problem-solving techniques through shared stories. Most importantly for bereaved adolescents, they learn that they have peers with whom they are able to identify, thus lessening their sense of feeling alone.

Children's Bereavement Programs and Interventions

The Dougy Center, the first center in the United States to provide peer support groups for grieving children, was founded in 1982 in Portland, Oregon (www.dougy.org). It was part of a grassroots effort to provide a safe space for grieving families to share their loss experiences after bearing witness to the positive impact a local boy had by connecting with other dying children before his death from an inoperable brain tumor. Currently, the National Alliance for Grieving Children, a national non-profit membership organization that connects professionals and organizations who are engaged in providing advocacy, education, and direct support services to bereaved children through its professional network, lists more than 500 bereavement support providers in its online directory (retrieved from http://childrengrieve.org/local-support, March 27, 2015). While service delivery models vary amongst the providers, their missions generally aim to normalize grief for children through social support.

Many types of bereavement interventions exist for youth (Schreiber & Spear, 2014). Some bereaved youth attend individual or family therapy, and others participate in peer-based support groups. Some programs may provide support services solely to bereaved youth of specified ages, while others incorporate all ages, including adult caregivers. Theoretical models and guiding ideas may differ based on service delivery providers' overall organizational goals. For example, some interventions rely on peer-based support groups facilitated by trained volunteers without professional mental health backgrounds, while others rely on licensed mental health professional facilitators. Service delivery logistics also differ due to space limitations, funding, and personnel. Some interventions are offered in time-limited, closed sessions, while others provide ongoing, open sessions. This substantial variation represents a strong interest in this area of intervention, but also suggests a wide breadth of approaches based on good intentions and perceived benefits rather than empirical evidence. While this does not reduce the importance of this work or the positive effects programs and interventions may achieve, it is unclear if these interventions have significant measurement outcomes, work across diverse populations, have efficacy in a variety of settings, and/or rely on a certain level of skilled practitioner or other program or setting factors. The efficacy of bereavement interventions, particularly for youth, is an understudied area of interest. Empirical research into childhood bereavement programs is crucial for creating the most effective interventions that have the potential to improve the lives of the diverse population of bereaved children.

Empathy and Containment: Relevant Factors of Bereavement Programs that Impact Change for Adolescents

Attachment Theory is strongly embedded as an influential construct in empathy. The neuroplasticity of the brain suggests that weak attachments can be made stronger or "rewired" and mirror neurons can be measured and changed, thereby enhancing empathy (Gerdes, Segal, Jackson, & Mullins, 2011). This factor is very important in that shared grief experiences provide the opportunity for strong attachments, especially for adolescents who rely on peers for self-identity formation.

Turner (2009) described mindfulness techniques as a way to foster empathy. This technique has been successfully incorporated into activities at bereavement programs as a way to enhance well-being, foster connections, and alleviate suffering. For example, a 13-year-old boy reported that he continuously had difficulty sleeping because "I shared a room with my brother and now I lie in bed for hours thinking about him." Many of his peers reported similar challenges with sleep, so a group facilitator led them through a visual imagery exercise and provided a printed copy of the exercise that they could use at home. Doing this exercise as a group (as opposed to individually) normalized the negative feelings associated with sleep challenges (and stereotypes that boys should not cry and should be strong, etc.), creating a bond and empathic connections between the boys. Through a narrative lens, Babits (2001) introduced the concept of metaphor as a tool to provide containment or holding in the therapeutic relationship. Therapeutic metaphor fostered a new way of understanding and feeling heard by the client from the therapist, which created an empathic connection. At bereavement programs, therapeutic metaphors are both explicitly and implicitly incorporated into the fabric of programs. For example, "The Human Knot" is an icebreaker activity where all the adolescents grab hands with anyone in the circle other than the person beside him or her, and then they attempt to unknot themselves. The experience of being tangled in a "knot" is used as a metaphor for grief, and then the participants brainstorm ways to "get out or loosen some of the knots."

Henshelwood (1997) reflected on the use of psychic containing in group therapy and how it is used as a bridge between the inner world of the individual and the group process. The group itself becomes the container of the individual's world. Many grieving adolescents report that the program he or she attends is the only place where he or she feels "safe" and welcomed to share feelings and thoughts related to the death. The sense of isolation with non-bereaved peers can be overwhelming; peer-based programs provide a "container" or "holding environment" for their grief experiences. As one 16-year-old girl exclaimed when describing her journey during the year she attended a grief group for teens following the accidental death of her older brother, "Everything has changed, everything is different, I'm different, but I'm still me. I didn't get that before I came here." A 14-year-old boy turned to her and shook his head in agreement, quietly stating, "I'm not alone in this world."

Key Points

Adolescence is one of the most challenging, and exciting, times of growth and change an individual will encounter. For grieving adolescents, this can be more pronounced than their non-grieving peers. Since adolescents often define themselves based on how they feel that they are perceived by others, being different than their peers, due to the death of a sibling, may create negative outcomes. Adolescents who participated in a peer-based support group for bereaved siblings recommended the following to adults working with sibling-bereaved adolescents:

- We may give the impression that we are adults and don't need support, but we try to protect our family and friends by not always sharing how we feel. Ask, but give us space, too.
- Don't tell us how to feel. Don't tell us "it will be okay." Respect how we feel.
- Be patient as we try to find our own sense of self. Unless we're being unsafe, respect our choices.
- Just because I may not want to talk about my brother or sister who died does not mean I don't think about him or her (probably more than you think)!

References

Adams, D. (2001). The grief of male children and adolescents and ways to help them cope. In D.A. Lund (Ed.), *Men coping with grief* (pp. 275–308). Amityville, NY: Baywood.

Babits, M. (2001). Using therapeutic metaphor to provide a holding environment: The inner edge of possibility. *Clinical Social Work Journal*, 29, 1, 21–33.

Balk, D. (1991). Death and adolescent bereavement: Current research and future directions. *Journal of Adolescent Research*, 6, 1, 7–27.

Balk, D.E. & Corr, C.A. (Eds.). (2009). *Adolescent encounters with death, bereavement, and coping*. New York: Springer Publishing Company.

Blos, P. (1979). *The adolescent passage: Developmental issues*. New York: International Universities Press.

Corr, C.A. & Balk, D.E. (Eds.). (1996). *Handbook of adolescent death and bereavement*. New York: Springer Publishing Company.

Corr, C.A. & McNeil, J.N. (Eds.). (1986). *Adolescence and death*. New York: Springer Publishing Company.

Doka, K.J. & Martin, T.M. (2010). *Grieving beyond gender: Understanding the ways men and women mourn*. New York: Taylor & Francis Group.

Elkind, D. (1981). *Children and adolescents: Interpretive essays on Jean Piaget* (3rd ed.). New York: Oxford University Press.

Erikson, E. H. (1963). *Childhood and society*. New York: W.W. Norton and Co.

Erikson, E.H. (1994 [1968]). *Identity: Youth and crisis*. New York: W.W. Norton & Co.

Gerdes, K.E., Segal, E.A., Jackson, K.F., & Mullins, J.L. (2011). Teaching empathy: A framework rooted in social cognitive neuroscience and social justice. *Journal of Social Work Education*, 47, 1, 109–31. doi: 10.5175/JSWE.2011.200900085.

Henshelwood, L. (1997). The effect of sudden sibling loss on the adolescent or young adult. *International Journal of Palliative Nursing*, 3, 6, 340–4.

Lawrence, E., Jeglic, E.L., Matthews, L.T., & Pepper, C.M. (2005). Gender differences in grief reactions following the death of a parent. *Omega: Journal of Death and Dying*, 52, 4, 323–37.

Noppe, I.C. & Noppe, L.D. (1996). Ambiguity in adolescent understandings of death. In C.A. Corr & D.E. Balk (Eds.), *Handbook of adolescent death and bereavement* (pp. 25–41). New York: Springer Publishing Company.

Noppe, I.C. & Noppe, L.D. (2004). Adolescent experiences with death: Letting go of immortality. *Journal of Mental Health Counseling*, 26, 2, 146–67.

Oltjenbruns, K. (1991). Positive outcomes of adolescents' experience with grief. *Journal of Adolescent Research*, 6, 1, 43–53.

Schreiber, J. & Spear, C. (2014). The magic of grief camps: The impact on teens. In K. Doka (Ed.), *Coping with loss in adolescence* (pp. 305–22). Washington, DC: Hospice Foundation of America.

Turner, K. (2009). Mindfulness: The present moment in clinical social work. *Clinical Social Work Journal*, 37, 2, 95–103. doi: 10.1007/s10615-008-0182-0.

chapter 7

Michelle's Story

Rose Planer

The phone rang at 7 a.m. on a Tuesday morning. I was a sophomore in college at the time; I jumped out of bed...alarmed. Who would be calling this early? I picked up the phone...my limbs went numb, as I listened to my mother's panicked voice on the other end of the phone.
"Mom? Is everything ok?"
"Rose, are you sitting down? I have some horrible news...
Michelle was killed last night in a car accident. She's dead."

The above conversation is all I remember of that terrible morning of April 2, 2002. I was 19 years old. I had my whole life in front of me. Yet at that moment, I struggled to breathe.
Michelle was my only sibling: a beautiful, smart, creative, and compassionate 16-year-old girl. She loved life unconditionally. She cherished her family, friends, and faith.
I sincerely admired my younger sister. She fiercely clung to her belief that every human deserves to be treated with dignity and respect. She celebrated diversity and embraced people of different faiths, religions, and ethnicities. Her friends lovingly described her as their *sage elder* for she challenged bullying and confronted adversity.
In addition to her compassionate spirit, Michelle possessed many artistic gifts. Through her love of painting, she could bring a boring, white canvas to life as if by magic. Her artwork was always displayed throughout the high school hallways and on our home refrigerator. At a young age, Michelle found a new medium: dance. She dazzled us all as we watched her

gracefully glide across the stage. We would marvel at her and say "Michelle will do something remarkable with her life."

On the evening of April 1, 2002, Michelle was riding in the back seat of a car, returning from a friend's house. The teenage driver, a high school acquaintance, lost control of the car and barreled it into a tree. The impact tragically killed my sister and another teenage boy.

One can have such high expectations for life. When asked, Michelle knew she wished to pursue a career in the arts. The day she died, the world seemed to drain of its color for the vibrant, beautiful soul humanity had lost forever.

I returned home from college and we buried Michelle four days after her death. I remember the feeling of emptiness as if the world had swallowed me whole. I wondered if I would ever feel anything other than numbness again.

As a Jewish family, we sat *Shiva* as part of the mourning ritual. For seven days, I watched family and friends emerge as surrogate caretakers of our lives. For a whole month, my parents and I never cooked a meal or cleaned the house. The outpouring of love from the community reminded me of my sister's faith in the power of the human spirit. Ultimately, it was my parents' love for one another that helped me recognize the importance of confronting my grief and moving forward with my life.

During their darkest days, I watched my parents' love for one another strengthen. Each morning, they would embrace and remind each other that Michelle would want them to continue living their lives. Through their love and support coupled with grief counseling, I began to emerge from the black hole that threatened to keep me in the darkness forever.

There is something unnatural about the death of a child – a horrific, twisted occurrence that can never be explained. I could never fully understand the trauma my parents experienced when Michelle died. However, I felt alone in the sense that they could not fully comprehend my suffering. My only sibling was dead. I had to now face the world without an automatic best friend.

As I started grief counseling, I recognized that I felt anger for the fact that the universe had robbed my parents of a daughter and me of a sister. I had to first process the anger before I could understand the depth of my sorrow.

It was through journaling that I felt a connection to Michelle. Shortly after her death, I began writing letters to her in my journal. In the early letters, I expressed my anger at her for getting in the car with someone whom she did not know well. However, as the days drifted into weeks, the angry tone in my letters faded. My tears began to spill onto the pages, as I would apologize to Michelle for the fights we experienced or for my failures in serving as a model older sister. I continued to journal for a year after she died. Through writing my letters to Michelle, I began to understand and accept the reality of my new life – a life without my sister.

Michelle will always remain my greatest role model. Through her actions and teachings, she helped shape the individual I am today. Several years ago, I decided to start my journey toward becoming a grief counselor. I know she would be proud of my decision to help others confront difficult life transitions and traumatic losses.

After Michelle died, it was challenging to see the world without a future filled with pain and suffering. As time moved on, happiness once again entered my life. I married a wonderful man, who Michelle would have been proud to call a brother-in-law.

One of the happiest days of my life occurred on December 10, 2013, when I gave birth to a beautiful baby boy. It is customary in the Jewish faith to name a child after someone who has died. It seemed only fitting to name my son, *Max*, after his radiant Aunt Michelle. As Max grows, certain personality traits have emerged that remind me of Michelle. Max is a sweet child who greets me every morning with a smile. He lovingly ensures that his stuffed animals receive ample hugs and kisses throughout the day. He is a bright and compassionate soul just like Michelle.

Michelle DID do something *remarkable* with her life.

In her short 16 years, she touched the lives of everyone who knew her with her gracious and forgiving nature and her unshakeable belief in the capacity for human goodness. Michelle's legacy will continue to endure as we teach Max the importance of treating others with respect, kindness, and unconditional love. Our family will never forget the compassionate, artistic soul who once dazzled us with her beauty and taught us to value every moment of our precious lives.

chapter 8

Losing My Brother at 14

Elizabeth DeVita-Raeburn

On a rainy day in May, 2002, 23 years after my older brother's death, I went back to see his room at the National Institutes of Health (NIH). In family parlance, it is referred to as The Room. It wasn't just any hospital room. It was a special sterile enclosure. My brother, Ted, had an illness that had destroyed his immune system. He lived out the second half of his nearly 18 years in the sterile room, divided from the world, and from us, by a clear plastic curtain that kept germs away from him. He was known as Washington, DC's "Bubble Boy."

I had expected it to be the same. I don't know why. There'd been at least three renovations in that hospital since my brother died, in 1980. After 9/11, NIH, the seat of government research in the US, had changed its walk-in policy. Now you had to be invited in by someone, your name added to a list, your car gone over by men with bomb sniffers. It was a different world now than it was in 1980. In so many ways.

Our family saga, the one that would define all of our lives, began one September night when my brother was 9 and I was 6. My father spotted bruises on Ted's legs while we sat at dinner. Huge purple bruises that my father, an oncologist, immediately recognized as a sign of a blood disorder. He suspected leukemia, which was just beginning to be treatable in the early 70s. My dad saw and treated kids with leukemia all the time at the National Institutes of Health, where he worked, a mile away from our house. It was a horrible diagnosis but now, thanks to the research of my father and others, kids had a shot.

Aplastic anemia, my brother's diagnosis, was much grimmer. No functioning immune cells. You could prop patients up with transfusions, for a time, but that didn't save their lives. People with aplastic anemia had exactly one shot – and it was a long one. In some cases, their immune systems might mysteriously start working again. If not, they died, usually within a year.

My father's colleagues at the NIH convinced him that the best way to give my brother a chance to be in the survival group was to place him in one of the sterile "bubble rooms" the NIH had created for cancer patients whose bone marrow had been wiped out by what was then very experimental chemotherapy. There were no other options. So one night, when my brother had spiked a frightening fever, my parents put him in.

The sterile room worked...sort of. My brother, who was almost ten at the time, did not die within a year, but his immune system didn't start to function again, either. He was stuck. No immune system, a room to protect him. His life was confined within an 8x8 foot room. Our lives circled around his.

This continued for eight years. Any semblance of family life that involved the four of us took place in his hospital room, where my mother, father, and I stayed on the non-sterile side of the clear plastic curtain that divided the room in half.

You might think that, with the duration of his illness, I was prepared for my brother's death. But I wasn't. To me, it was as shocking as if he'd been run over by a car. That's because, over time, his illness became my normal. I was 6 when he was diagnosed, and 14 when he died. I didn't remember life any other way.

What's more, my parents, in trying to protect me from the grim possibilities, had never prepared me for the fact that my brother might die. They talked only in terms of "when Ted gets out." I suppose I knew, in a vague way, that death was a possibility. But my brother had been a constant in my life – there when I opened my eyes to the world, and ever present ever since, even in the hospital. His absence did not seem possible.

Having him wrenched away was like shearing away a psychological skeleton, an inner scaffolding that propped me up in ways I didn't even understand. And neither did anyone else, it seemed. Again and again, I was met with the same response, from people who became aware of my family's loss: "How terrible for your parents." "How are your parents?" "You have to be good for your parents, they're going through a lot."

This last line was delivered to me by a well-meaning woman who'd accosted me at the side of my brother's grave, where I stood looking helplessly at my brother's coffin, which rested on straps over the hole that would soon consume it. She meant well. So did the others. But their words made me feel horrifyingly self-indulgent in my grief, and ultimately drove me inward. For years, I would perceive my brother's death as my parents' loss.

Losing a sibling at 14, these were my struggles:

- The horror of friends too young to understand, who just want you to act normal and fun. I tried, but always felt like I was play acting in my own life.
- A struggle with independence. Normally, teens pull away in the process of attempting to become independent adults. My bereft parents, however, became overprotective and smothering after Ted's death. I was torn between not causing them more grief and pursuing my own normal development.
- An identity crisis. Losing a sibling, I would realize many years later, is something of an identity crisis – we define ourselves, in part, in contrast to our siblings. I didn't know who I was anymore, much less who I was in the family. My parents looked to me, for instance, to be the hub of the family in my brother's absence. But I had long since learned to be invisible and give my brother center stage. The pressure was awful.
- Other people's discomfort in the face of my story – and not having the social tools, yet, to handle the situation. I learned not to mention that I'd had a brother to strangers, and to avoid the now awful question – Do you have brothers and sisters? But this also felt like a betrayal of my brother, denying his existence.
- The horror of guilt – why him and not me? Because my brother had been so focused upon, I felt like the lesser sibling, the less worthy one. I felt he should have survived, rather than me, and that everyone would have been happier had that been the case.
- For me, as the younger sibling, there was also the disorientation of losing a leader, the person who showed me the way. My brother, even from his hospital room, had shown me the way – from how to act and joke to what to read and what music to listen to. Teenagers are susceptible to suicidal ideation, anyway. For me, this was worsened by how lost I felt without my brother. How was I to know how to go forward?

This amidst the usual teenage angst. It wasn't pretty. On the surface, I seemed okay, if withdrawn (which was interpreted as normal). I had to be. I was being strong for my parents, not causing them any more pain. Inside, I carried it all. Never allowing myself to grieve – it wasn't my loss, it was my parents' loss – never learning how to truly go on.

By the time I was 27, it was apparent that things in my life weren't working. Not my job as an editor, at which I was unhappy, though I loved to write. Not my relationships, which always failed somehow. Nothing.

I functioned well enough. I had a job. I paid my rent. But I knew that I was depressed. Not can't-function depressed. But subdued. As if my volume had been turned down somehow.

But I was now living in New York City where, by everything I'd learned from Woody Allen movies, everyone had a therapist. This was big, because I did want to fix whatever was broken. Not only because I didn't feel well, but because, in addition to everything else I carried about my brother, I felt an obligation to live life extra well on his behalf. And I knew that I wasn't.

So I found a therapist – referred from a friend. When my soon-to-be therapist returned my first call to ask what it was I'd like to work on, I had no idea how to respond. "The usual stuff," I said haplessly, hoping that would fly. There was a pause on the other end of the phone, and then she told me what day and time to show up.

When I did finally show up at that appointment, I sat down on the couch and immediately began to cry. When I finally could speak, five words I had not planned to say, or even been conscious to be true, slipped out. "I am my brother's death."

I had not known this. Had not anticipated saying it. But there it was, and it was true. I was a solid block of frozen grief. Stuck. Unable to move forward. And so, more than ten years after my brother's death, I began to claim his loss as mine and to learn how to mourn. When I revisited The Room, it was different. It was no longer a sterile bubble. The curtain that had stretched across the room was gone. It was no longer a place where someone might spend years awaiting a cure. The Room had changed. The hospital had changed. And so had I.

Emerging Adulthood (18–30)

chapter 9

Living the Moment... Envisioning the Future

Ann Laverty

Writing is a conversational process between author and reader. As I write, I am curious about how you understand my words as they fall on the page and extend past the margins. While actual conversation between us is not possible, I believe we each have interpretations in this process, shaped by our histories and imagined conversational turns that invite new understandings. As such, I will be transparent with you, the reader, about aspects of my history that influence my interpretations of sibling bereavement in emerging adulthood.

As a psychologist in post-secondary counseling, I have listened to many stories of emerging adults. I have witnessed profound changes over time about what it means to grow up, to navigate changing relationships, to find hope in a seemingly uncertain future, and to draw upon resilience in the face of overwhelming loss. By attending to those narratives, my understandings about emerging adults and bereavement are shaped.

I am also a bereaved sibling. My youngest sister, Beth, died nearly 20 years ago when I was just beyond emerging adulthood. Her death transformed me and the way I live to this day. I now know with greater assurance that death can interrupt any day of my living without permission or notice. I also now live with greater intention with as few regrets as possible. These learnings also inseparably shape my interpretations of this experience.

Yet for these noted qualities, I also need to be clear that I do not believe this gives me final insight or authoritative voice for psychologists, emerging adults, or bereaved siblings. I merely highlight these elements because in some way they influence how I make sense of this experience and converse with you, the reader.

In preparing to write this chapter, I faced a number of challenges. Emerging adulthood is a recent theory of development with limited research applying it to diverse populations and life experiences (Arnett, 2007; Lane, 2015). As well, research about sibling relationships and bereavement in emerging adulthood is sparse (Balk, 2001; Servaty-Seib & Taub, 2010; Scharf, Shulman, & Avigad-Spitz, 2005). In essence, what is presented as "known" about sibling bereavement in emerging adulthood in this chapter is speculative, drawing upon threads of what is understood about emerging adults, sibling relationships, and sibling bereavement. As such, I have positioned this chapter to highlight possible ways developmental experiences and sibling bereavement in emerging adulthood might intersect and influence lived experience.

Emerging Adults and Sibling Relationships

Emerging adulthood, roughly 18–29 years of age, was identified as a new life stage near the end of the 20th century as normative patterns of adolescence and young adulthood in Western society challenged existing psychosocial models (Arnett, 2000; Erikson, 1968). It is as a period of living somewhere in-between adolescence and adulthood where a fluidity of attending to present and future life issues can occur simultaneously (Arnett, 2000; Gutierrez & Park, 2015; Schwartz, Zamboanga, Luyckx, Meca, & Ritchie, 2013; Summer, Burrow, & Hill, 2015). Greater emphasis is placed on relative freedom to try on new relational patterns and life directions (Living in the Moment) as well as focusing on identity development and shifting worldviews (Envisioning the Future). It is viewed as the most heterogeneous life period as illustrated by the variety of ways life is lived by emerging adults (Arnett, 2007).

Sibling relationships are impacted by developmental transitions in emerging adulthood. As greater freedom and independence occur, emerging adults can experience a major recentering of family relationships. Sibling relationships become more voluntary than during previous developmental periods and siblings can begin to move toward more egalitarian relationships in order to facilitate potentially closer bonds later in life (Aquilino, 2006; Conger & Little, 2010). Transitions such as one sibling moving away from home can shift power differentials and the possibility of rebound positivity following conflict and disconnection can emerge (Scharf et al., 2005; Whiteman, McHale, & Crouter, 2011). As well, there can be a shifting of adolescent sibling experiences to make room for a different relationship to be established as each sibling develops new understandings of themselves and each other (Lindell, Campione-Barr, & Greer, 2014). In addition, sibling relationships contribute to evolving identities and worldviews due to their shared histories (Devita-Raeburn, 2004). Past experiences can be taken up as one considers their emerging identity and worldview, at times in consultation with a close sibling. In addition, an active re-examination of religious and spiritual beliefs common during this period can also contribute to emerging identities and worldviews (Gutierrez & Park, 2015).

The nature of a sibling relationship prior to death can shape grieving and familial relationships (Packman, Horsley, Davies, & Kramer, 2006). Surviving siblings can feel as if they have lost a part of themselves and continuing bonds can persist and contribute ongoing influence (Devita-Raeburn, 2004; Marshall & Davies, 2011; Packman et al., 2006). As siblings grieve, they may examine their lives to look for purpose, make meaning out of loss, and determine how to go on despite the death of their sibling (Forward & Garlie, 2003). Greater compliance with social norms and responsibilities during emerging adulthood might also factor into life changes (Arnett, 2007). In balance with the challenges, siblings with securely attached relationships can exhibit more flexible coping and higher post-traumatic growth following periods of challenge which may include greater maturity, personal strength, relational awareness, and compassion (Cohen & Katz, 2015).

Living the Moment–Envisioning the Future is a conceptual process for how I have come to understand emerging adulthood. There is a fluid movement wherein bridges are built between adolescence and adulthood with time for freedom, self-focus, exploring possibilities, and determining life direction. When a sibling dies during emerging adulthood, relationships can change, maturity can accelerate, identity can shift, and worldviews can alter. The individualistic nature of this process requires room for the diversity of emerging adult experiences to be present. To illustrate the possibilities of this experience, I have created four imaginary emerging adults navigating different aspects of Living the Moment–Envisioning the Future following the death of their sibling.

Living the Moment

Changing Relationships

Sarah died in a skiing accident three months ago. Her older sister Jennie, 25, can still remember the frantic phone call from her father as she walked to the bus after her shift as a nurse at the local hospital. Jennie and her toddler, Chloe, lived with Sarah and their parents and after years of sibling rivalry their relationship was getting closer. Jennie laughs when she admits her little sister was no longer a tag along but someone she enjoyed including in activities with her friends and she was a special aunt to Chloe. Jennie feels cheated that just as she was beginning to appreciate Sarah, it all ended. While her supervisor was supportive of her taking time away from work, Jennie finds the structure and sense of accomplishment important to her grieving process. It also seems to be a helpful distraction when she finds herself trying to understand what it means to be an only child. Jennie's parents immigrated to Canada from China 20 years ago and work at a local manufacturing plant. As they do not speak English, Jennie has sole responsibility for dealing with legal matters and insurance companies related to Sarah's death. At night, she often talks with Sarah, laughing and crying about being left to carry the care of both their parents and Chloe on her own. She knows her skills as a nurse to multitask and remain flexible will help her get through; yet, she feels overwhelmed and struggles to find ways to uphold the family values of loyalty and honor in all life circumstances.

Forcing Maturity

Martin, 19 and the youngest of three siblings, finished high school, decided to get a job, make some money, and move out of the family home with some buddies – finally having his own space. He landed a job framing houses in the construction industry and quickly earned a promotion due to his work ethic and teamwork skills. Martin's brother, Sean, died last year in a car accident due to impaired driving and lately times have gotten tough. While Sean was never overly reliable and had a distant relationship with Martin, he did help out by still living at home and bringing in some extra income to help the family make ends meet. Martin's sister, Diane, the middle sibling, has a developmental disability that necessitated their mother staying home to care for her. While Martin's father has a good job, the cost of everything is increasing and Sean's death brought not only a huge loss but increased financial pressures. It is weird for Martin to see his father cry as his anger moves to tears when pressures mount. His mother seems to just keep busy and does not talk about Sean. Martin is not sure what to do about all of this as he has never known anyone who died before – all of his grandparents and even the family dog, Sparky, are still alive. Sean's death was a wake-up call for Martin. He resolved to never again drink and drive and volunteers to be the designated driver when needed. Although his boss has offered to pay for his schooling to apprentice as a carpenter, Martin is worried about the cut in pay. He knows moving home would help his cash flow and support of his family but he struggles as his freedom and lack of responsibility to anyone but himself seems to be evaporating.

Envisioning the Future

Shaping Identity

Raina, 28, just completed her PhD in civil engineering. She acknowledges feeling like a "work in progress" far longer than her friends who have settled into jobs and parenthood. The culmination of all those years of study has been to fulfill her dream of moving to the west coast from the small prairie town of her birth to work and find a life partner. Her older brother, Amir, was her strongest supporter when she came out as lesbian to her Muslim family and extended community. She will forever hold Amir's love within her as his support and acceptance of her true self helps her live with transparency. She remembers his call three years ago to tell her his wife, Priya, was expecting twins. A year later Amir was diagnosed with leukemia and died within 18 months, leaving the family devastated. Recently, Raina is rethinking what it might mean to set aside her dream of moving in order to be closer to help Priya raise the twins. She feels torn as she knows finding a life partner in their small town is not likely and even if she met someone online, it would be complicated to navigate where and how this relationship might be viable. She cannot imagine them living with three generations in one house yet as her family adapted in the past, perhaps this might be possible in the future. While her career is important to her, she can also envision her role as auntie as more central to her future identity and life purpose. Despite her own needs, she knows Amir's death is changing her future as she tries to figure out her own identity and lifestyle in balance with the needs of their family in the years to come.

Changing Worldviews

Paul, 22 and the second of four siblings, grew up with parental expectations to take over the family business after completing a finance degree at university. Three generations have overseen the growing success of the business and entrepreneurial ventures are highly valued. Devout in their evangelical Christian faith, the family relied heavily on their church community following the death of Paul's sister, Bethany, after a lengthy illness. As Paul nears the end of his degree, he recognizes more clearly how significantly Bethany's death has transformed him. He silently questions his faith as he struggles to understand how a God could exist in the midst of his sister's protracted pain and suffering. When he asks these questions out loud, he is encouraged to trust the faith of his childhood and pray for guidance, suggestions he finds hollow in the face of his searching. Paul also recognizes more fully the fragility of life and his own mortality. He often thinks of conversations with Bethany where she encouraged him to live his life to the fullest and not take time for granted. Her encouragement and strength invites him to now consider doing what is right for him rather than just what is expected. He wants to make a positive difference in the world but has yet to figure out what that means to him. He is certain about his decision to travel abroad for a year and maybe find employment in Europe in order to expand his horizons. Knowing his parents are looking forward to partial retirement when he graduates and enters the family business, Paul struggles under the weight of this expectation. He realizes he has to figure out a way to tell his parents he might never want the life they envision for him.

Future Directions

Death of a sibling in emerging adulthood can bring forth transitions and transformations in relationships, maturity, identity, and worldviews. It can also bring forth other changes not identified in this chapter. Grieving is not a straightforward process with static and defined parameters. The same can be said for developmental experiences of emerging adults. Remaining attentive to these processes requires a position of openness to the possible shifts while also drawing on present knowledge of what we believe is true at this point in time about grieving and growing up.

I have never lived in a family where my cultural identity necessitates me to consider my role and obligation as a sibling. I have not been responsible for the financial well-being of my family or the care of young children following the death of a sibling. Nor have I experienced a significant shift in my worldview after a sibling dies that impacts the pressure of parental expectation mismatched with my own life priorities. Yet Jennie, Martin, Raina, and Paul brought these worlds and other complexities into this chapter to open up our thinking to what might be relevant and important to consider about sibling bereavement for emerging adults. Their stories do not illustrate the complete picture of all that is possible as many other stories exist that are shaped by the uniqueness of culture, family, and sibling relationships. Considering the fluidity of what is understood about sibling bereavement in emerging adulthood, our challenge is to raise questions that matter, to remain open to multiple answers, and to continue to draw upon constructed knowledge and lived experience to guide our research moving forward.

References

Aquilino, W. (2006). Family relationships and support systems in emerging adulthood. In J. Arnett & L. Tanner (Eds.), *Emerging adults in America: Coming of age in the 21st century* (pp. 193–217). Washington, DC: American Psychological Association.

Arnett, J. (2000). Emerging adulthood: A theory of development from the late teens through the twenties. *American Psychologist*, 55, 5, 469–80.

Arnett, J. (2007). Emerging adulthood: What is it, and what is it good for. *Society for Research in Child Development*, 1, 2, 68–73.

Balk, D.E. (2001). College student bereavement, scholarship, and the university: A call for university engagement. *Death Studies*, 25, 67–84.

Cohen, O. & Katz, M. (2015). Grief and growth of bereaved siblings as related to attachment style and flexibility. *Death Studies*, 39, 158–64.

Conger, K. & Little, W. (2010). Sibling relationships during the transition to adulthood. *Child Development Perspectives*, 4, 2, 87–94.

Devita-Raeburn, E. (2004). *The empty room: Surviving the loss of a brother or sister at any age*. New York: Schribner.

Erikson, E.H. (1968). *Identity: Youth and crisis*. New York: W.W. Norton & Company.

Forward, D. & Garlie, N. (2003). Search for new meaning: Adolescent bereavement after the sudden death of a sibling. *Canadian Journal of School Psychology*, 18, 1/2, 23–53.

Gutierrez, I. & Park, C. (2015). Emerging adulthood, evolving worldviews: How life events impact college students' developing belief systems. *Emerging Adulthood*, 3, 2, 85–97.

Lane, J. (2015). Counseling emerging adults in transition: Practical applications of attachment and social support research. *Professional Counsellor*, 5, 1, 30–42.

Lindell, A., Campione-Barr, N., & Greer, K. (2014). Associations between adolescent sibling conflict and relationship quality during the transition to college. *Emerging Adulthood*, 2, 2, 79–91.

Marshall, B. & Davies, B. (2011). Bereavement in children and adults following death of a sibling. In R. Neimeyer, D. Harris, H. Winokuer, & G. Thornton (Eds.), *Grief and bereavement in contemporary society: Bridging research and practice* (pp.107–16). New York: Taylor & Francis.

Packman W., Horsley, H., Davies, B., & Kramer, R. (2006). Sibling bereavement and continuing bonds. *Death Studies*, 30, 817–41.

Servaty-Seib, H. & Taub, D. (2010). Bereavement and college students: The role of counselling psychology. *Counseling Psychologist*, 38, 7, 947–75.

Scharf, M., Shulman, S., & Avigad-Spitz, L. (2005). Sibling relationships in emerging adulthood and in adolescence. *Journal of Adolescent Research*, 20, 1, 64–90.

Schwartz, S., Zamboanga, B., Luyckx, K., Meca, A., & Ritchie, R. (2013). Identity in emerging adulthood: Reviewing the field and looking forward. *Emerging Adulthood*, 1, 2, 96–113.

Summer, R., Burrow, A., & Hill, P. (2015). Identity and purpose as predictors of subjective well-being in emerging adulthood. *Emerging Adulthood*, 3, 1, 46–54.

Whiteman, S., McHale, S., & Crouter, A. (2011). Family relationships from adolescence to early adulthood: Changes in the family system following firstborns leaving home. *Journal of Research on Adolescence*, 21, 461–74.

chapter 10

Making Clinical Sense of Sibling Bereavement
Ordinary People as a Case Study

Simon Shimshon Rubin

The loss of a child at any stage in life is a powerful and catalytic process for the family (Rubin, Malkinson, & Witztum, 2012). The artistic portrayal of family and sibling bereavement in the film *Ordinary People* (Schwary & Redford, 1980) allows for the education of clinicians and the engagement of bereaved siblings and families. Considering a fictional case accessible to all allows for nuanced discussion amongst clinicians and families (Rubin, 2001).

Succinctly, *Ordinary People*, directed by Robert Redford, is based closely on the novel (Guest, 1976). The story revolves around the struggles of 18-year-old Conrad Jarett (Timothy Hutton) who must deal with the young adult's age-appropriate issues of identity consolidation, individuation, self-acceptance, and renegotiation of family ties, at a time when both his individual and the familial "secure base" have been upended. Two factors stand out here. The first is traumatic bereavement. Conrad went sailing with his brother Buck but they capsized and Buck drowned whilst

Conrad was rescued. The second is Conrad's attempted suicide which resulted in his psychiatric hospitalization for four months. He is repeating the 11th grade, while his former classmates are in their final year of school. These two experiences set in motion forces that impact Conrad's parents, Calvin (Donald Sutherland) and Beth (Mary Tyler Moore), as well as the school friends of the boys. Conrad is confused, traumatized, and emotionally lost.

Orienting to the Story with the Two-Track Model of Bereavement

Every significant loss sets in motion a process of adjustment and change. From the perspective of the Two-Track Model of Bereavement (Rubin, 1999; Rubin et al. 2012), the consideration of adjustment and change focuses us on two tracks or domains. The first is biopsychosocial functioning and looks to understand Conrad's strengths and difficulties with particular attention to the adaptive and maladaptive aspects of his day-to-day existence. Along this first track, Conrad's emotional and behavioral functioning indicate that he is having a difficult time generally functioning and modulating his feelings. Emotionally, he is anxious and depressed. Interpersonally, he is unable to reconnect with friends and is relatively isolated. Within his family, he is estranged from his mother and unwilling to share much with his father. He suffers from traumatic flashbacks of the boating accident and the struggle to stay alive. His school work and his athletic abilities have not returned to their pre-loss levels. His suicide attempt following the death was a major breakdown in his management of his emotional homeostasis. From an attachment perspective on his relationships, we would see him as basically insecure in his current relationships with elements of avoidance more predominant and anxiety present as well.

Conrad's attempted suicide and subsequent hospitalization mean that although he is back at school, the return is not an easy one. King and Merchant (2008) indicate that social support and integration, communication with parents, and improved emotion regulation mitigate suicidality. Conrad is socially awkward, limited in his social relationships, unable to communicate with his parents, and having difficulty modulating anxiety and physical reactivity. Former areas of accomplishment, such as academic and athletic success in his school, are now much more difficult for him. All these fall under the rubric of our Track I consideration.

The second focus of interest, Track II in the model, relates to Conrad's past and ongoing relationship with Buck, and how he manages to assimilate and narrate the death story. Buck and Conrad grew up together and formed a strong attachment bond between them. Both were members of the swim team and shared activities and friends. Buck had been the instigator for the fatal outing. Conrad is unable to think about Buck without emotionally overwhelming reactivity to the traumatic nature of the death and the acute pain of loss. From the perspective of Track II, an adaptive response to Buck's death should include the ability to process and hold onto a range of memories of the relationship and to maintain the continuing bond to him.

All losses of significant others are difficult to process. The death of a sibling loss amongst brothers and sisters very close in age pierces their basic sense of security, protection, and safety. The event of his brother's death in the sailing accident, where Conrad was concerned both for his own life and his brother's, meets the criteria for a stressor event sufficient to trigger PTSD (Malkinson, Rubin, & Witztum, 2000). However, the relief at his own survival cannot come without a variety of emotions stimulated by his brother's drowning and the aftermath as the family will never be the same. Guilt at his survival is a cognitive-emotional response, and his dysfunctional extreme "survivor guilt" will need to be addressed at some point so as to allow him to embrace his life and its possibilities while distancing him from suicidal ideation and depression (Malkinson, 2007). These themes are heavily rooted along the organization of the relationship to the deceased brother and the death story, but they also extend to features of the relationship with his parents and friends that we focus on in our consideration of biopsychosocial functioning (Track I).

The Family's Response to Bereavement

From the early scenes to the conclusion of the film, we are exposed to a family system whose members are having trouble meeting and communicating with each other. Overall, Calvin, the well-meaning father, is unsure of how to relate to his son, and unable to assist or mitigate the problematic bond between mother and son. He shares his feeling that he is losing them as well as the sense of family they had shared before the death. From an attachment perspective, we could say that he is showing elements of an anxious attachment, and a dearth of being able to understand the "theory of mind" of himself, his wife, and his son. On Track I, his work is suffering, but it is unclear how much of this is related to the death of Buck, and how much stems from the problems with Conrad and the tensions within the family. On Track II, we see him remembering his children playing together and his intervening, but we are not really treated to very much knowledge of how he thinks about Buck, his relationship with that son, and the nature of his longing and grief experience.

Conrad's mother, Beth, is portrayed as a woman whose need to have matters under control has been severely shaken due to the death of one son and the attempted suicide by the surviving son. A very attractive woman, she is pleased to bask in the social limelight on her terms, but not at all comfortable with loss of face, privacy, or uncontrolled emotion. From an attachment perspective, she appears to be open to relationships, up to a point, with sharing and intimacy aspects that she is less comfortable with. Her defensiveness results in outright avoidance of upsetting matters, and this is part of the estrangement between mother and son, and as the film develops, also a source of distance between the parents.

From the perspective of the Two-Track Model, we would see her initially as a model of high functioning on Track I and she would fall into the category of resilient responders in many conceptualizations of response to loss. She did not manifest a deterioration in biopsychosocial functioning on many of the domains typically assessed following loss. As the story unfolds, however, we would revise our estimation and pay more attention to the rigidity of her emotional responses, her limited range of responsiveness to her husband and son, and the lack of insight she manifests as indicating brittleness and lack of emotional flexibility.

On her relationship to Buck, Track II, there is a great deal of connection. He was the son whose outgoing personality, athletic success, and social standing were gratifying to her. Throughout the film, we see evidence of her connecting with memories of her son, but due to her need to control her emotions, she is unable to share this with those closest to her. The scene where she sits down in Buck's room to gaze at the trophies, memorabilia, and photographs conveys the grief and longing for Buck that she can allow herself in private. Conrad's arrival is disruptive to this private reverie, and she shuts down. Comparing her relationship with Conrad to that of her relationship to Buck, we get a sense of her disappointment, her anger, and her embarrassment at what he has put her through.

On her theory of mind, we do not see curiosity or empathy with Conrad, and a lack of insight or curiosity about her own responses and their meaning for the family system. Her coping style of avoidance of unpleasant material was put to the test during Conrad's hospitalization, and she proved herself unwilling and/or unable to visit him during his weeks of hospitalization. Her mode of emotional regulation is via control and avoidance of the unpleasant. Beth's style of holding onto control is to maintain appearances and not relating or sharing emotion beyond protest when being challenged to move out of her comfort zone.

Within the first 20 minutes, we have met most of the characters, their difficulties, their personal styles, and will watch them evolve. Throughout the film, the psychotherapy is portrayed as the major vehicle for Conrad's increasing opening up to his feelings, disappointments, and moving from constant anxiety and avoidance of change or seeking out what he wants to facing and growing through engagement.

As a matter of foresight as well as hindsight, we should ask the question of when and how to involve the parents (at least) in therapy when a family member has been lost (Rubin & Malkinson, 2001). Meeting with the entire nuclear family can be a valuable way of understanding family-system dynamics, and the impact of the individual grieving styles on the bereavement. In the Jarett family, the responses of each of the family members to the crises of bereavement and the suicide attempt in its aftermath would suggest the value of an initial consultation. Therapy begins with Conrad alone, however, and yet it becomes catalytic for the entire family. After therapy has begun, Calvin will seek out the therapist to "talk about himself" and this will leave Beth even more isolated.

Formulation

Psychotherapeutic intervention for Conrad, and attention to the family communication post-loss are indicated. Conrad as a grieving, traumatized, and confused adolescent/emerging adult is first and foremost in need of a supportive relationship where he can unburden himself and share his overwhelmingly difficult thoughts and feelings. If successful, the formation of such a relationship can help him reach a more secure attachment style. What else should we hope for in therapy? At a minimum, the goals for Conrad on Track I of the Two-Track Model include: reduction of emotional flooding, anxiety, and depression, establishment of better peer relationships, improved communication within the family, assistance with the anxiety triggered by memories of the accident, and greater emotional comfort with his thoughts and feelings. The goals for Conrad on Track II include: the ability to talk about his relationship with Buck more broadly and to access a range of their lives together, the ability to narrate the story of the death without being flooded by unreasonable guilt or too strong negative emotion, and exploration of the ambivalent side of their relationship.

The family struggle to manage life following the death of a son and brother is not working well. Three individual styles of adaptation prove unsuccessful for both the individual and for the family system. Conrad's suicide attempt earlier in the response to loss, and his current attempt to go through the motions of living his life without sharing his inner world leave him vulnerable, isolated, friendless, and adrift. He is repeatedly assaulted by his traumatic memories of the accident and his brother's death – but does not have interest, opportunity, or a relationship that will allow him to talk about this. Beth's desperate attempt to maintain the appearance of normalcy while keeping her grief and longing for Buck in check focus her on control and a shallow range of emotion and connection. Calvin's loss of his first son, his fears for his second son, and his personal style of avoiding confrontation and conflict leave him anxious, preoccupied, and alone. The potential for psychotherapy to begin a process of communication and healing is something we shall look for in the intervention.

Psychotherapy and Authenticity in the Relationship

Conrad contacts Dr. Berger (Judd Hirsch) as part of his post-hospitalization planning. Berger fills the role of a genuine, engaging, and warm person who seeks to reach his adolescent client in an authentic manner. Despite much tension in the initial session, their moments of shared wry humor and connection in the session hint at the possibilities for their work together. Although Berger has an unconventional and quirky style, his caring and support are evident throughout the course of the therapy.

The evolution of the relationship between Dr. Berger and Conrad unfolds over the span of several months. From their earliest tentative human encounter until their emotion-laden engagement around Conrad and Buck's struggle to stay alive, the evolving connection between these two people is striking. In the sessions with Dr. Berger, Conrad has the freedom to explore his emotions, to listen to himself, to discover his anger and disappointment with his father and his mother, and to feel his sense of estrangement from his peers. The freedom and sense of friendship in his relationship with Berger gives him the strength to reach out to his friend (and "sibling" stand-in) from the hospital, Karen, and to his choir mate and romantic interest, Jeannine Pratt.

Connecting to aspects of his authentic and emotionally present self leads Conrad to increasing awareness of his mother's limited ability to be emotionally present for him, his father's emotional ineptitude, and a growing sense of self-worth and power. Rather than suppressing his anger and rage, Conrad becomes more combative at home and with peers and much the freer for it.

Over the course of psychotherapy, Conrad becomes increasingly attuned to the emotional world. His focus on the feelings and motivations of others, the so-called theory of mind, will encompass his parents and himself. In the final climactic encounter, it will expand to include Buck, and allow Conrad a sense of release and emotional relief.

The climax of the film occurs when Conrad telephones Karen to share his positive feelings following his growing involvement with Jeannine – only to discover that Karen has taken her own life. This "sibling" death throws Conrad back into the place where he has been before – unable to forgive himself for surviving when he did not save his brother – and face to face with a guilt that is too hard to bear. With his parents away, staying with grandparents with whom he cannot communicate, he begins to segue into the wrist-cutting process that almost killed him the year before. What is different this time is the relationship and his outreach to his therapist. With Conrad highly emotional, Berger is able to learn from Conrad the trigger for his emotional storm, and links Buck and Karen's deaths – and Conrad's assumption of responsibility for both at various times in the discussion.

Moving from talking about the present to experiencing the accident past as occurring in the present, the opportunity to explore emotions and thoughts heretofore inaccessible arises. When Berger assumes the role of Buck to respond to Conrad's angry accusations in the here and now, a significant and catalytic change occurs. While Conrad shouts at Buck for "screwing around until it's too late" and "I'm supposed to take care of it," Berger/Buck accepts the anger and the unfairness of it all. By the end of the angry outburst and the discussion about Buck and Karen, there is a release from the impossible expectation that Conrad's survival was at the expense of Buck's or that he could/should have saved Karen. Conrad's confrontation with his brother leads him to identify those parts of Buck's personality that placed both of their lives at risk, and of Buck's responsibility for the danger to them both. As this crisis session subsides, the two-person authentic relationship between Conrad and his therapist – couched in the language of "friendship" – allows for the consolidation of the secure interpersonal base needed for Conrad to move forward intrapersonally and interpersonally. Conrad's successful struggles are but one of the significant changes of this family. While Calvin has moved to be more demanding, in touch with his feelings, and more present, Beth has not yet clarified her response to the changes in her husband and son. Emotionally controlled and choosing to take time off from the family, her future remains unknown.

Closing

Ordinary People focuses on sibling and family bereavement in a story that addresses issues relevant for many adult bereaved siblings living with their family of origin. In line with the Two-Track Model of Bereavement (Rubin, 1999), I would encourage clinicians and counselors working with bereaved individuals to a) evaluate the areas of strengths and weaknesses in current biopsychosocial functioning (Track I); b) assemble a full narrative of the pre-loss and current relationship with the deceased along with the story of the death and how it is perceived and integrated by the deceased (Track II); and c) attend to the broader family dynamics (and to consider inviting in the broader family) as part of assessment and intervention considerations that are of particular importance for emerging adults. Our understanding of sibling loss can be enriched by exploring material from film and literature accessible to all. This writer's brief analysis of this "case" is shared to open dialogue and invites multiple perspectives from trainees, therapists, families, and adolescents. Ultimately, discussion of particular portrayals of bereavement allows for the creation of a transitional space for exploration. Bereavement challenges individuals and families, clinicians and the community. Let us talk about these challenges together.

References

Guest, J. (1976). *Ordinary people*. New York: Ballantine.

King, C.A. & Merchant, C.R. (2008). Social and interpersonal factors relating to adolescent suicidality. *Archives of Suicide Research*, 12, 3, 181–96. doi: 10.1080/13811110802101203.

Malkinson, R. (2007). *Cognitive grief therapy: Constructing a rational meaning to life following loss*. New York: W.W. Norton.

Malkinson, R., Rubin, S.S., & Witztum, E. (2000). *Traumatic and nontraumatic loss and bereavement: Clinical theory and practice*. Madison, CT: Psychosocial Press.

Rubin S.S. (1999). The Two-Track Model of Bereavement: Overview, retrospect and prospect. *Death Studies*, 23, 8, 681–714.

Rubin, S.S. (2001). Ethical dilemmas, good intentions and the road to hell: A clinical-ethical perspective on Yalom's depiction of Trotter's therapy. *Psychiatry*, 64, 2, 146–57.

Rubin, S.S. & Malkinson, R. (2001). Parental response to child loss across the life-cycle. In M. Stroebe, R. Hansson, W. Stroebe, & H. Schut (Eds.), *Handbook of bereavement research*. Washington, DC: American Psychological Association.

Rubin, S.S., Malkinson, R., & Witztum, E. (2012). *Working with the bereaved: Multiple lenses on loss and mourning*. New York: Routledge.

Schwary, R.L. (Producer) & Redford, R. (Director) (1980). *Ordinary People*. USA: Paramount.

chapter 11

The Happiness of Moving Forward
Sibling Suicide Loss 20 Years Later

Michelle L. Rusk

When I married in June 2015, I was faced with a decision of how to handle the deaths of my younger sister and both my parents. My sister Denise had died in 1993, just a few weeks before her 18th birthday, my dad in 2006, and my mom in spring 2015. At first I thought I would leave the first pew empty and lay flowers for each of them. However, I realized that I needed to focus on what I still had, not what was missing from my life. And that is much how I have approached the loss of half my family. Instead of leaving the first pew empty, I filled it with the people I call family.

When my sister died, I was 21 and a college student. I didn't feel as if my world had ended so much as I just couldn't believe that my sister, who I thought valued life so much, would end her life. But as someone who has held onto a dream of becoming a published writer since I was 6 years old, I couldn't relate to her pain.

While we shared a room for ten years and she knew more about me than anyone else, we were vastly different people. My dreams always kept me going and she was my biggest supporter despite the sibling rivalry that we endured, with me even putting tape down to separate our halves in the room. I detested that she was messy and that I had to share a room with my younger sister.

As I continued through my life after her death, everything was different and I found myself needing to make sense of what I had been through but also looking for a way to help others in ways that weren't available for my own experience. What began with my first book, *Do They Have Bad Days in Heaven? Surviving the Suicide Loss of a Sibling* (Linn-Gust, 2001), eventually led to more experiences and opportunities: speaking around the world, becoming president of the American Association of Suicidology (AAS), getting a doctorate in family studies, and working with Native American populations in New Mexico where I made my home following my master's degree from the University of New Mexico. Then there were several more books about coping with suicide loss.

Around 2010 I began to realize that I had changed. I felt like one of those aging country singers still singing the same songs that made them famous in their teens even though they were now in their 40s. I had a sense that I had done what I was supposed to do for the field and it was time for me to start other projects. And in all this, having always felt my sister by my side following her death, I could see her saying, "I appreciate all you've done for sibling survivors around the world but don't forget who you are, who you were before I died, and what's most important to you."

At the same time I stepped into my presidency of AAS, my first fiction novel was published, *The Australian Pen Pal* (Linn-Gust, 2011). And in this time, I began to see that the road was not unfolding as I thought it would. When Denise died, someone told me that I would always be the same Michelle I was before she died. I was insistent (which is documented in *Bad Days in Heaven*) that that Michelle was gone, never to return. This person said, "You'll always be the same Michelle. You'll like the same things and do the same things." I thought it was a joke. After all, he hadn't lost a sibling, especially one to suicide. He had no idea what I was going through. But he was right. In August 2011, a surfing lesson confirmed it. I always loved surfing but as a girl growing up in the late 1980s it wasn't something that girls did. And living in Illinois didn't provide many opportunities to do it. Instead, I admired it from afar.

In those same years, I also developed a sense of style that revolved around wearing bright colors and Benetton. I love wearing skirts and I always had my hair cut in some funky asymmetrical 80s way. As I started college though none of this was important. It was almost as if life was preparing me for a new road and when my sister died, I had already begun to travel on it without realizing what was happening.

Yet all these years after her death, I found myself returning to that person. I think of it as Michelle 2.0, a new improved version. When I was speaking and other people noticed my bright color dresses, I began to see the connection to the Michelle of all those years ago. I also saw that running track and cross country had prepared me for grief. I had coping skills that many people didn't possess. My years of competitive running, time spent motivating myself, taught me how to process grief, although in a different form. In times when I thought I couldn't push anymore, I reached inside myself and did, just as I would do later when I coped with Denise's death. These lessons took form in my book *Conversations with the Water: A Memoir of Cultivating Hope* (Linn-Gust, 2012), what I call the bookend to *Bad Days in Heaven* and my memories of water with my sister woven with surfing lessons and a divorce that same year.

As the suicide part of my life began to take a lesser role, I found myself working with separated and divorced women through the Catholic Church, helping them find hope again. I also gained a new perspective regarding my faith and the importance of prayer. Each part of my life was teaching me something that I could use to help others. I realized that I was taken down roads and taught lessons that I could pass onto people struggling with many of the same challenges I was.

It's hard for me not to think about how in many ways we were a family of four because my older brother and sister are at least six years older than me. Many of my memories of my family are of the four of us because Brian and Karen had graduated, were working, were out in the world with their friends. Instead it was the four of us who took trips together. I remember sitting in the kitchen late one afternoon near the end of the school year when I was in high school. A storm came over us and we were simply...together.

But I realize their deaths freed me from the past. I have the memories, I carry them with me, but I am no longer bound to them. And that meant at the time of my marriage it was also time to let go of my last name. I no longer needed to be Michelle Linn-Gust. I wasn't changing my name because I am embarrassed by my past or because I want to be someone new. Instead, becoming Michelle L. Rusk was about realizing I didn't have to fear losing my past or who I was. It was about filling the pew in the church with the people who are alive in my life while knowing my parents and my sister were watching from a front row in heaven.

References

Linn-Gust, M. (2001). *Do They Have Bad Days in Heaven? Surviving the Suicide Loss of a Sibling*. Atlanta, GA: Bolton Press.
Linn-Gust, M. (2011). *The Australian Pen Pal*. Albuquerque, NM: Chellehead Works.
Linn-Gust, M. (2012). *Conversations with the Water: A Memoir of Cultivating Hope*. Albuquerque, NM: Chellehead Works.

chapter 12

Brother And Sister Always

Rayna Vaught Godfrey

Colored leaves fluttered along the ground as students scurried about, preparing for midterms. Nothing in the crisp evening air on the college campus indicated that something was not right. Even when my friend stopped by my tutoring job to tell me people were looking for me, it didn't occur to me that this would turn out to be the darkest day of my 20-year-old existence.

As I left work, two sorority sisters came running up, "You've got to come back to the house right away!" they ordered in bursts between gasps, trying to catch their breath. "I'm going there now. What's going on?" I asked, shrouded in a cloud of unknowing. They both looked at me intensely, with faces I couldn't discern, and said "Just come on!" I trailed after them, walking as fast as I could, asking again, "What is it?" But they wouldn't answer. One word popped into my head at that moment: Wesley. Something was wrong with my 16-year-old brother and best friend. He was sick. He was hurt. He had run away. I never thought that he might be dead. I entered the sorority house and saw several family members, including my mother and father who were divorced and avoided one another as much as possible. I looked at the semi-circle of faces and knew someone was missing, but my brain wouldn't register who it was. My mother and father encircled me in their arms. "Mom, Dad, what's wrong?" I barely managed to whisper. In echoing pain my dad replied, "We've lost Wes." He had been killed in a car accident earlier that afternoon, dying instantly when his car slammed sideways into a tree.

My parents held me while I screamed, my knees buckling under the weight of this horrific news. I couldn't comprehend it. Wes was dead? My only sibling was gone? We had certainly had our share of normal sibling rivalry in childhood, but we had grown to be true companions. We enjoyed one another's company, reveled in the same sense of humor. We were attuned to the other's needs and connected to the other's pulse of life. We shared in triumph and sorrow. Wes was quiet but fierce in the way that he loved me. His brown eyes would light up at seeing me, his face breaking into a boyish grin. He was good-natured and even-tempered; sensitive and patient. He made me laugh. He was my co-conspirator, my friend, my confidant. With him I felt safe, even in the midst of the storm of adolescence and divorce and family tragedies. I could not imagine a life without him. Yet I was thrown into such a life with no warning.

It has been 25 years since the world as I knew it changed in an instant. The life that I once could not imagine became the life that I have lived. Actually, these 25 years have not been without Wes. He hasn't been here physically, of course. I cannot call my brother and laugh with him about something. I do not have the pleasure of seeing him and sharing in his pursuits. I can't hear him play the saxophone or delight in a warm hug. But Wes is still a constant presence in my life. A day does not go by that I do not think of him or feel him with me in some way. I wonder what he would say or I instinctively know how he would react. "Wes would love this! That would make him laugh! We would roll our eyes at that!" Sometimes I page through a well-worn memory of us together or I remember something in a given moment that connects me to him. I often think of him in the context of my work as a psychologist specializing in grief and loss. Thoughts of him flow through my stream of consciousness, as natural as breathing. I feel a sense of security and well-being that emanates from him. His presence is warm and nurturing, a loving current of energy that surrounds me daily. I'm not always aware of this energy, but I've learned over time that tapping into it is as simple as getting quiet and focusing on it. Wes is always near.

In the first few years, thinking of him could release waves of sadness. The well of piercing grief seemed infinite then. There are still times I feel sad, times I miss him like mad and ache to be able to see him or get an email from him. I will never stop trying to dream into existence the reality I once knew. Sadness is less frequent and less intense, though. It doesn't overwhelm me or derail me anymore. I have been a bereaved sibling longer than not; grief is familiar and tender. It is woven into the fabric of my life, stitched with enduring love.

The night before Wes died, we had talked on the phone, sharing news, ideas, and advice. We ended the call as we always did, saying, "I love you! I love you, too!" Those were the last words we ever said to one another, a touchstone to remind me of how connected we were when he was alive.

From this touchstone, I have found many ways to connect with him, to experience his presence, to continue our bond. My brother remains one of the most significant relationships in my life.

Therapy helped me explore ways of fostering this relationship. I didn't go to therapy until seven years after Wes died and I didn't go to deal with grief specifically. I was in graduate school and felt I needed to do my own time on the couch if I were to be a good psychologist. I didn't realize going into it how helpful it would be to me in my grief and how powerfully it would feed my connection to my brother. I didn't work through any steps or stages; there were no tasks to complete, no grief "work." I simply told my story. I didn't talk about Wes every session; there were other issues to cover, such as the stress of graduate school. When I did talk about him, my therapist listened. She validated the importance of my relationship with Wes. She understood that he was not *just* my brother, as so many people had said to me in trying to minimize my grief. She created a safe place for me to express my grief and integrate the loss into a new narrative.

"This might sound weird," I said to her as the eighth anniversary of Wes' death approached, "but I anticipate the day almost like it's Christmas. It's the one day that I have permission to grieve." She nodded in understanding and said, "Maybe you could come up with a way to celebrate this year." This had never occurred to me and I loved the idea. My husband and I went to a nearby national park for the day. My brother loved the outdoors and doing something in nature seemed the perfect place to celebrate him. As we drove through the park toward the hiking trail, I kept seeing a flash of brilliant turquoise in the trees. "Look at that exquisite bird!" I exclaimed. "It's so beautiful! I have never seen anything like it!" I delighted each time I saw it flitting through the branches, following us along the road. On our hike, before we lit a candle in honor of Wes, I heard squawking and turned to see the indigo and turquoise bird flying straight toward me, at eye level. Our gazes locked and I stood perfectly still, holding my breath. The bird came within inches of me and swooshed upward at the last minute, fanning my face with air from its wings. My heart soared with joy: Wesley! From then on, I called the stellar jay the "Wesley bird." I continue to use rituals to connect with Wes, to honor him, and to experience him in extraordinary ways.

My new narrative expanded my understanding of who I was and who I wanted to be. I focused my doctoral research on sibling loss in adulthood. I presented at conferences and taught graduate courses on grief and loss. I realized Wes could have an impact from beyond the grave. Together, we could help others who were grieving. There could be some meaning in his death.

More than his death and my grief, the hallmark of my experience has been his continued presence in my life. Our narrative encompasses how we remain connected and how our sibling bond never wavers. We are brother and sister still. We are brother and sister always.

PART IV

Adulthood (31–59)

chapter 13

Sibling Loss in Adulthood
Narrative Reflections

Brenda J. Marshall

WILLIAMS, Anna
    In loving memory of our dear sister who departed nineteen years ago today. We think of you often and remember your kind ways. You are always with us.
    Missed with such deep sadness.
    Alan, Debbie & Michael

(Obituary in newspaper)

I was pulling out place cards for Easter the other day and there are these Easter hats I'd made for Brian, his wife, and each of his three kids...I thought, come on...throw them out. But I put them back in the box. I don't know why I want to keep them. I just think that every Easter I'd like to open up the box and see them...and remember there was a time when we had Easters together.

(Karen, bereaved sibling)

> We are holding a memorial service this evening. If you would like your loved one to be honored at this event, please complete the information below and submit your card in the drop box.
>
> Please remember my _____ (Mother, Father, Husband, Wife, Spouse, Significant Other, Son, Daughter, Grandmother, Grandfather, Friend, Other....)
>
> My loved one's name is: _____

Figure 13.1 Memorial card

Each of the above represents a story in motion. First there is a memoriam placed for a sister on the 19th anniversary of her death. The words are simple but the gesture powerful. One wonders if this is a ritual that has been repeated annually. Second are the words of Karen, a bereaved sibling whose brother died suddenly in a house fire. More than 8 years after his death, she holds onto a box that reminds her of how her family used to be. Her poignant words point to some of the unique layers of loss presented when a sibling dies in adulthood. She misses her brother. And she misses her brother's children, now no longer part of family gatherings. Lastly, there is a memorial card – one given to me at a conference where I was speaking about sibling loss (Figure 13.1). A careful reading of the card reveals something very telling. "Siblings" are absent. And for me, also a bereaved sibling, it is the juxtaposition of this absence with the deep sadness expressed by so many bereaved siblings (Berman, 2009; Ellis, 1993; Wray, 2003) that speaks to the very essence of this loss. We are simply not on the card – of society, researchers, clinicians, friends, or support organizations. We are the forgotten grievers (Marshall, 2009; Rostila, Saarela, & Kawachi, 2012) and it is this "outsiderness" that colors our experiences so deeply.

To frame this conversation, I begin with a brief review of what we know of the adult sibling relationship in life. Next, using themes culled from my own research (Marshall, 2009, 2013) we'll look at the features of sibling bereavement that are unique to this age group. And finally, I'll close with some thoughts on what we've learned about sibling loss in this age group and where we might focus future efforts.

Sibling Relationships in Adulthood

"If not for death, they [siblings] would be with us longer than anyone else on earth" (Godfrey, 2006, p. 7). Longer than parents, spouses, or friends, the relationship one has with a sibling has the potential to be lifelong. Siblings know each other in ways friends and other blood relatives do not. We have shared bedrooms, bathrooms, holidays, school days, family milestones, meals, and a way of growing up that people outside the family do not understand. It is unique in its longevity, intimacy, historical connections, and the nature of how it is formed (Cicerelli, 1995). And unlike selecting a friend, spouse, or life partner, a sibling simply arrives and there is no choice but to be in a relationship.

Goetting (1986) provides a framework for understanding this relationship from a life-cycle perspective. Within early and middle adulthood, the second life-cycle stage, she identified three major developmental tasks. First was companionship and emotional support as siblings related to one another as friends and confidantes while building their own families and careers. A second major task was cooperation in the care of elderly parents, noting that it was most often in this age group where siblings came together to deal with the changing support needs of their aging parents. And finally, aid and direct services. Siblings come to one another's assistance during illness, marital breakups, and often to assist with child rearing.

Connidis' (1992) study of the *adult sibling tie* offers similar findings. For the majority of those in her study, siblings remained an important and valued connection throughout life. And, though there were times when their frequency of contact ebbed and flowed, the closeness of the sibling tie was something they felt could be rekindled or mobilized when needed. "Siblings remain lifelong parts of most adults' social networks" (White, 2001, p. 566). White noted that the average adult had contact with a sibling once or twice a month for 60 or 70 years *after* leaving home. Nearly two thirds (White & Riedmann, 1992) considered at least one sibling to be among their closest friends and about 30 percent would call upon a sibling first for emergency help. Fast forward to today where social media makes staying in touch even easier, the potential for even more frequent contact and connection with siblings is evident.

When an Adult Sibling Dies

Given the importance of this relationship and the ongoing nature of its development (Cicerelli, 1991, 1995), the irony of the memorial card that opens this chapter is stark. As Wright (2015) notes "adult sibling loss has only recently become a topic of research interest" (p. 2). Indeed some of the more detailed accounts of the impact of *adult* sibling death come from the trade literature (Berman, 2009; McCurry, 2001; Wray, 2003). Although there is newer research connecting sibling bereavement with adverse health consequences for adult surviving siblings (Rostila et al., 2012, 2013, 2014), prior to this, studies on this specific age group were few (Eaves, McQuiston, & Shandor, 2005; Pretorius, Halstead-Cleak, & Morgan, 2010; Robinson, 2001).

A theme that runs through all of these studies and accounts is the lack of recognition and support siblings receive after their brother or sister's death. Indeed, it was my own experience with "outsiderness" and "silencing" that led me to the research (Marshall, 2009, 2013) that frames this chapter. Using a narrative approach (Clandinin & Connelly, 2000), I worked with 3 bereaved siblings; Rena (sister Cookie), Karen (brother Brian), and Catherine (brother James) over an 8-month period to uncover their experiences of bereavement. We completed more than 35 hours of interviews which were used to create a series of stories and short vignettes about each woman's experience. At the time of their siblings' deaths, each was married, had children, and had busy careers. And while their experiences of loss were unique, there are common themes that run across their stories to which I'll now turn. I invite the reader to consider these themes against the backdrop of "outsiderness" noted earlier.

Profound Loss

> It's a hole and you just can't fill it. You move on, you figure out ways to [go on] but it's always going to be there…
>
> (Catherine)

> I don't remember anything. I don't remember taking pictures at Christmas, I don't remember Christmas shopping. I was just beside myself…It was the loneliest time of my life.
>
> (Karen)

> And sometimes I see sisters together having lunch or they're going shopping together or they're walking together or even in the hospital, sisters are with each other at appointments when they're elderly and that was the way it was supposed to be.
>
> (Rena)

"'You can never fill the gap that's left': Expressions of brotherly loss in the Second World War" is the title of Maynard's (2015, p. 57) review of the personal accounts of men whose brothers died. More than 75 years ago, a sibling gave voice to a feeling that resonates today. For Rena, Karen, and Catherine, their sibling's death was devastating. In the early days, they missed the phone calls, check-ins, and just the feeling of connection they had to their brother or sister. "I would come home from work and want to pick up the phone and call her and suddenly I'd catch myself" (Rena). Karen refused to believe the human remains found in her brother's burnt-out home were his. Instead, she convinced herself he was simply away on a trip, delaying funeral plans for several weeks, hopeful he'd soon return. All three women spoke in detail of the incredible pain of loss and how difficult it was to continue with their daily lives. And the lack of understanding and acknowledgment from both family and friends heightened their grief.

Rosenblatt (1996, p. 50) says, for most people, "all that is lost is not realized at one point in time. There is, instead, a sequence, perhaps extending over one's lifetime, of new losses or new realizations of loss." The loss of a future together was a particularly powerful and painful theme repeated many times. "We were supposed to grow old together" was something I heard from each. Goetting (1986) notes that two key developmental tasks of siblingship in later life are "companionship and emotional support" and "shared reminiscence and perceptual validation" (p. 712). For these women, the sad recognition of their lost shared future with their sibling was as painful as their absence on a daily basis. For Karen, the death of her father and the birth of Brian's grandchild brought new layers of sadness. She wished her brother was present, knowing that he would have stood with her to present the eulogy. She felt sad imagining how excited Brian would be to have a grandchild. For Rena, her ordination as a rabbi was a key moment she missed sharing with her sister. For Catherine, her daughter's wedding was bittersweet. James and his niece had a special connection and his absence on such a happy occasion was difficult. This knowledge of missing out on "what should have been," both happy and sad, was something each felt acutely and was a reminder of how intertwined their lives once were.

Protect My Parents

> I would kind of tread lightly because I was afraid of upsetting her. That if I would bring it up...she would be upset. On the other hand, sometimes, I wanted us to just be able to talk about her...
>
> (Rena)

> The funeral place...had a tree planting for everybody that had passed away in that year...My mom didn't want to go. She couldn't deal with it. So we never went...
>
> (Catherine)

> Here's a cassette tape of the funeral. And you know what's funny? Is that my mom keeps asking for it and I keep saying no. I won't give it to her...I just don't want her to be playing it over and over...it's almost like I think I'm protecting her.
>
> (Karen)

Just as young children (Davies, 1999) want to alleviate their parents' despair, adult children do as well. Buckle and Fleming (2010) noted parents experienced "almost a role reversal or a blurring of the boundaries between parent and child" (p. 99). Said one parent of her surviving daughter, "She tries to protect us, which means not saying anything" (p. 100). One of the challenges adult siblings face is they have both the cognitive and emotional ability to glimpse the magnitude of their parents' grief. Many siblings have children themselves, and can imagine the pain.

Protecting parents takes different forms. Many try to fill the gap created by the deceased sibling through their actions. Judy, a bereaved sibling (Marshall, 2012), described how after her two sisters died, she uprooted her life to move closer to her parents. "I felt like I had to be there to bring sunshine to my parents' lives...I was the daughter for three" (p. 14). Karen, Rena, and Catherine also took on more extensive roles in their parents' lives, visiting more frequently, taking on additional tasks, all designed to "fill the gap" left by their sibling. And they also tried to protect their parents with their silence. If their parents couldn't speak of their deceased child, they wouldn't speak of their sibling.

This need to try and make things better for parents comes at a cost for the surviving adult children. It can create a "delayed mourning" (Pretorius et al., 2010, p. 2) and for some, a feeling of resentment at being left to sort through painful emotions alone. As one described, she and her surviving brother became the de facto parents of the family after her sibling's death. Ford Sori (2003) notes "my mother became wrapped permanently in a dark cloak of grief, closed off and unable to enjoy life, so I really lost my mother as well as my sister...I took on the role of maintaining all the family rituals" (p. 307).

Changed Family

> So that was a huge shift because when the kids got together, there was 7 kids and then we went down to 4...
>
> (Karen)

> So she was really the hub. She was really central to the family. And sometimes that whole matrix that gets rearranged doesn't quite work and that's exactly what happened in our case. It just didn't quite work.
>
> (Rena)

> It's really difficult to get past that bitterness of wanting everybody to grieve the way that you're grieving and interpret – and trying not to interpret it as, well, I'm grieving more than you, I must have loved him more...
> (Catherine)

Pretorius et al. (2010) studied the experiences of 3 young adults (24–39 years) whose siblings were murdered. "Sibling grief appears to be compounded by the actual loss of a sibling, the resultant experiential loss of their significant parent and the fragmentation of their family as they knew it" (p. 10). This notion of family fragmentation resonates. For Karen, the loss of contact with her brother's wife and children was especially difficult. They spent years celebrating family milestones together and suddenly the entire family was absent. For Rena, she continued contact with adult nieces and nephews for several years but gradually, over time, it faded. The image of a "ghost family" now sitting at the table during holiday functions comes to mind. Consistent with developmental milestones in this age group, the role of aunt and uncle are all part of a normal trajectory. Bereaved adult siblings often now contend with the added loss of this role and their connection to nieces and nephews – another layer that is unlikely to be acknowledged.

And finally, there is fragmentation amongst surviving siblings. There is a "holding back" of information and reluctance to dive too deeply into the loss out of a perceived need to protect others from more pain. Van Riper's (1997) paper about the death of her sister 36 years prior describes the experience so well. "Over the years, our family never really talked much about the events surrounding Shelley's death...Maybe it just hurt too much to talk about it. Maybe we didn't want to make each other cry" (p. 587). Moss and Raz (2001) encountered a similar phenomenon in their analysis of a therapy group. Three surviving sisters of a murdered sibling often attended the group together. One week when the eldest sister was present without her younger siblings, she shared graphic details about her sister's death that she'd never shared with her family members. She'd always kept them to herself "to protect everyone from this horrible description" (p. 399).

Our families are not well equipped to deal with such trauma and so often each member attempts to deal with the pain on their own. Neither Rena nor Karen discussed their siblings' deaths with surviving brothers and sisters. They never shared their pain or talked through the experience. In fact both acknowledged that the most they'd ever talked about their siblings' lives and deaths was in our interviews.

Concluding Remarks

The death of a sibling in adulthood represents the loss of a relationship at a pivotal moment in its development. By this age, a sibling is often a friend and a key part of our support network. Our children are cousins and we've added the role of aunt or uncle to our lives. It is our brothers and sisters who step in for us during health crises and marital breakups and stand with us as our children marry and move on with their lives. And, we come together to make difficult decisions about the care of our aging parents. Siblings expect to grow old together and face what the next years bring with someone who knows what "growing up" was like in our family. They are likely the only person who has known us our entire life. When a sibling dies in adulthood, it is an "off-time" loss which is further amplified by the lack of support and recognition siblings feel from others. I believe our greatest opportunity to make a difference lies in education. Making adult sibling loss part of the curriculum in schools, hospitals, and community support organizations would bring it into the conversation in a way that it currently is not. And this alone would make a tremendous difference for bereaved siblings.

References

Berman, C. (2009). *When a brother or sister dies: Looking back, moving forward.* Westport, CT: Praeger Publishers.

Buckle, J.L. & Fleming, S.J. (2011). *Parenting after the death of a child: A practitioner's guide.* New York: Routledge.

Cicirelli, V. (1991). Sibling relationships in adulthood. *Marriage and Family Review*, 16, 3–4, 291–310.

Cicirelli, V. (1995). *Sibling relationships across the life span.* New York: Plenum Press.

Clandinin, D.J. & Connelly, F.M. (2000). *Narrative inquiry: Experience and story in qualitative research.* San Francisco, CA: Jossey-Bass.

Connidis, I.A. (1992). Life transitions and the adult sibling tie: A qualitative study. *Journal of Marriage and the Family*, 54, 4, 972–82.

Davies, B. (1999). *Shadows in the sun: The experiences of sibling bereavement in childhood.* Philadelphia, PA: Brunner/Mazel.

Eaves, Y., McQuiston, C., & Shandor, M. (2005). Coming to terms with adult sibling grief. *Journal of Hospice and Palliative Nursing*, 7, 3, 139–49.

Ellis, C. (1993). There are survivors: Telling a story of sudden death. *Sociological Quarterly*, 34, 4, 711–30.

Ford Sori, C. (2003). Legacy of loss and "re-membering." *Family Journal: Counselling and Therapy for Couples and Families*, 11, 3, 306–8.

Godfrey, R.V. (2006). Losing a sibling in adulthood. *Forum*, 32, 1, 6–7.

Goetting, A. (1986). The developmental tasks of siblingship over the life cycle. *Journal of Marriage and the Family*, 48, 4, 703–14.

Marshall, B.J. (2009). Silent Grief: Narratives of bereaved adult siblings. PhD thesis, University of Toronto, Toronto. Retrieved from http://hdl.handle.net/1807/19153.

Marshall, B.J. (2012). Adult sibling loss: Stories revised through art. Paper presented at the annual conference of the Association of Death Education and Counselling, March, Atlanta.

Marshall, B.J. (2013). *Adult Sibling Loss: Stories, Reflections and Ripples.* New York: Baywood Publishing.

Maynard, L. (2015). "You can never fill the gap that's left": Expressions of brotherly loss in the Second World War. *Journal of War and Culture Studies*, 8, 1, 57–71.

McCurry, A. (2001). *Letters to Sara: The agony of adult sibling loss.* New York: 1st Books.

Moss, E. & Raz, A. (2001). The ones left behind: A siblings' bereavement group. *Group Analysis*, 34, 395–407.

Pretorius, G., Halstead-Cleak, J., & Morgan, B. (2010). The lived experience of losing a sibling through murder. *Indo-Pacific Journal of Phenomenology*, 10, 1, 1–13.

Robinson, L. (2001). Adult grief reactions following a sibling's death from AIDS. *Journal of the Association of Nurses in Aids Care*, 12, 2, 25–32.

Rosenblatt, P.C. (1996). Grief that does not end. In D. Klass, P.R. Silverman, & S.L. Nickman (Eds.), *Continuing bonds: New understandings of grief* (pp. 45–58). Philadelphia, PA: Taylor & Francis.

Rostila, M., Saarela, J., & Kawachi, I. (2012). The forgotten griever: A nationwide follow-up study of mortality subsequent to the death of a sibling. *American Journal of Epidemiology*, 176, 4, 338–46.

Rostila, M., Saarela, J., & Kawachi, I. (2013). Suicide following the death of a sibling: A nationwide follow-up study from Sweden. *BMJ Open*, 3, 4. doi: 10.1136/bmjopen-2013–002618.

Rostila, M., Saarela, J., & Kawachi, I. (2014). "The psychological skeleton in the closet": Mortality after a sibling's suicide. *Social Psychiatry and Psychiatric Epidemiology*, 49, 6, 919–27. doi: 10.1007/s00127-013-0780-1.

Van Riper, M. (1997). Death of a sibling: Five sisters, five stories. *Pediatric Nursing*, 23, 6, 587–93.

White, L. (2001). Sibling relationships over the life course: A panel analysis. *Journal of Marriage and the Family*, 63, 2, 555–68.

White, L. & Riedmann, A. (1992). Ties among adult siblings. *Social Forces*, 71, 85–102.

Wray, T.J. (2003). *Surviving the death of a sibling: Living through grief when an adult brother or sister dies.* New York: Three Rivers Press.

Wright, P.M. (2015). Adult sibling bereavement: Influences, consequences, and interventions. *Illness, Crisis, and Loss*. doi: 10.1177/1054137315587631.

While the World Mourned a Hero, I Mourned My Murdered Brother
The Case of Barbara, a Bereaved 9/11 Sibling

Cori Bussolari and Heidi Horsley

Background

In the United States today, most siblings will spend 80–100 percent of their lifespans with each other (Packman, Horsley, Davies, & Kramer, 2006). This is more time than they spend with parents, friends, or teachers (Kim, McHale, Osgood, & Crouter, 1996). Consistent with what we know about sibling loss in childhood, the death of a sibling in adulthood is significant and life changing (Marshall & Davies, 2011), a primary source of bereavement in very old age (Lalive d'Epinay, Cavalli, & Guillet, 2010), and may also impact mortality and health (Rostila, Saarela, & Kawachi, 2012).

Although the sibling relationship is a rich and powerful one, research regarding the impact of sibling loss in adulthood is minimal. Given the importance of this specific relationship, with approximately 2 million people becoming bereaved siblings each year (Hogan & DeSantis, 1992), it is ironic that sibling death is one of the *least* investigated and understood adult crisis experiences (Hogan & DeSantis, 1992; Packman et al., 2006). Cicirelli (1991) has asserted that attachment, or the "lasting psychological connectedness between human beings" (Bowlby, 1969, p. 194) can be observed beyond the parent–child relationship to the siblings throughout old age. In fact, the sibling relationship is quite close to the mother–child relationship (Gold, 1989) and the loss can be shattering. It is clear that a sibling death at *any* age has a profound impact on surviving siblings.

Similar to what younger children face, bereaved adult siblings must also deal with shifting family dynamics. Their parents are often reluctant or unable to speak of their deceased child (Marshall, 2013) and can be emotionally unavailable. Relationships with their other siblings may also be strained. New relationships with their deceased siblings' surviving family must be negotiated which becomes even more complex if and when the surviving partner remarries (B. Marshall, personal communication, February 8, 2013).

Consequently, bereaved siblings frequently feel invisible in the aftermath of death, and the term "forgotten bereaved" has been used to describe this particular and challenging experience (Wray, 2003). Too often, their pain is overlooked or minimized (Horsley & Horsley, 2007). A key struggle bereaved adult siblings face is a lack of societal recognition for the significance of their loss. In fact, most community-based bereavement support organizations focus their support on other losses, such as the death of a child, parent, or partner, with very few offering adult sibling loss groups (Marshall, 2013).

The term "Disenfranchised Grief" is used to describe a situation where the loss is not readily acknowledged (Doka, 1989) and exemplifies many bereaved siblings' experiences. This has never been more apparent than among those people who traumatically lost siblings in the 9/11 World Trade Center attack. It is hard to imagine that the bereaved siblings were, in fact, not even given permission to read the names of their deceased loved ones at the World Trade Center Memorial Commemoration until 2005. Clearly, the public did not consider their grief to be as valuable.

In our clinical experiences working with grief, bereaved siblings have often found their process qualitatively different than other family members because of perceived disenfranchisement and changing roles. Within this chapter, we will discuss the case of Barbara, a bereaved 9/11 sibling, in order to highlight this population's specific grief phenomenology through the lens of her family system and then offer some clinical suggestions.

The Case of Barbara: The Death of the Family Hero

Barbara, a 36-year-old female, initially sought therapy three years after her firefighter brother Joe died when the second tower fell on September 11, 2001. Joe was born only 18 months before Barbara and they grew up in the same working-class New York City neighborhood as her parents and grandparents. He was her only sibling. She and Joe were always very close even though he was considered the "shining light" of their family. Barbara joked, "C'mon! He was the first-born, male, and we are Italian. My parents could only have loved him more if he became a priest."

At the time of his death, Joe was 38 years old. He was married for almost 15 years to his "college sweetheart" and they had three young children. Barbara was briefly married and immediately divorced after her daughter was born. Barbara reported that they were "very close" to her brother's family, spending at least one day a week with them. On September 11, Joe was not supposed to be working, but picked up an extra few shifts that week. He ended up being one of the earliest responders. According to Barbara, "He would have gone no matter what. He was just that kind of guy."

Over the course of therapy, several themes related to sibling bereavement emerged.

Disenfranchised Grief: "I am not as important"

Barbara was "feeling sad, angry and invisible" because she had not been offered the supportive mental health services like her parents and brother's family. According to Barbara, "Everything was given to everyone else; I was just sort of left out." She wasn't sure about seeking help for herself because she began to believe that she was undeserving, noting with sarcasm, "After all, I was *just* his sister."

Even though she was initially inundated by media, Barbara believed that her loss wasn't considered valuable. Her grief was trumped by the loss of her "parents' child" or "sister-in-law's husband." She minimized her feelings, stating, "I began to give people what they wanted and just told them I was fine when I really wasn't." This deliberate effort by surviving siblings to keep their feelings secret to protect their parents has been frequently reported as "prohibited mourning" (Rosen, 1985). She commented, "No one ever told me that my feelings also counted" and she frequently heard, "Be strong for your parents" or "This must have been really hard for your parents."

Survivor Guilt: "The wrong child died"

Drawing upon Bowenian theory, Carter and McGoldrick (1980) noted that families engage in a "family projection process" (p. 227), which influences the importance that each child has within the emotional functioning of the family. In the context of Barbara's family, it was understood that Joe was "special." Research (Flomenhaft, 2007) suggests that several bereaved 9/11 siblings acknowledged their deceased siblings as their parents' favorite children due to their achievements and leadership within the family. Barbara's public and familial narrative was that "Joe was a first responder who ran into the building to save people when everyone was running out," adding, "The family hero had died. You can't compete with that." Barbara felt like she had done "nothing" with her life compared to her brother and believed that it would be easier for her parents (and for others) had she died instead of him. Joe was a true extension of his parents' future hopes and expectations, and his loss reverberated throughout the family.

Double Losses: "I was left behind"

Barbara didn't just experience the loss of her brother, but she also experienced secondary losses such as the loss of her parents, sister-in-law, and brother's children. Barbara realized that her parents' lives had been forever altered and recognized how difficult it was for them to lose a child. At the same time, they began to pull away from her, wanting to spend increasingly more time with Joe's family. Barbara reflected, "I think it was their way of staying connected to my brother, but it's so hard for me."

The term *multigenerational transmission process* is used to describe the intergenerational emotional legacy of families (Kerr, 2003). More specifically, the level of competence an individual develops within his or her family is often informed by both the multigenerational transmission as well as the family projection process. Barbara was always viewed, in her opinion, as having to work harder or not be as talented as her brother. Consequently, Barbara relied upon her family, especially her older brother, for extended support for herself and her daughter.

Barbara's sister-in-law also recently became engaged to another firefighter and Barbara and her daughter began to spend less time with them. Barbara worried that she would not be included in her sister-in-law's new family. Not only had Barbara's brother died, but her immediate and extended family were moving on without her, resulting in secondary and unanticipated relational losses.

Roles

Joe's death created a huge familial and systemic void. Families primarily function through role engagement (Worden, 2009) and alliances (Bowen, 1978). Not only was Joe the oldest, but he was the person all the family relied upon. In her opinion, he was the "one person who really got me." Barbara questioned her "identity" since her brother's death, specifically her roles as sister and daughter. In essence, she lost her one ally and didn't feel capable of connecting with anyone else in the same way. The sibling loss has been shown to be "magnified for those who were now an only child and had no one who shared their history, who could reminisce with them, and validate their family story" (Godfrey, 2002, p. 124).

Barbara felt "lost" within her own emotional framework, especially regarding how she could make meaning around an unreclaimable role. At the same time, within her new role as "only child," she felt the brunt of her parents' grief. Flomenhaft (2007) noted that within a sample of 9/11 bereaved siblings, there was a lack of acknowledgment of their grief as well as increased role demands. Of importance, they felt expected to attend to the profound grief of their parents without concern for their own emotional well-being.

Barbara's biggest concern was the unspoken expectation of taking care of her parents all by herself. Although they were currently spending most of their time with their daughter-in-law, Barbara knew that when their health began to decline, she would have to "step up." According to Barbara, "This was Joe's job," and she was not prepared for this familial role shift.

Getting Real with the Relationship: "My brother wasn't perfect"

Although very close when they were growing up, Barbara and Joe often disagreed or argued, and didn't always see eye to eye. Sibling rivalry is quite natural within most family structures and can include feelings of jealousy, envy, and resentment even in the closest sibling relationships. According to Neubauer (1983), the rivalry emerges from "the competition among siblings for the exclusive or preferred care from the person they share" (p. 326). Barbara admitted to feeling "jealous" of Joe and how "effortlessly he went through life." This has been especially hard for Barbara, given the nature of his death and the very public response. Because Joe was now considered a national hero, she found it very challenging to say anything that *wasn't* positive about her brother who she noted, "could be an absolute shit at times." She also realized that she didn't make a consistent effort to spend more time with him when he was alive, and felt a great deal of guilt over this.

Specific to 9/11 – Trauma/Global Shared Experience: "He was MY brother and I have to share him with everyone"

The very public and global circumstances of her brother's death brought up an array of difficult and situation-specific issues for Barbara. She felt as though there were constant reminders of his death and was also increasingly angered that she had to share her grief. Most striking was Barbara's reaction when the therapist initially tried to empathize with her "loss." She strongly replied, "Loss? What do you mean loss? He wasn't lost, he was murdered." While the loss of a child through violence is readily thought of as the most devastating parental experience, there is only minimal recognition of how this loss affects surviving siblings (Fanos, 1996) or the "co-victims," as they have been described (Spungen, 1998). Of significance, she couldn't accept the way her brother died and the fact that they might never have a body to bury.

Suggestions When Working with Bereaved Siblings

While there are specific experiences unique to those adults whose siblings died on 9/11, our clinical practice has illuminated that most bereaved adult siblings encounter common challenges. Based upon current research and best practices, as well as the authors' clinical experiences, we propose three important strategies for clinicians to best support bereaved siblings with their monumental grief.

1. *Validation of the loss*: It is essential that siblings feel that their grief is important. Barbara experienced a profound sense of loss that reverberated throughout all areas of her life. Yet, whether spoken or not, she felt her loss was "lesser" and disenfranchised. Clinicians are encouraged to listen with compassion and respond without judgment. The surviving sibling often needs to share the story of their relationship with the deceased, but often doesn't have anyone to do this with, especially their family. Barbara learned to ignore and minimize her grief, which caused her great distress. Only through consistent external validation, specifically validating Barbara's considerable grief and concurrent feelings of "otherness," was Barbara finally able to confirm that her feelings and relationship with her brother were valuable. Of importance, she became better able to talk about the reality of their relationship, not just the positive aspects.
2. *Foster continuing bonds*: A major shift within bereavement research and practice focuses upon supporting ongoing connections with the

deceased and, thus, using continuing bonds expressions as a means of coping (Packman et al., 2006). Due to internalized feelings of disenfranchisement and often consequential disengagement with their deceased sibling, it would be helpful for clinicians to find ways for surviving adult siblings to nurture their connection and not separate from the relationship. At one point, Barbara stopped talking about her brother and was reticent to do anything that might imply she was grieving. Over time, however, Barbara displayed additional photos of her brother in her house, and even developed a weekly ritual where she scheduled time to think or write about him. By the time she completed therapy, Barbara had a private memorial where she buried a picture of she and Joe together as children. This helped her create some emotional closure, as his remains were never discovered.

3. *Use a family systems framework*: When doing therapy with bereaved adult siblings, it is often difficult to physically include families of origin. Without this systemic framework, bereaved adult siblings are left to feel isolated and alone, especially regarding their role within the family. Whenever possible, clinicians should include the family system in therapy. Of importance, Barbara's family never actually came to therapy, but we continually talked about them and framed her issues as a "family challenge," which seemed more accurate. This helped her shift from the negative belief that something was wrong with *her* to a place where she could describe her family grief process and the interactions. As she began to differentiate from her family's grief, she was better able to self-validate and make personal meaning around her brother's death. At one point, she even began to spontaneously reach out to her parents and sister-in-law without the need for reciprocation.

References

Bowen, M. (1978). *Family therapy in clinical practice*. New York: Jason Aronson.

Bowlby, J. (1969). *Attachment and loss: Vol. 1. Attachment*. New York: Basic Books.

Carter, E. & McGoldrick, M. (Eds.). (1980). *The family life cycle: A framework for family therapy*. New York: Gardner Press.

Cicirelli, V.G. (1991). Sibling relationships in adulthood. *Marriage and Family Review*, 16, 3–4, 291–310.

Doka, K.J. (Ed.). (1989). *Disenfranchised grief: Recognizing hidden sorrow*. Lexington, MA: Lexington Books.

Fanos, J.H. (1996). *Sibling loss*. Mahwah, NJ: Erlbaum Associates.

Flomenhaft, D. (2007). The forgotten ones: The grief experience of adult siblings of World Trade Center victims. Unpublished doctoral dissertation, New York University School of Social Work, New York.

Godfrey, R.V. (2002). Losing a sibling in adulthood. Unpublished doctoral dissertation, University of Denver, Denver, CO.

Gold, D.T. (1989). Generational solidarity. *American Behavioral Scientist*, 33, 1, 19–32.

Hogan, N. & DeSantis, L. (1992). Adolescent sibling bereavement: An ongoing attachment. *Qualitative Health Research*, 2, 159–77.

Horsley, H. & Horsley, G. (2007). *Teen grief relief: Parenting with understanding, support, and guidance*. Vernon Hills, IL: Rainbow Books, Inc.

Kerr, M.E. (2003). *One family's story: A primer on Bowen theory*. Washington, DC: Bowen Center for the Study of the Family.

Kim, J., McHale, S.M., Osgood, D.W., & Crouter, A.C. (1996). Longitudinal course and family correlates of sibling relationships from childhood through adolescence. *Child Development*, 77, 5.

Lalive d'Epinay, C.J., Cavalli, S., & Guillet, L.A. (2010). Bereavement in very old age: Impact on health and relationships of the loss of a spouse, a child, a sibling, or a close friend. *OMEGA*, 60, 4, 301–25.

Marshall, B. (2013). *Adult sibling loss: Stories, reflections, and ripples*. New York: Baywood.

Marshall, M. & Davies, B. (2011). Bereavement in children and adults following the death of a sibling. In R.A. Neimeyer, D.L. Harris, H.R. Winokuer, & G.F. Thornton (Eds.), *Grief and bereavement in contemporary society: Bridging research and practice* (pp. 107–16). New York: Taylor & Francis.

Neubauer, P.B. (1983). The importance of the sibling experience. *Psychoanalytic Study of the Child*, 38, 325–36.

Packman, W., Horsley, H., Davies, B., & Kramer, R. (2006). Sibling bereavement and continuing bonds. *Death Studies*, 30, 817–41.

Rosen, H. (1985). Prohibitions against mourning in childhood sibling loss. *Omega*, 15, 307–16.

Rostila, M., Saarela, J., & Kawachi, I. (2012). The forgotten griever: A nationwide follow-up of mortality subsequent to the death of a sibling. *American Journal of Epidemiology*, 176, 4, 338–46.

Spungen, D. (1998). *Homicide: The hidden victims*. Thousand Oaks, CA: Sage.

Worden, J.W. (2009). *Grief counselling and grief therapy: A handbook for the mental health practitioner* (4th ed.). New York: Springer.

Wray, T. (2003). *Surviving the Death of a Sibling*. New York: Three Rivers Press.

chapter 15

Honoring Donna

Lyn Prashant

"My sister and my best friend"

My beloved sister Donna S. Brown was a gentle, loving, caring soul. She was my trusted confidant, my witness, my cheerleader, and my best friend. She died September 6, 2002, at age 49. Donna was born three and a half years after me. We were giddy and vulnerable with each other. At only 6 years old I nostalgically remember walking down the street, holding her hand, thinking about how lucky I was to have her as my very own precious sister. A glance into her sparkling onyx-colored eyes affirmed my joy. Donna was always loyal and true. As we matured our commitment and sense of knowing one another deepened.

I'd already been widowed, having lost my young husband, Mark, to cancer at age 36. Then, Donna at 36, received her first diagnosis of breast cancer. The words sent electrifying shock waves through me once again. I remember feelings of disbelief at the sound and implications of the doctor's communication; immediately producing physical sensations of numbness, shortness of breath, dry mouth, and a profound inability to think clearly. Everything felt so ephemeral. Donna's first yearlong debilitating barrage of chemotherapy and radiation put the cancer into remission. Donna's doctors told her at that time that if she stayed cancer free for five years, she would be cured forever. Believing that to be true, she lived fully, freely, and fantastically. She left a confining marriage, sold her house, changed her business card from "hospital based" to "traveling" speech and swallowing evaluation specialist. Accepting temporary assignments all around the USA,

Donna, an animal lover extraordinaire, enjoyed traveling with her devoted German shepherds, mama and son, Molly and Charlie Brown. We'd often rendezvous and camp out under the stars in glorious national parks.

The Reoccurrence

Donna, a graceful woman of few words, was an introvert with beautiful dark eyes. Papa called her gypsy. Nana called her "black-eyed Susie." She told me she became a speech pathologist because it gave her a reason to talk. The reoccurrence of the cancer was diagnosed 11 years later. She was fiercely angry that they lied to her about the "5 year cure theory." Donna felt betrayed by the medical establishment and vehemently vowed to beat the cancer. This treatment plan included integrative therapeutic modalities supporting conventional treatments.

We left the doctor's office silently stunned. Humbly, she asked, "Lyn, as my older sister, can you be my advocate? Please understand, I do not need you to be in charge of me. I need you to hear me and give feedback." She then added, "What I really need from you *is to be responsible TO me...NOT for me*."

My jaw dropped. Her simple request indelibly imprinted in my mind and on my heart. Donna's words changed my role as a sibling, friend, family member, therapist, caregiver, companion, and lover. So simply stated; so eloquently transformative.

"Yes, Donna, I'll practice and promise to do my best." Knowing I was losing her caused me unthinkable pain and no one else, including and especially Donna, was ready to hear that. After her treatments we often slept side by side, face to face, holding hands. Too many times I'd awaken to shrieks of pain emerging from the depths of sleep, wrecking the needed reprieve, shocking her nervous system. The cancer found its way through the barriers of opiate meds. Neurological breakthrough pain is hot, searing, and relentless, causing her body to violently bolt upright. In response a scream would escape her unwavering private internal demeanor in horror, shock, and shame. As the disease progressed so did the pain. The metastases unmercifully squeezed, strangled, and suffocated the brachial plexus in her right shoulder, killing the nerves and leaving her right arm dangling unresponsively.

Like most professional caregivers, Donna found asking for help was quite foreign. Donna was highly skilled, devoted, independent, and strong willed. Cancer was not going to stop her. She always strove to raise the bar of integrity. She was motivated and determined. She learned to write left-handed, ordered her affairs, balanced her checkbook, sorted papers, and donated books to designated colleagues.

An Unexpected Lesson

My professional work, Degriefing®, is in truth an oxymoron. There is truly no way to *DEGRIEF*! Degriefing is about normalizing and then using our grief as fuel. By engaging in verbal expression and then choosing specific integrative activities for transforming the pain of our grief (physical, emotional, mental, and spiritual), this work can assist each of us in making peace with our grief. As a psychologist, a grief and loss somatic specialist, for years I have worked with the concept of somatic resonance. What I was dealing with was similar, yet distinctly specific. In empathic communion I can sense what is going on with the other individual. This was beyond that, and occurring frequently. I began to identify and explore the concept of "genetic resonance."

The internal cellular gut-wrenching pain that I experienced caring for my sister was inexplicably different. With the death of my husband I lost my projected future, the father of the children I would never have. As I compare the experience of losing Mark to cancer; it was *his* parents and siblings who reeled with excruciating distress as I continued to be, as promised to Mark, their steadfast emotional support.

That was not the case with my family of origin. Their pain and horror exponentially exacerbated my experience of losing Donna. When she ached, so did I. When she suffered, so did I, when her parents cried, so did mine. The lengthy experience of losing my sister caused my flesh, blood, and bones to ache.

My pain echoed and reverberated from organ to organ and tissue to tissue. I could not calm the internal quaking as well as I had been able to, while being in service to Mark's family. Shared parents offer the gift of genetic bonds. Donna knew secrets of my soul from early childhood. It was her birthright. My life's most authentic reference point was disappearing. When she died a trusted reflection, an irreplaceable piece of my identity died too. Since my beloved husband Mark died, my path of healing involved "making peace with my own grief." Absolutely no person is ever replaceable. Yet socioculturally "a husband" is said to be replaceable. A sister just cannot ever be replaced.

I experience a sense of personal purpose and find meaning presenting the degriefing work in Donna's honor. It keeps her alive in my heart as her love and wisdom guide me from within. Both Donna and Mark's spirits live in that "metaphoric 5th chamber" of my heart. Loss and grief are part of the human condition. "Grief is the most available, untapped emotional resource for personal transformation" is something I often say. So might I be in training for the captain of the Spiritual Olympics team? The two who knew me best would slyly smile at such a question. Donna was the best thing in my life for 53 years. She enhanced my well-being. As my friend she was kind, honest, and steady. As my sister she was genuine, generous, loving, and supportive.

Donna, your beautiful smile lives within me forever. With gratitude and infinite appreciation for your presence, I light a candle in your honor.

Poem Written Weeks before Donna's Death

My sister is dying,
I recognize it.
My sister is dying
and it leaves me
suspended
questioning
Why does my longtime companion suffer so before my very eyes?

So that my heart aches
and my tears
are just a decision to allow

The inevitable lip quivering period after
we
she
me
we, all do
what we can
do to cope
and grow
and stay glued together
by the fierce intension
to honor,
Donna.

She said she felt invisible.
she said She got used to it.

The dignified and gracefully
contained image
of a life
in process.
My sister
my teacher
my greatest loving critic –
She really got me.

She loved me always
for reasons
and for
no reason.

Donna blesses me with her
steady, beaming support.
She held space for me before I ever defined it.

she got me, up and out of bed on depressed Sunday afternoons
to meet her
for lunch. Just because we could.
so I did.

I could make her laugh, and that, made me smile.
She models integrity.
Is bright, caring, kind, determined, willful, and genuine.

"I feel that I am letting you all down."

You don't let people down, you meet them at eye level.
You have dark sparkling, intensely communicative, gorgeous eyes.

I sit in your home
while you lie in the hospital bed
at the palliative care Center,
I miss
sleeping near you.

I look around at the walls of the house you've made yours,
Your presence is everywhere.

it will always be everywhere.

I have grown so nurtured by the resonance of our love.
my soul aches, my heart is breaking, it cries to hold you.

I tremble at the thought of the sensation,
of the emptiness
I am certainly to feel so devastatingly,
should I outlive you.

Thank you Donna, for being Donna.

You are my best friend.
You are my sister.
You are my hero.
You are love.

The quote and poem are both published in my Degriefing manual: both original and both mine.

Reference

Prashant, L. (2002). *Transforming Grief: Degriefing Training Manual*. San Francisco, CA: Self-published.

chapter 16

On My Only Brother's Death

H.D. ("De") Kirkpatrick

It was difficult to determine which angle to take on this subject, because death exhibits many sides and exhibits some seriously cruel angles. The angle for this story is called "loving with grief."

I never understood why some people just seemed to dwell in endless grief. My brother's sudden death almost 14 years ago at 64 from cancer and surgical complexities changed my mind and heart about that lack of understanding. I was 53. He went into the hospital for exploratory surgery. Now there's an oxymoron if ever I heard one. He never came out.

There is a loving grief that keeps my brother alive. His removal from my life robbed me of having a full measure of life with him. I think about him almost daily. His wife (my sister-in-law) Pamela and I talk with and through loving grief about her husband, my brother, her children's father – Robert Galloway Kirkpatrick. I have equally loving conversations wrapped in a mixture of sadness and joy with my niece Mela and my nephew Kirk. We miss him. Pamela and I agree that loving grief doesn't end.

In a state of loving grief, all bets are off about predictable, time-framed stages of grief. Plus, death gets to be talked about. It loses some of its sting when its identity is clarified. It helps to have conversations about and with death.

Despite his mild protestations, I was authorized to call him "Bobby." Kinda Kennedy-esque, don't you think?

A full measure with Bobby would have been deeply serious and involved more seriously funny conversations about how to write a good whodunit. He could tell me what he thinks of my two efforts. He could have helped me design our Irish coat of arms incorporating his favorite compliment: "Pretty good. What there was of it," now in Irish: "An-mhaith! A raibh ann de." He used to occasionally tell me a very funny dirty joke. He's missing the ongoing impact on our family of Jimmie Lee Kirkpatrick's revelation to me about our family history and slave ownership. Bobby would have loved the *Observer* stories. We could plumb the ARP (Associate Reformed Presbyterian Church) issues together. What fun! I miss that I cannot analyze with him the biblical support for American slavery. You cannot imagine how much he would have to say about it.

He's missed his son's wedding and he's gonna miss his daughter's. He missed the birth of his grandson and is gonna miss more grandchildren. He'll never know his daughter-in-law or son-in-law. We can't have dinner conversations with him. We can't poke fun of him wearing his crown and making pronouncements. I can't talk to him about the University of North Carolina sports and African American studies program scandal. He had called it.

Bobby had a wonderful sense of humor that can only be obtained if you convince yourself that you actually live in the 19th century. Not FROM the 19th century. IN it. As a child, he met regularly with two imaginary friends, Bonhubbard and Lallalibloomsted, the latter being Jewish I think. He was an original beatnik. To get away from it all, one summer he worked in the Jolly Green Giant pea factory in Washington State.

Most older brothers offer you some of their favorite cereal as a token of love. My brother offered me things like, "What happens when an object that cannot be stopped strikes an immovable object?" Then he would fix me a gourmet meal so we could discuss this conundrum. I was about 7. You can't stop missing a guy like that.

He assured me I was not adopted and that he had been present at my birth. I found this comforting when I was feeling out of sync with my roots.

Just recently, I was informed by a relative that our Scottish Presbyterian ancestors' castle, Closeburn, contains a secret Catholic chapel, a so-called "priest's hole." Who knew! Bobby, as well as his wife and daughter are Catholic. Bobby apparently had foreknowledge about this hidden room of hidden faith, for he convinced our ARP parents to let him attend a Catholic elementary school. These were parents who believed the Pope would control the White House if Kennedy was elected. He'd chuckle if I had been able to tell him that he had a hidden Catholic chapel in Chalmers. I think he'd favor a trip to Closeburn to see this for himself. His other favorite pronouncement was "Important if true."

Bobby paired deliciously with food. He loved good food, but most enjoyed serving it to others. As all southerners can tell you, food goes arm in arm with grief. I had the audacity to say, "I will grieve for food" at my brother's funeral. He laughed at most of my jokes. He would have thought that was funny. How cool was that? We each thought of the other as funny. The man could cook. I miss our weekly dinners, when we lived next door to each other in Chapel Hill. I can't drive to Fearrington to eat with him and Pamela.

I want to share life with him. That opportunity on a physical plane was ripped from me. Loving grief keeps him alive. The dead depend upon the living. Our love for each other keeps us both alive. I'll try to let you know what happens after I die, because, if possible, I truly want to resume some conversations and jokes with him. I am decidedly curious about heaven and/or the afterlife. I know he will already have taken a complete tour and acquired celestial artifacts, so finding him early on will be important. Who wouldn't miss a brother like that?

PART V

Late Adulthood (60 Plus)

chapter 17

Clinical Issues Related to Sibling Loss in Older Adulthood

Jason M. Holland and Vincent Rozalski

The study of sibling bereavement in older adulthood has received relatively little attention, despite a growing body of anecdotal and empirical evidence suggesting that the loss of a brother or sister in later life can have a significant impact on one's sense of well-being, self-identity, and mortality (Cicirelli, 2009; Hays, Gold, & Pieper, 1997; Moss & Moss, 1989; Rostila, Saarela, & Kawachi, 2012). In some ways, this lack of attention is perhaps not surprising, given that few older adults live with a sibling, provide substantial care to a sibling, and/or seek counseling after the death of a sibling (Cicirelli, 1985; Connidis, 1994; Moss & Moss, 1989). However, in this chapter we review the existing literature on sibling loss in later life and, in light of the provocative findings that have emerged thus far, argue that more research on this topic is sorely needed. We begin by examining the mental and physical health implications of sibling loss in older adulthood, followed by a discussion of possible risk factors, protective factors, and clinical strategies for working with older adults who have lost a sibling. Throughout the chapter, key points are illustrated through the case example of Alice – an 89-year-old woman who over the course of her lifetime experienced the loss of all five of her siblings.

Mental Health Implications

The existing evidence suggests that the loss of a sibling in later life is a relatively common experience (exceeding the rate of spousal loss by a factor of 3:1; Hays et al., 1997), and a sizable minority of older adults show significant increases in psychiatric symptomatology afterward. For example, in a recent epidemiological study of Dutch older adults, roughly 13 percent of those who reported having lost a sibling exceeded the clinical cutoff for elevated complicated grief – a form of intense and chronic grief that has been proposed as a new diagnostic label in the International Classification of Diseases, Volume 11 (Maercker et al., 2013; Newson, Boelen, Hek, Hofman, & Tiemeier, 2011). Other studies have similarly shown a modest, but significant, association between the loss of a sibling (or other non-spousal family member) in older adulthood and increased depressive symptoms (Cicirelli, 2009; Williams, Baker, & Allman, 2005).

Several mediating variables have been proposed that may help explain the link between sibling loss in later life and increased psychiatric symptomatology. In a study conducted by Cicirelli (2009), fear of death was shown to statistically mediate the association between sibling loss and depressive symptoms, whereby older adults who had experienced the loss of one or more siblings were more likely to report fears about death, which in turn were significantly associated with increases in depression. Of course, the link between sibling loss in later life and perceived mortality is likely complex, as illustrated by the qualitative work of Moss and Moss (1989). In their study of 20 older adults who had lost a sibling at age 60 or later, they found that when asked if the loss changed the way they thought about their own death, roughly one third of participants denied any shift in their perceptions. Of those who reported some change in the way they viewed their own death, several themes emerged highlighting both greater resignation and acceptance of death as well as a more life-affirming sense of survival that stemmed from outliving one or more siblings (Moss & Moss, 1989).

From an Attachment Theory standpoint, relationships with siblings in later life may play an important role in terms of evoking feelings of safety, belongingness, and connection with one's parents and family of origin (Cicirelli, 1982; Connidis, 1989; Moss & Moss, 1989). Thus, when an older adult loses a sibling, he or she may simultaneously experience a loss of personal identity and family history (Moss & Moss, 1989). Loss of identity and a diminished sense of footing in the world have been shown in a number of studies to lead to poorer bereavement outcomes (Holland, Currier, & Neimeyer, 2014; Neimeyer, 2001). This link is poignantly illustrated in the case of Alice, which is discussed further in the chapter. After her younger and last remaining sister, Helen, died of a stroke, Alice was struck by the realization that she suddenly had "no one left to laugh with" about cherished family stories – an activity that had always served to validate and affirm her life story.

Older adults who have experienced the loss of one or more siblings are also subject to other secondary losses, such as the loss of emotional support. Findings suggest that older adults may actually experience greater relational intimacy with siblings in later life compared to earlier stages of adulthood (Gold, 1996; Ross & Milgram, 1982), or at least maintain levels of intimacy during this period (Moss & Moss, 1989). This level of closeness and reliance on siblings for support in later life can be seen in the work of O'Bryant (1988). In her study of more than 200 conjugally bereaved older women, support from siblings was found to play a crucial role in the adjustment process for many of these widows.

Siblings may be particularly well positioned to provide support in these situations, given that most are close in age and have experienced similar types of losses, facilitating a deeper level of empathic understanding and validation (O'Bryant, 1988). Unlike adult children who are likely to be experiencing their own grief reactions when a parent dies, siblings in older adulthood may be better able to serve as a holding environment for difficult feelings that may emerge during these kinds of life crises (Winnicott, 1965). Although many older adults report receiving little instrumental support from their siblings, most believe that their sibling is available to provide emotional support in times of need (Connidis, 1994). Of course, when a sibling dies, this unique form of support is no longer available, and this void may be experienced as an additional loss (Moss & Moss, 1989). In cases where the loss of siblings is accompanied by other significant losses, one may experience a sense of "bereavement overload" (Neimeyer & Holland, 2006, p. 166), which has been shown to be a risk factor for complications in the grieving process (Mercer & Evans, 2006; Neugebauer et al., 1992).

Physical Health Implications

Older adults who have lost a sibling have been found, on average, to be in poorer physical health compared to other bereaved groups (Hays et al., 1997). Specifically, in Hays et al.'s (1997) study, bereaved brothers and sisters were more likely to report difficulties with activities of daily living and scored lower on a test of general cognitive function compared to older adults who had lost a friend. Likewise, aging men and women who had lost a sibling rated their own health lower than other bereaved groups, including those who were widowed. These findings are, of course, likely influenced by shared genetics among siblings. Others have also pointed out that older adults may engage in a complex form of mental arithmetic when estimating their life expectancy and current physical well-being, and the health status of siblings may be weighted heavily when deriving such estimates (Marshall, 1975).

A third explanation for these findings is that perhaps the stress of sibling bereavement itself poses health risks. Notably, recent studies provide strong evidence for increased mortality rates due to sibling bereavement. For example, both natural and unnatural causes of sibling death have been shown to be associated with increased mortality during a 20-year period (Rostila et al., 2012). In addition, increased mortality following sibling loss has been shown to be due to a variety of causes, including stroke (Rostila et al., 2013a), cardiac problems (Rostila et al., 2013b), and suicide (Rostila et al., 2013c). Mortality risk is also increased for discordant causes of death (e.g. sibling death from cancer increasing risk for subsequent myocardial infarction among a bereaved sibling), highlighting that shared genetics alone is unlikely to fully account for these results (Rostila et al., 2012).

Risk and Protective Factors

Although it is not feasible here to provide an exhaustive review of all known bereavement risk and protective factors (see Lobb et al., 2010 for a review), we focus on three that seem particularly relevant to the issue of sibling loss in older adulthood, namely age, nature of the relationship, and circumstances of the death.

Studies examining the association between age and bereavement outcome have yielded mixed results, with some finding that younger adults fare worse than older and middle-aged adults (Ball, 1976), others finding that advanced age is associated with poorer outcomes (Futterman et al., 2010; Sanders, 1980), and yet others finding more complex associations (e.g., curvilinear effects; Perkins & Harris, 1990; Ringdal, Jordhøy, Ringdal, & Kaasa, 2001). One tentative conclusion to draw from these conflicting results is that advanced age may serve as both a risk and protective factor in the context of bereavement. For example, adults tend to become more efficient and invest less energy in coping with life stressors from late middle age to older adulthood (Brennan, Holland, Schutte, & Moos, 2012). However, many older adults no longer have access to resources (e.g. due to physical, cognitive, and social losses) that may help them cope with life stressors, such as the death of a sibling, forcing them to find ways to creatively compensate for these lost resources (Baltes & Baltes, 1990).

Aside from age, one's relationship with a sibling in life is also likely to influence the bereavement process following his or her death. Gender and ethnicity may play an important role in determining the nature of this relationship and the grief reactions that follow from it. In one study, sisters who lost a brother in later life were found to report greater distress following their loss, compared to older women who lost a sister (Hays et al., 1997). Likewise, older men who lost a brother were more likely to experience financial difficulties, perhaps suggesting a greater degree of financial entanglement among brothers in later life (e.g. having joint ownership over the family business; Hays et al., 1997). Although subject to multiple interpretations, these findings may stem from the traditional gender roles (e.g. with men typically assuming a patriarchal role) that pervaded many of these older adults' families of origin (Mintz & Kellogg, 1988), and it is possible that these gender differences may not hold for future generations of older adults.

Though preliminary, Moss and Moss' (1989) study found that ethnic minority older adults were somewhat more likely to report being close to their sibling and substantially affected by his or her death. This finding is consistent with other bereavement research, showing that ethnic minority individuals may grieve more intensely following the loss of family members that are not typically regarded as primary attachments, perhaps due to more flexible family structures (e.g. having a variety of family members assume caretaking responsibilities; Laurie & Neimeyer; 2008). Whether motivated by gender or cultural factors, when the relationship with the deceased is characterized by greater closeness and/or dependency, the grieving process may be more likely to present challenges and strain existing family relationships (Bonanno et al., 2002; Moss & Moss, 1989; Servaty-Seib & Pistole, 2006).

Circumstances regarding the death of a sibling are also likely to influence an older adult's grieving process. For example, older adults who perceive that they were not prepared for a loved one's death show elevations in complicated grief symptoms that persist even nine months after the loss (Barry, Kasl, & Prigerson, 2002). Other notions of a *good death*, such as being treated with dignity, maintaining good relationships with caretakers, and having a sense that important life tasks were completed, have also been shown to decrease anxiety at the end of life and lead to better bereavement outcomes (Carr, 2003; Chochinov et al., 2002; Steinhauser et al., 2000). Although no studies to our knowledge have explicitly examined these factors among aging bereaved siblings, there is little reason to believe that the importance of a good death would be any less salient for this population of grievers. In the case of Alice, the death of her second-eldest sister, Doris, was complicated by the perception that her terminal cancer diagnosis was acknowledged too late and that she died in pain without loved ones around her – all of which was exacerbated by Alice's feeling of guilt and belief that she "should have done more."

Clinical Strategies

Many of the same guidelines for working clinically with bereaved individuals in general likely also apply to older adults who have lost a sibling. For example, meta-analytic findings suggest that bereavement interventions are primarily effective when delivered to those who have shown signs of serious difficulties with the loss (Currier, Neimeyer, & Berman, 2008). Thus, a thorough assessment may be needed first to determine if a bereavement-focused intervention is even warranted. Assessment tools such as the Inventory of Complicated Grief (ICG) and the ICG-Revised can be used for this purpose, and cutoff scores have been identified to assess the severity of problems and need for treatment (Boelen, van den Bout, de Keijser, & Hoijtink, 2003; Prigerson et al., 1995; Prigerson & Jacobs, 2001). For aging bereaved siblings, clinicians would do well to pay particular attention to issues related to secondary losses (e.g. financial losses and/or loss of support), loss of family history and personal identity, and the nature of the sibling relationship itself (e.g. the level of closeness and/or dependency).

Among those with significant difficulties following a loss, several approaches have been found to be helpful, with some slight advantage for those that incorporate cognitive and behavioral components (Currier et al., 2010). Given the loss of history and diminished sense of identity that may accompany sibling loss in older adulthood (Moss & Moss, 1989), life-review techniques may be particularly relevant for this population. Specifically, life review may be used to make sense of difficult memories, validate aspects of one's life story that are perceived to have no living audience left, and integrate seemingly disparate narratives into coherent themes that allow for a more hopeful and purposeful future (Jenko, 2012; Neimeyer, 2014).

Consistent with the dual-process model of bereavement (Stroebe & Schut, 1999), some focus on helping bereaved siblings to restore their lives in the wake of secondary losses experienced after the death may often make sense as well. Notably, flexible forms of behavioral activation have been proposed for bereaved older adults that involve strategically planning important tasks of grieving (e.g. journaling about the loss) and restoration-oriented tasks (e.g. organizing one's finances) during the week, both of which are interspersed with activities geared toward self-soothing and increasing positive emotion (Holland & Diliberto, 2012).

Some perception of *unfinished business* (e.g. the belief that something was unsaid, unresolved, or incomplete in the relationship) may occur after the death of the sibling, particularly if the relationship was characterized by closeness and complexity (Klingspon, Holland, Neimeyer, & Lichtenthal, 2015).

These unresolved issues may be addressed in the context of empty chair work with the deceased or other similar techniques (e.g. writing letters to the deceased; Neimeyer, 2012; Paivio & Greenberg, 1995). In cases where one's own fear of mortality has been activated by the loss of a sibling, more existential work that focuses on clarifying values and meaning in life may be appropriate (Yalom, 1980).

Case Example

When Alice was 80 years old, she learned that her brother Harold had died of a heart attack in the airport while returning home from a cruise ship vacation. This loss occurred only a year after the death of her older sister, Doris, who still prompted feelings of guilt, as Alice believed she should have intervened to ensure that her sister's final needs were met. Having already lost two other older sisters several years before, the loss of Harold suddenly left Alice with only her younger sister, Helen.

Harold had played an important role in the family, as the "happy-go-lucky" jokester, guardian of family memorabilia, and coordinator for family events and reunions. For Alice, in particular, Harold's light-hearted and positive nature, even in the face of hardship, served as a model of strength and resilience. Thus, his sudden loss coupled with other prior losses left Alice feeling confused, lost, and incomplete. Alice initially coped with the loss of her brother by reaching out to her younger and last remaining sister, Helen. However, these efforts were largely rebuffed, perhaps due to Helen's own distress and preference to avoid reminders of their siblings' deaths. Though Alice felt supported by her husband of many years, there was a sense that no one was left who could truly understand what she had lost. At the urging of one of her adult children, Alice ultimately sought counseling to work through her feelings of sadness and grief.

Treatment with Alice initially focused on assessing for symptoms of complicated grief and depression and carefully reviewing her family history, including previous losses. This assessment revealed that Alice was in fact experiencing clinical levels of depression, which she largely attributed to the loss of her brother. Through the course of a more in-depth life review, two prominent themes emerged: 1) guilt and responsibility toward her siblings (particularly her older sister, Doris, who had died under less than ideal circumstances) and 2) disconnection with the "playful" and light-hearted part of herself, which Harold had always nurtured.

Alice's unresolved feelings of guilt related to Doris' death were addressed in the context of empty chair dialogues with her sister. Initially, this dialogue centered on Alice's extreme regret for not "doing more" for Doris during her final weeks as well as the belief that she had been a "bad sister." After these negative thoughts and beliefs were given full expression, Alice was encouraged to switch to the empty chair and give voice to her sister. With only a few prompts from her therapist, which invited Doris' perspective on the matter, Alice was able to speak from her sister's chair and begin reconstructing her narrative of the loss. Through this process, Alice had the insight that several people had contributed to the circumstances of Doris' death, including Doris' husband, her adult children, and even Doris herself who had a tendency to not want to deal with "unpleasant" matters. She was also able to recall numerous examples in which she had in fact helped to take care of her sister and express her love, not only at the time of Doris' death but throughout their lives together.

As Alice's feelings of guilt subsided, treatment turned to addressing Harold's death and the loss of the important role he had played in helping Alice to get in touch with her "playful" side. This phase of treatment began with continuing bonds work that focused on exploring the ways in which Harold and his light-hearted spirit were still alive within her and could be shared with others. Alice was inspired by this possibility, which initially took form in a modified behavioral activation exercise. In keeping with more conventional approaches to behavioral activation, Alice and her therapist collaborated to develop a list of activities that were considered either pleasant or meaningful, and she was encouraged to set daily goals for completing activities and monitor her progress. As part of this plan, Alice was also encouraged to consider activities that helped her to feel closer to Harold and/or share some part of him with others. After several weeks of practicing her behavioral activation plan and consolidating the gains that she had made, Alice left therapy with a renewed sense of siblinghood that allowed her to continue to appreciate, connect, and learn from her lost brothers and sisters.

Conclusions and Future Directions

The existing literature suggests that the loss of a brother or sister in later life can be quite impactful for a subset of grievers. However, more research is clearly needed in this area to better understand the difficulties aging bereaved siblings face and learn how to best intervene when indicated. We would advocate for research with greater methodological rigor (e.g. studies with larger samples and a prospective longitudinal design) that aims to: 1) examine unique risk/protective factors (e.g. birth order, level of intimacy/dependency in the relationship), 2) develop and test treatments that are geared specifically for older adults who have lost a sibling, and 3) assess contemporary models of grief (e.g. Dual Process Model; Stroebe & Schut, 1999) with this unique population of grievers. Notwithstanding these future possibilities, this chapter has offered some preliminary evidence-based guidelines for conceptualizing and managing issues of sibling loss in older adulthood that may emerge in clinical practice.

References

Ball, J.F. (1976). Widow's grief: The impact of age and mode of death. *Omega, 7*, 307–33. doi: 10.2190/WEEF-NoHD-0CQ5-18TY.

Baltes, P.B. & Baltes, M.M. (1990). Psychological perspectives on successful aging: The model of selective optimization with compensation. In P.B. Baltes & M.M. Baltes (Eds.), *Successful aging: Perspectives from the behavioral sciences* (pp. 1–34). New York: Cambridge University Press.

Barry, L.C., Kasl, S.V., & Prigerson, H.G. (2002). Psychiatric disorders among bereaved persons: The role of perceived circumstances of death and preparedness for death. *American Journal of Geriatric Psychiatry, 10*, 447–57. doi: 10.1097/00019442-200207000-00011.

Boelen, P.A., van den Bout, J., de Keijser, J., & Hoijtink, H. (2003). Reliability and validity of the Dutch version of the Inventory of Traumatic Grief (ITG). *Death Studies, 27*, 227–47.

Bonanno, G.A., Wortman, C.B., Lehman, D.R., Tweed, R.G., Haring, M., Sonnega, J., ... Nesse, R.M. (2002). Resilience to loss and chronic grief: A prospective study from preloss to 18-months postloss. *Journal of Personality and Social Psychology, 83*, 1150–64. doi: 10.1037/0022-3514.83.5.1150.

Brennan, P.L., Holland, J.M., Schutte, K.K., & Moos, R.H. (2012). Coping trajectories in later life: A 20-year predictive study. *Aging and Mental Health, 16*, 305–16. doi: 10.1080/13607863.2011.628975.

Carr, D. (2003). "A good death" for whom? Quality of spouse's death and psychological distress among older widowed persons. *Journal of Health and Social Behavior, 44*, 215–32. doi: 10.2307/1519809.

Chochinov, H.M., Hack, T., Hassard, T., Kristjanson, L.J., McClement, S., & Harlos, M. (2002). Dignity in the terminally ill: A cross-sectional, cohort study. *Lancet, 360*, 2026–30. doi: 10.1016/S0140-6736(02)12022-8.

Cicirelli, V.G. (1982). Sibling influence throughout the lifespan. In M.E. Lamb & B. Sutton-Smith (Eds.), *Sibling relationships: Their nature and significance across the lifespan* (pp. 267–84). Hillsdale, NJ: Erlbaum.

Cicirelli, V.G. (1985). The role of siblings as family caregivers. In W.J. Sauer & R.T. Coward (Eds.), *Social support networks in the care of the elderly* (pp. 93–107). New York: Springer.

Cicirelli, V.G. (2009). Sibling death and death fear in relation to depressive symptomatology in older adults. *Journals of Gerontology Series B: Psychological Sciences and Social Sciences, 64*, 24–32. doi: 10.1093/geronb/gbn024.

Connidis, I.A. (1989). Siblings as friends in later life. *American Behavioral Scientist*, 33, 81–93. doi: 10.1177/0002764289033001008.

Connidis, I.A. (1994). Sibling support in older age. *Journal of Gerontology*, 49, S309–18. doi: 10.1093/geronj/49.6.S309.

Currier, J.M., Neimeyer, R.A., & Berman, J.S. (2008). The effectiveness of psychotherapeutic interventions for bereaved persons: A comprehensive quantitative review. *Psychological Bulletin*, 134, 648–61. doi: 10.1037/0033-2909.134.5.648.

Currier, J.M., Holland, J.M., & Neimeyer, R.A. (2010). Do CBT-based interventions alleviate distress following bereavement? A review of the current evidence. *International Journal of Cognitive Therapy*, 3, 77–93. doi: 10.1521/ijct.2010.3.1.77.

Futterman, A., Holland, J.M., Brown, P.J., Thompson, L.W., & Gallagher-Thompson, D. (2010). Factorial validity of the Texas Revised Inventory of Grief-Present scale among bereaved older adults. *Psychological Assessment*, 22, 3, 675–87. doi: 10.1037/a0019914.

Gold, D.T. (1996). Continuities and discontinuities in sibling relationships across the lifespan. In V.L. Bengston (Ed.), *Adulthood and aging: Research on continuities and discontinuities* (pp. 228–43). New York: Springer.

Hays, J.C., Gold, D.T., & Pieper, C.F. (1997). Sibling bereavement in late life. *Omega*, 35, 25–42.

Holland, J.M. & Diliberto, R. (2012). Behavioral activation with bereaved older adults: Unique clinical considerations. *Clinical Gerontologist*, 35, 303–15. doi: 10.1080/07317115.2012.680685.

Holland, J.M., Currier, J.M., & Neimeyer, R.A. (2014). Validation of the Integration of Stressful Life Experiences Scale – Short Form in a bereaved sample. *Death Studies*, 38, 4, 234–8. doi: 10.1080/07481187.2013.829369.

Jenko, M. (2012). Life review. In R.A. Neimeyer (Ed.), *Techniques of grief therapy* (pp. 181–3). New York: Routledge.

Klingspon, K.L., Holland, J.M., Neimeyer, R.A., & Lichtenthal, W.G. (2015). Unfinished business in bereavement. *Death Studies*, 39, 397–8. doi: 10.1080/07481187.2015.1029143.

Laurie, A. & Neimeyer, R.A. (2008). African Americans in bereavement: Grief as a function of ethnicity. *Omega*, 57, 173–93. doi: 10.2190/OM.57.2.d.

Lobb, E.A., Kristjanson, L.J., Aoun, S.M., Monterosso, L., Halkett, G.K., & Davies, A. (2010). Predictors of complicated grief: A systematic review of empirical studies. *Death Studies*, 34, 673–98. doi: 10.1080/07481187.2010.496686.

Maercker, A., Brewin, C.R., Bryant, R.A., Cloitre, M., Reed, G.M., van Ommeren, M., ... Saxena, S. (2013). Proposals for mental disorders specifically associated with stress in the International Classification of Diseases – 11. *Lancet*, 381, 9878, 1683–5. doi: 10.1016/S0140-6736(12)62191-6.

Marshall, V.W. (1975). Age and awareness of finitude in developmental gerontology. *Omega*, 6, 113–29.

Mercer, D.L. & Evans, J.M. (2006). The impact of multiple losses on the grieving process: An exploratory study. *Journal of Loss and Trauma*, 11, 3, 219–27. doi: 10.1080/15325020500494178.

Mintz, S. & Kellogg, S. (1988). *Domestic revolutions: A social history of American family life*. New York: Simon & Schuster.

Moss, S.Z. & Moss, M.S. (1989). The impact of the death of an elderly sibling: Some considerations of a normative loss. *American Behavioral Scientist*, 33, 94–106. doi: 10.1177/0002764289033001009.

Neimeyer, R.A. (2001). Reauthoring life narratives: Grief therapy as meaning reconstruction. *Israel Journal of Psychiatry and Related Sciences*, 38, 171–83.

Neimeyer, R.A. (2012). Correspondence with the deceased. In R.A. Neimeyer (Ed.), *Techniques of grief therapy* (pp. 259–61). New York: Routledge.

Neimeyer, R.A. (2014). Chapters of our lives. In B.E. Thompson & R.A. Neimeyer (Eds.), *Grief and the expressive arts: Practices for creating meaning* (pp. 80–4). New York: Routledge.

Neimeyer, R.A. & Holland, J.M. (2006). Bereavement overload. In N.J. Salkind (Ed.), *Encyclopedia of human development* (pp. 166–7). Thousand Oaks, CA: Sage Publications.

Neugebauer, R., Rabkin, J.G., Williams, J.B., Remien, R.H., Goetz, R., & Gorman, J.M. (1992). Bereavement reactions among homosexual men experiencing multiple losses in the AIDS epidemic. *American Journal of Psychiatry*, 149, 1374–9.

Newson, R.S., Boelen, P.A., Hek, K., Hofman, A., & Tiemeier, H. (2011). The prevalence and characteristics of complicated grief in older adults. *Journal of Affective Disorders*, 132, 1, 231–8. doi: 10.1016/j.jad.2011.02.021.

O'Bryant, S.L. (1988). Sibling support and older widows' well-being. *Journal of Marriage and the Family*, 50, 173–83. doi: 10.2307/352437.

Paivio, S.C. & Greenberg, L.S. (1995). Resolving "unfinished business": Efficacy of experiential therapy using empty chair dialogue. *Journal of Consulting and Clinical Psychology*, 63, 419–25. doi: 10.1037//0022-006X.63.3.419.

Perkins, H.W. & Harris, L.B. (1990). Familial bereavement and health in adult life course perspective. *Journal of Marriage and the Family*, 52, 233–41. doi: 10.2307/352853.

Prigerson, H. & Jacobs, S.C. (2001). Traumatic grief as a distinct disorder: A rationale, consensus criteria, and a preliminary empirical test. In M.S. Stroebe, R.O. Hansson, W. Stroebe, & H. Schut (Eds.), *Handbook of bereavement research: Consequences, Coping, and Care* (pp. 613–45). Washington, DC: American Psychological Association. doi: 10.1037/10436-026.

Prigerson, H.G., Maciejewski, P.K., Reynolds, C.F., Bierhals, A.J., Newsom, J.T., Fasiczka, A., ... Miller, M. (1995). Inventory of complicated grief: A scale to measure maladaptive symptoms of loss. *Psychiatry Research*, 59, 65–79. doi: 10.1016/0165-1781(95)02757-2.

Ringdal, G.I., Jordhøy, M.S., Ringdal, K., & Kaasa, S. (2001). Factors affecting grief reactions in close family members to individuals who have died of cancer. *Journal of Pain and Symptom Management*, 22, 6, 1016–26. doi: 10.1016/S0885-3924(01)00363-3.

Ross, H.G. & Milgram, J.I. (1982). Important variables in adult sibling relationships: A qualitative study. In M.E. Lamb & B. Sutton-Smith (Eds.), *Sibling relationships: Their nature and significance across the lifespan* (pp. 225–49). Hillsdale, NJ: Erlbaum.

Rostila, M., Saarela, J., & Kawachi, I. (2012). The forgotten griever: A nationwide follow-up study of mortality subsequent to the death of a sibling. *American Journal of Epidemiology*, 176, 338–46. doi: 10.1093/aje/kws163.

Rostila, M., Saarela, J., & Kawachi, I. (2013a). Fatal stroke after the death of a sibling: A nationwide follow-up study from Sweden. *PloS One*, 8, e56994. doi: 10.1371/journal.pone.0056994.

Rostila, M., Saarela, J., & Kawachi, I. (2013b). Mortality from myocardial infarction after the death of a sibling: A nationwide follow-up study from Sweden. *Journal of the American Heart Association*, 2, e000046. doi: 10.1161/JAHA.112.000046.

Rostila, M., Saarela, J., & Kawachi, I. (2013c). Suicide following the death of a sibling: A nationwide follow-up study from Sweden. *BMJ Open*, 3, e002618. doi: 10.1136/bmjopen-2013–002618.

Sanders, C.M. (1980). Comparison of younger and older spouses in bereavement outcome. *Omega*, 11, 217–32. doi: 10.2190/AHER-PDC7-VAW1-FYPX.

Servaty-Seib, H. & Pistole, M.C. (2006). Adolescent grief: Relationship category and emotional closeness. *Omega*, 54, 147–67.

Steinhauser, K.E., Clipp, E.C., McNeilly, M., Christakis, N.A., McIntyre, L.M., & Tulsky, J.A. (2000). In search of a good death: Observations of patients, families, and providers. *Annals of Internal Medicine*, 132, 825–32. doi: 10.7326/0003-4819-132-10-200005160-00011.

Stroebe, M. & Schut, H. (1999). The Dual Process Model of coping with bereavement: Rationale and description. *Death Studies*, 23, 197–224. doi: 10.1080/074811899201046.

Williams, B.R., Baker, P.S., & Allman, R.M. (2005). Nonspousal family loss among community-dwelling older adults. *Omega*, 51, 125–42. doi: 10.2190/BUBQ-J0VP-EVPW-V95V.

Winnicott, D.W. (1965). *The maturational processes and the facilitating environment: Studies in the theory of emotional development*. London: Hogarth Press.

Yalom, I.D. (1980). *Existential psychotherapy*. New York: Basic Books.

chapter 18

A Letter to My Brother

Carol L. Sachs

Dear Ken,

    I want to share with you the events of the weekend of March 8, 2002 and how my life changed so suddenly. The phone rang about 10:00 A.M. that Friday morning. It was your son saying something rather incoherent about his dad, something about the doctors saying the family should come and that something terrible had happened. My brain could not wrap around the fact that his dad was you, my brother, my only sibling. I thought he was talking about one of his grandfathers but that could not be because both had died in 1995. My mind could not accept that he was really talking about you, my big brother, five and a half years older than I. But it was you and you were lying in a hospital 100 miles away from me near your home and were on life support.

    We (my husband and I) drove to the hospital and learned that you were found unconscious that morning and taken by ambulance to the hospital where you were put on life support. There was no hope. You probably had a massive stroke that destroyed your brain. My brilliant lawyer brother was basically gone, so suddenly. You were 69½ and I was almost 65. We have longevity in our family so how could you die at 69? I went into your room a number of times, not believing what I was seeing. The shock was enormous. Late that night, the family decided to take you off life support. Everyone left but me. I refused to go. The radiology technician and the physician both wanted me to leave but I would not let you die alone. I have never regretted being there with you. It was very important to me to do that for you and for me.

That whole weekend is seared in my memory. I can recall every moment. Sometimes I wish I could forget; other times I am grateful I remember even though I was in shock. Your funeral was on Sunday since in Judaism we don't bury on Saturday. I was in a daze. There was no chance to say goodbye. I, for the first time in my life, defined myself as an only child. You were always there as my protector. You never told me in words that you would always be there if I needed you but I just knew this was true. And now suddenly you were gone.

Six weeks later, our mom died at the age of 95. Though she was old and fragile, I knew she could not survive your death. I had to become mom's executrix, your job, but you weren't there to do it. I spent a year dealing with probate. Many of the people I dealt with were difficult and asked over and over for the same proof of her death and my official executrix papers. This was your job. You were the lawyer and you had handled all of her finances. I knew very little and it was such a struggle. I sometimes cried on the phone to these faceless people that they had to be kind to me. I had lost two important members of my family of origin within six weeks of each other. There were times I didn't know who I was grieving for but I knew that mom was at an age that I would expect her to die but not you. There were people who would say to me that it was fortunate that you died suddenly so you would never suffer. But what about me and your wife and your son? We suffered and still do. You know that I am a family therapist and a bereavement counselor. But the only part of my profession that helped me was that I knew it was OK to feel this incredible pain in the very depths of my being and I knew that it was OK to take whatever time I needed to go on my own path of sorrow. There was no time limit for me.

We did not see each other a lot but we talked. And we always spent Thanksgivings together except for the eight years we lived far away. I remember my first Thanksgiving back here in Massachusetts without you. Because we had no family anymore except for my children to invite, we asked some friends to join us. That morning, I sat for a long time on the couch sobbing and wishing that no one was coming. Yet when our children arrived and the friends came, I seemed to be OK and I did get through the day and was glad everyone was there. Getting through these past 13 years has softened the pain. But there can still come suddenly the sense of loss. The grief overtakes me but I know I will survive.

There have been events in our family that were bittersweet because you weren't there. The weekend your son married a beautiful, kind young woman gave me such mixed emotions. I said a few words at the rehearsal dinner. I was your son's closest blood relative on our side and I wanted to identify myself as your sister. I agonized for weeks how to introduce myself. Do I say "I was Ken's sister, I'm Ken's sister, Ken was my brother, or Ken is my brother?" I chose to say that I am your sister because I am even though you died.

In February 2014, you became a grandfather. Your grandson carried your name as his middle name. You would have loved being with that little boy. I wish you could share in his life.

The years have helped me. But I think there is and always will be a deep sadness. I have a full life, a husband, a career (now retired), two daughters, two grandchildren, a son-in-law, and many Siberian Huskies who have brought me great joy. Yet with all of this, there will always be a deep hole in my heart. I am now a number of years older than you were when you died. For many years, I was afraid that when I went to sleep, I would not wake up just as you didn't that fateful Thursday night.

I think what I wish most of all is that our society would recognize adult sibling loss as the major event that it is. I have no one to talk to about our years of growing up in our family, of events that I don't remember well because I was younger than you. I tried to find a support group soon after you died for adult sibling loss in my area. Here I was a professional and I couldn't find such a group. It was suggested that I start a group but my grief drained me of any ability to do that. I still had to treat my families and do my bereavement work.

I find that now, this many years later, I no longer let the loss of you define me anymore. I miss you with all that I am and all that I have. I had a brother. No matter how I aged, I remain your "little sister." I will always be grateful for you; I will always miss you.

Your "little sister"

Carol

chapter 19

The Death of a Sister and a Brother

Gloria Horsley

The call came in the early morning from my niece Patty. She was sobbing and said, "Aunt Gloria, My Mom is dead." I had been anticipating the call for several days. My big sister, Marilyn, age 82, had been on hospice for a month and was finally out of pain.

Upon hearing the news I began to reflect on our life together. Growing up as the youngest of four children was always a fun thing for me. Having a big sister nine years older was frustrating, maddening, and thrilling. Both my parents worked full time, and my sister Marilyn was given the task of managing her three younger siblings during the summer. She would assign us chores around the house, while she sunbathed in the backyard in her white two-piece swimming suit, which in the 1950s was daring. As a young sister I loved watching my big sister make paper dolls, and I remember visiting her at college and thinking I wanted to be just like her. She was my first sibling to get married, and she had my parents' first grandchild, and my first nephew. Later, when I had four kids of my own, she welcomed me into her home for weeks at a time during the summer. She was my children's beloved Aunt Marilyn and loved by all. We called her the mayor of her small town in Perry, Utah. In her later years her husband had a stroke and she became his caregiver, never complaining and always keeping a positive attitude. As she reached her 80s her task as a caregiver became more and more demanding and her health suffered. Her small-town hospital was not able to handle her health issues such as kidney failure and pneumonia following gallbladder surgery. Like so many caregivers, she died before those for whom she was caring.

It is amazing to think that I spent 73 years with my oldest sister in my life. After her death, a part of my family history died and I wondered who would identify the pictures in the family album. I wish I had asked her more about my grandfather as he died before I was born. She had seven kids so when I called her there was always a lot to talk about, now I can no longer call her to find out about my nephews and nieces. She not only had grandchildren but great grandchildren. We are having a family reunion this summer and I will miss her a lot. She won't be there to organize the event. She won't be there with an open door to serve homemade bread and a pot of stew. She won't be there with open arms to give us all hugs and kisses. My big sister will never be there again, and although I am poorer for having lost her I am so much richer for having her in my life for 73 years.

Death of a Brother

The last family reunion my family had was three years ago. Little did I know at the time that three years later at this year's family reunion, both my brother and my sister would be dead. My brother, Bill, was six years older than me. Growing up, I had a crush on all my brother's friends and wanted to play with them. As a boy in the 1940s Bill had a lot more freedom than I did. He and his friends were able to go on camping and hunting trips on their own. My dad would drop them off in the canyon and pick them up three days later. My mother of course adored her only son and catered to him until he reached puberty and discovered girls, and then she would chase him around with a broom threating to hit him if he didn't get his chores done. After a year of college Bill joined the Navy. I was really sad to see him go. When he packed to go to boot camp I slipped a letter into his suitcase telling him how much I loved him. I was 12 and he was 18. On Christmas Eve he gave his girlfriend a diamond ring and they were married that next summer. He had three boys, Chad, his oldest son died at one year old, of an enlarged heart. Little did I know that years later I would also lose a son. After Bill got married, I had to share my big brother with his new wife and her family. Through the years we had contact but were not as close as we had been growing up. The last time I saw my brother Bill was at a family reunion, he told me that he was going to have hip surgery. During the operation, the surgeon found that the hip was worn away not by age, but by cancer. While I lived in California he lived in Utah. Having contacts at the University of Utah I volunteered to help my sister-in-law find a highly regarded hospice program. I visited him at the nursing home where he had rehab for his hip surgery and spoke with his family daily when he went home on hospice until his death three months later. My big brother who I had adored growing up, and who I had wished I had been closer to, had died.

Losing Family Contact

Losing my sister and my brother has caused me to feel concern that I am losing contact with their families. My nephew's wife was just diagnosed with cancer and is having chemotherapy. My sister-in-law Mary keeps me informed, but she is in her early 80s and suffers serious heart problems. I have learned that if you don't have a sibling to keep you informed you not only miss the big things but the smaller ones like graduations, achievements, and a window into people growing up.

Putting Things into Perspective

I had a sister for 73 years and a brother for 71 years and now both are gone. My last living sibling, my sister, is 79 years old and lives in Arizona; we try to talk weekly. Thankfully, she and I are both in good health. We both golf and she spends a couple of weeks with me in California in the summer to get out of the Arizona heat. It is strange to think that one day one of us will be an only child.

As a senior I am reconciled to the fact that a natural part of the life cycle is death and I realize that as I age my circle of family and friends will continue to get smaller and smaller. I keep busy and engaged and have a terrific husband and three wonderful daughters along with friends that share my passion for golf and help with my work. I think that dealing with the loss of my siblings has been made easier because they both lived long and productive lives, and did not die before their time. I also had a comfortable relationship with my sister and brother having few if any unresolved conflicts. My heart goes out to those whose siblings left with unresolved issues. I also believe that the death of my son Scott at age 17, when I was 44, has impacted my understanding of loss and the grieving process. Scott's death was like climbing Mount Everest. I have taken the trip to hell and back and I am here to tell you that not only can you survive, but you can eventually thrive even after devastating losses. I think I am lucky as both of my siblings died with dignity and courage with their families at their side. They died of "natural causes." I honor them in their lives and their deaths. They have left me a grand legacy.

Keys to Surviving Sibling Loss

I believe there are several keys to surviving sibling loss and regaining equilibrium. One is gratitude for what our siblings brought into our lives and the second is love for the beautiful world and people that live with us today. You might have liked a closer relationship with one of your siblings, for me it was my brother, but I have come to accept the fact that our relationship was perfect just the way it was. I am grateful for having known Marilyn and Bill, the siblings who taught me how to deal with the world. We fought, envied each other, played together, forgave each other, and loved one another. I count myself lucky to have had my brother and sister in my life for three quarters of a century.

PART VI

Special Topics

chapter 20

Sibling Grief after Suicide

Diana C. Sands

This chapter addresses adult sibling grief after suicide with reference to a relational, meaning-making model of suicide bereavement: the *walking in the shoes* model (Sands, 2009; Sands, Jordan, & Neimeyer, 2011). Adult sibling bereavement is the least researched familial relationship of loss. However, available research stresses that siblings occupy an irreplaceable position in each other's lives and that, importantly, this connection is potentially one of the longest relationships in a person's life (Forward & Garlie, 2003; Robinson & Mahon, 1997; Rostila, Saarela, & Kawachi, 2012). As children move from childhood to adolescence and adulthood, siblings are a companion and witness to family dynamics and events over an extended period of time. In general, siblings hold unique perspectives and many-layered memories of each other's lives that authenticate a sense of self (Hogan & deSantis, 1992; Riches & Dawson, 2000).

Consideration of the fundamental role of siblings in terms of self-identity, and the inevitable changes in family relationships and structure following the death of a family member, provides insight into the nature and significance of sibling grief. However, when a sibling dies due to suicide the grief process is frequently complicated by additional issues. Suicide is a sudden and often violent and traumatic way for a family member to die and can leave families and individuals trapped in disrupted grief processes, struggling to come to terms with why, and how, this death could have happened (Neimeyer & Sands, 2011; Rynearson, 2001). Memories of the deceased are frequently shrouded by the horror of the death and tainted with complicated issues of stigma, guilt, blame, anger, and the trauma associated with a suicide death (Jordan, 2011). Importantly, these concerns can disrupt efforts to construct an adaptive, healing story that repairs the griever's sense of self, relationships between family members, and the ongoing relationship with the deceased (Neimeyer & Sands, 2011; Rynearson, 2001). Of further concern is a significant body of research that has documented an increased risk of mental health issues, suicidal behavior, and completions, in those bereaved by suicide (US National Guidelines, 2015).

The walking in the shoes model (Neimeyer & Sands, 2011; Sands, 2009; Sands et al., 2011) identifies meaning making and relational themes in a non-linear, three by three matrix model. Significant relational themes identified in the model are the relationship with *self*, *the deceased*, and *significant others*. The relationship with the deceased is also termed the *continuing bond* (Klass, 2006; Klass, Silverman, & Nickman, 1996). These relationship themes interact with three dominant meaning-making themes, designated in the model as *trying on the shoes*, *walking in the shoes*, and *taking off the shoes*. Trying on the shoes attempts to make sense of whether the death was accidental, preventable, or intentional, and who, or what, was responsible or to blame. Walking in the shoes focuses on reconstructing the imagined or known pain the deceased experienced during their life and, in particular, the events leading up to the death. Importantly, those bereaved by suicide often spend a significant amount of time in anguished cogitations about their loved one implementing his or her death. As the beginnings of adaptive reconstructed meanings emerge, taking off the shoes themes become more prevalent. These themes are concerned with the integration and construction of an adaptive story and for some, but not all, the development of new perspectives and post-traumatic growth through grief (Calhoun & Tedeschi, 2006; Sands et al., 2011; Sands & Tennant, 2010).

The following case study draws on the relational, meaning-reconstruction perspectives outlined in the model, using expressive arts interventions, as a guide in counseling "Jessica," 28 years old, who lost her only sibling, "Mark," 26 years old, to suicide. Jessica had moved to Australia from Britain in response to a career opportunity shortly before Mark's death. Jessica shared photos of herself as a little girl with a cheeky grin, her arms wrapped around an angelic child with golden curls. Jessica was on an interstate work trip when her father phoned sobbing and repeating over and over, "he's gone...he's gone." It took a number of phone calls for Jessica to piece together what had happened. Mark had gone to a nearby expressway flyover, a gathering place for local youth, where they sat to smoke and drink as they watched cars speed past. Mark, a suicide note in his pocket, had stabbed himself several times and jumped to his death. An early morning jogger found his body lying in the wasteland below the flyover.

Through tears, Jessica recounted the story of her long flight home, the intense physical pain in her heart, and thinking repeatedly, "My life is ended." Later, they found out from the police that Mark had for months been using his computer to research ways to take his life. It was evident that her sibling's suicide presented a foundational assault on Jessica's assumptive world (Janoff-Bullman, 1992). It was Jessica who took care of the funeral arrangements and looked after her mother and father. However, after returning to Sydney Jessica worried about her mother who suffered from bipolar disorder, an illness that had taken a toll on family life and worsened in the aftermath of Mark's death. In the period after the funeral hurtful things were said and these arguments had not been resolved. Communications within the family were severely impaired.

The clinician noted a number of complications and in particular the mental health issues embedded within the family dynamics. Unfortunately, Mark's tragic death added to existing family dysfunction provoking a descent into blame, guilt, and isolating behavior. Jessica's family found themselves unable to offer support and comfort to each other. Many researchers have noted the effect of suicide loss on family communications (Cerel, Jordan, & Duberstein, 2008; Linn-Gust, 2004; Sands & North 2014). Jessica was grieving the loss of her brother, the person she was closest to in the world. Every day brother and sister had texted or emailed each other, using a sibling shorthand, nicknames, and humor with references to events and family dynamics developed over their growing-up years – an intimate language only they understood. It had been Jessica's way of staying close and supporting Mark with his illness and difficult home environment. Jessica's plan had been to help Mark come to Australia where she believed a new life was possible for him. However, her intense grief for Mark was all but eclipsed by her fear another tragedy could claim her mother, who threatened that she was going to end her life. Fears for family members and a sense of not being safe are well documented in survivor research (Jordan 2011; Linn-Gust, 2004).

In a clinical intervention, Jessica was invited to imagine having her family in the counseling room. In this way their response to conversations she could not have with them in real life could be intuited. Jessica sketched onto paper symbols or figures that represented those people who comprised her relational world: her parents, Mark, her two best friends, a small group of work friends, and a sad canine face representing the family dog, Jack. Jessica joked that Jack, a terrier, knew everything that went on in her family. The clinician, drawing on Family Systems Theory, asked questions about the relationships between family members, and changes in patterns of behavior since Mark's death.

Afterwards, visibly upset, Jessica talked of how her mother's feelings had always "taken center stage" in the family. "Like now...only mum's grief is important...even though dad is suffering just as badly." Her father hated confrontation of any kind and his response was to withdraw, while Mark had used humor to cope. Jessica thought this was the way Mark protected himself from people feeling sorry for him. Frequently Mark's illness and her mother's illness caused difficulties and disruptions in the family. Despite these challenges, Jessica excelled at school and university; however, she avoided talking with her parents about her achievements and successful career in Australia. Mark had struggled from failure to failure, repeated relapses, and more medications. In effect, Mark was a prisoner of his illness and she suffered with him.

Jessica was asked if she would like to explore her insights further through creating a physical image using elements within the counseling room (Neimeyer & Sands, 2011; Sands, 2014). Jessica selected a red pillow to represent Mum, and a large yellow pillow placed to represent Mark, "our sunshine boy." Jessica placed over her mother and brother's pillows a black piece of material with gold sequins on the underside to represent her mother's grief, and her love. Jessica seated herself on a pink cushion and after being prompted about "the guilt" she placed a piece of heavy green velvet fabric trailing from her mother's pillow to wrap around her shoulders. The effect of this was to swamp Jessica almost completely. Jessica said, "this is the guilt, my guilt, my mother's guilt...it's heavy."

Jessica cried as she explained that after the funeral her mum screamed "It's your fault Mark's dead." Jessica explained that she believed her mother was referring to her moving to Australia or maybe, she pondered, it was because things had gone well for her. The clinician asked if mum had something to say to her now. After a long pause Jessica responded that her mum was silent, "but I know Mum feels bad for saying that...I know she doesn't really mean it...it's the illness makes her like that." Crying, Jessica explained, "She wasn't always like how she is now, she used to be such a good mum when we were small, before she got sick...there were happy times."

After Jessica deconstructed the belief that because Mark was unwell, she should not achieve her potential, the clinician asked Jessica to close her eyes and imagine what Mark would say. Given her mother's silence this was a critical moment in counseling. Mark's response, however, was decisive: "That's rubbish...don't listen to mum...I'm so proud of you, everything you've done Jess...and I'm so happy you got out of here." Then in reference to plans for Mark's relocation to Sydney: "I'm sorry I let you down...I couldn't do it...I just couldn't."

The clinician asked Jessica if she could change this picture of her family how would she like it to be different (Neimeyer & Sands, 2011). Thoughtfully, Jessica looked at the pillows and rolled up the green material and placed it to one side. Pausing as she reached for the black material, she held up the gold sequins and as if addressing her mother said: "See Mum... this is the good mum that I know is there." The clinician asked whether Dad had come out of his study to join them. Jessica said, "He's here listening too." Jessica reached for the blue pillow that represented her dad and moved it closer as she imagined her dad giving her a hug.

This was an emotional session; however, Jessica reported that she had found it helpful, explaining that she had never thought about her family in this way before and felt somehow less burdened. Jessica said she felt secure in knowing Mark understood and was an ally, Dad loved her, and, despite her illness, Mum loved her too. Prompted, she explained, "I could keep trying and trying...but I know there's nothing I can do to change the way Mum is."

Not long after this session, Jessica brought to counseling a lithograph of an expressway flyover, which she had done as part of a creative project at university a number of years prior to Mark's death. In a way Jessica found "weirdly synchronistic," this was the place Mark had chosen to execute his death. This place had become a recurring theme both in Jessica's daily ruminations and dreams, dreams that left Jessica exhausted, dreams in which Mark was present, but in a distressing way. Given the significant function of walking in the shoes themes in construction of an adaptive continuing bond, the clinician asked if Jessica could position the picture on a central chair, and if she could sit with Jessica in this place where her brother had died (Sands, 2012).

Having introduced self-soothing techniques to help Jessica self-regulate her emotions, the clinician asked what kind of things Jessica thought about when she was here. After a lengthy pause, with tears welling, Jessica said, "I think about him being alone and doing that to himself. I can't bear to think about him...scared and...alone." The therapy room was a safe crucible to hold Jessica's anguish, and to be acknowledged by an empathic other. The clinician asked whether there was something Jessica wanted to say to Mark. In a broken voice she said, "I'm sorry I wasn't there for you... so sorry I left...so sorry...[pause] I miss you so much." And Mark responded promptly, "You are the best sister, Jess...always with me...but this...this I had to do by myself...you have to give me that." After more tears, Jessica placed blue material around the expressway flyover picture and, with a whispered blessing for peace for her brother, placed stones around it. The stones represented a small part of her guilt that she felt ready to lay down. Jessica sighed as a faint smile transformed her face, "He was always like that you know – sometimes you just couldn't help him...he didn't want you to...[smiling fondly] he was such a Muppet."

Ensuing sessions continued to explore Jessica's conversations with her brother and the significant place of Mark's ongoing presence in her

Figure 20.1 Moon Dreamer

life. As time passed, Jessica began to connect with her sibling in places that recalled happier days. The quality of her dreams changed and Jessica painted *Moon Dreamer* to illustrate Mark now as a peaceful presence (Figure 20.1). As counseling continued, Jessica's resilience strengthened and she began to value herself, her special qualities, and her way of being in the world. Towards the end of counseling, taking off the shoes themes began to emerge through the long winter of her grief. Jessica noted a difference that was cause for laughter among her friends: she was now a magnet to strangers who sought her out and told her their sad stories. Jessica commented, "I guess it's because they feel I understand. I do feel my heart has changed…you know, grown bigger or something."

The case study has highlighted a number of pivotal counseling moments to illustrate adult sibling grief after suicide with reference to the walking in the shoes model as a clinical practice guide (Sands et al., 2011). The case study described the breakdown in family communications and functioning frequently noted in suicide bereavement literature. It also highlighted the disabling burden of responsibility, guilt, and anguish experienced by this sibling. Counseling is able to provide a place to unpack difficult issues and opportunities for imaginal conversations with estranged family members, and with the deceased, to support construction of an adaptive continuing bond. The horror and trauma often accompanying suicide death can be addressed supporting insight and opportunities for client growth through grief.

References

Calhoun, L. & Tedeschi, R.G. (Eds.). (2006). *Handbook of posttraumatic growth* (pp. 3–23). Mahwah, NJ: Lawrence Erlbaum.

Cerel, J., Jordan, J.R., & Duberstein, P.R. (2008). The impact of suicide on the family. *Crisis*, 29, 1, 38–44.

Forward, D.R. & Garlie, N. (2003). Search for new meaning: Adolescent bereavement after the sudden death of a sibling. *Canadian Journal of School Psychology*, 18, 1/2, 25–53.

Hogan, N.S. & DeSantis, L. (1992). Adolescent sibling bereavement: An ongoing attachment. *Qualitative Health Research*, 2, 159–77.

Janoff-Bullman, R. (1992). *Shattered assumptions: Towards a new psychology of trauma*. New York: Free Press.

Jordan, J.R. (2011). The principles of grief counseling with adult survivors. In J.R. Jordan & J.L. McIntosh (Eds.), *Grief after suicide* (pp. 179–223). New York: Routledge.

Klass, D. (2006). Continuing conversation about continuing bonds. *Death Studies*, 30, 843–58.

Klass, D., Silverman, P.R., & Nickman, S.L. (Eds.). (1996). *Continuing bonds: New understandings of grief*. Washington, DC: Taylor & Francis.

Linn-Gust, M. (2004). *Do they have bad days in heaven? Surviving the suicide loss of a sibling*. Albuquerque, NM: Chellehead Works.

Neimeyer, R.A. & Sands, D.C. (2011). Meaning reconstruction and bereavement: From principles to practice. In R.A. Neimeyer, D.L. Harris, H.R. Winokuer, & G.F. Thornton (Eds.), *Grief and bereavement in contemporary society: Bridging research and practice* (pp. 9–22). New York: Routledge.

Riches, G. & Dawson, P. (2000). *An intimate loneliness: Supporting bereaved parents and siblings*. Buckingham: Open University Press.

Robinson, L. & Mahon, M.M. (1997). Sibling bereavement: A concept analysis. *Death Studies*, 21, 1–13.

Rostila, M., Saarela, J., & Kawachi, I. (2012). The forgotten griever: A nationwide follow-up study of mortality subsequent to death of a sibling. *American Journal of Epidemiology*, 176, 4, 338–46.

Rynearson, E.K. (2001). *Retelling violent death*. Philadelphia. PA: Brunner-Routledge.

Sands, D.C. (2009). A tripartite model of suicide grief: Meaning-making and the relationship with the deceased. *Grief Matters: Australian Journal of Grief and Bereavement*, 12, 10–17.

Sands, D.C. (2012). The body of trust. In R.A. Neimeyer (Ed.), *Grief therapy: Creative strategies for counseling the bereaved* (pp. 76–9). New York: Routledge.

Sands, D.C. (2014). Restoring the heartbeat of hope following suicide. In B.R. Thompson & R.A. Neimeyer (Eds.), *Grief and the expressive arts: Practices for creating meaning* (pp. 215–21). New York: Routledge.

Sands, D.C. & North J.L. (2014). Family therapy following suicide. In D.W. Kissane & F. Parnes (Eds.), *Bereavement care for families* (pp. 154–70). New York: Routledge.

Sands, D. & Tennant, M. (2010). Transformative learning in the context of suicide bereavement. *Adult Education Quarterly*, 60, 99–121.

Sands, D.C., Jordan, J.R., & Neimeyer, R.A. (2011). The meanings of suicide: A narrative approach to healing. In J.R. Jordan & J.L. McIntosh (Eds.), *Grief after suicide* (pp. 249–82). New York: Routledge.

US National Guidelines (2015). *Responding to grief, trauma, and distress after a suicide: US National Guidelines Survivors of Suicide Loss Task Force.* Washington, DC: National Action Alliance for Suicide Prevention.

chapter 21

Sibling Grief and Its Effect on the Family System

Kathleen R. Gilbert and Rebecca J. Gilbert

The family, as a system, has received little attention in the study of sibling grief. The majority of research focuses on the grief of surviving siblings or the post-loss relationship between surviving siblings and parents. In this chapter, we draw from literature on Family Systems Theory to broaden the focus to the family level. For simplicity's sake, families of bereaved minor siblings will be the focus of the chapter.

The Family as a System

The family systems perspective considers the way relationships within the family and among family members, as well as the relationship between the family and other elements of the social environment, influence individual and family bereavement (Cook & Oltjenbruns, 1998). The family is characterized by wholeness, i.e. holism, with the system being made up of more than the sum of its parts; as such, it is comprised of individuals connected to each other through relationships. Both overt and covert rules govern behavior in the family and function to maintain a dynamic homeostatic balance between stability and change within the family. Family rules govern roles assigned to family members as well as necessary functions of the family. Families vary in their degree of openness to change, which significantly contributes to their capacity to adapt in the face of crisis (Cook & Oltjenbruns; White & Klein, 2008).

As a system, the family exists in paradox. The natural tendency of a system is to move toward homeostasis, an internal sense of balance. Family systems need the sense of continuity over time that stability provides so that family members know their roles and can carry them out with the security that they are "doing it right." At the same time, the system needs to be able to adapt to changes in and among family members (White & Klein, 2008). The result is a balancing act between constancy and change.

Family members have membership in multiple, interactive, sometimes conflicting subsystems within the family, with each of these subsystems maintaining its own boundaries, rules, and openness (Cook & Oltjenbruns, 1998). The sibling bond and the parent–child relationship are examples of such subsystems. The death of a child results in profound disruption of family processes/change in family dynamics. With the death, the family enters a state of disequilibrium, in which the rules and the roles of family members become unclear. Family identity changes and roles shift or are reassigned, and this can play an active part in reshaping the surviving siblings' identities (Shapiro, 1994).

Family Roles

Roles include social expectations and norms held regarding an individual's position and behavior within a group and are closely tied to identity (Stryker & Burke, 2000). Surviving siblings may experience some alteration to their identity within the family, for example, becoming an only child, with all that this means in the family. Such changes force reconsideration of what had been a fundamental part of their identity and their place in the family. This may also alter role behavior associated with that identity. While we typically think of roles as socially ascribed identities – mother, father, sister, brother – another way of looking at roles is in terms of the functions they serve: nurturer, disciplinarian, scapegoat, gatekeeper, charmer, troublemaker, etc. Roles help us understand what is expected of us in different situations, define status, and assign tasks responsible for the maintenance of the family. Following the death of a family member, roles that have served a function in the family need to be reassigned or shared, with role behavior apportioned to various family members (Walsh & McGoldrick, 1991). These new roles will then be accompanied by new expectations and demands. Thus, children may be pressured or feel an obligation to take on roles previously performed by a deceased sibling to maintain or reclaim a sense of equilibrium within the family.

Roles specific to a loss event (e.g. griever, supporter) may be ascribed to each family member in a specific form along with expectations regarding their own and others' performance, which can cause tremendous conflict in families. Loss affects assumptions about role performance, as we see with parents who were unable to fulfill the protector role for their child. They may see themselves as having failed in their role and either disengage from surviving children or become overly protective (McGoldrick & Walsh, 2004).

Family Development

The family life-cycle framework (McGoldrick & Walsh, 2004) is often used to explain normative changes/stressors (e.g. entering school, graduation) that occur in families. These are events that are anticipated and can be planned for. Regardless of any non-normative stressors/events, normal developmental change is ongoing in families. Thus, as a family works to cope with the aftermath of the death of a child and the behavioral changes in siblings, they must also cope with concurrent normative stressors that surviving siblings experience.

The family life cycle is interactive with individual development (McGoldrick & Walsh, 2004). Children at different developmental stages will experience grief in different ways. As children grow and move through different developmental stages, their conceptualization of death and how they ascribe meaning to a loss changes. Subsequently, they often re-experience the loss through this new lens. For instance, very young children may not recognize that death is permanent and their sibling will not return. As they age, they begin to understand permanence, and that they will not see their sibling again in their lifetime. The grief is fresh again, because their conceptualization and the meaning they ascribe to that loss has been altered by this new understanding (Oltjenbruns, 2001).

The effects of loss can be long-lasting, and pervade the future development of self and relationships with others (Deveau, 1997). Effects may be positive as well as negative. Children who suffer a loss may have more confidence in coping with adversity as well as greater access to personal and social resources as a result of their experiences. Positive outcomes are more likely in children who have stronger social support (Schaefer & Moos, 2001).

Grief is especially complicated for children and adolescents. As a normal part of their development, they are actively involved in the process of making meaning in their lives, a process that is tied to individual development and experience. They are working to establish their sense of self while also existing in a state of dependence. The disruption of meaning tied to the loss can be particularly devastating for them (Oltjenbruns, 2001).

Children are more likely than adults to experience fragmented recollection and a distorted understanding of the loss, attempting to make sense of the loss through their own perspective (Cook & Oltjenbruns, 1998). Both children and adolescents need an environment that is facilitative of their developing a coherent grief story, one that incorporates the recognition and acceptance of their emotions.

At the same time as they are coping with their own situation, children and adolescents must also cope with grieving adults, something that may frighten or unnerve them (Cook & Oltjenbruns, 1998; Deveau, 1997). Adults are the ones who are supposed to take care of and be available to them, not the other way around. Adolescents and children, especially older children, may feel that they need to take care of the adults. They may feel a desperate need for adults to get back to normal and stop being weird and scary.

Children and adolescents need to share their thoughts and feelings with others when they experience a loss, yet the ways in which they come to understand the loss and their techniques for grieving often are not understood or respected by adults. Their feelings may be overwhelming and frightening to them and to the adults (Cook & Oltjenbruns, 1998; Deveau, 1997).

Younger children are especially likely to want to talk and talk and talk, asking questions after adults don't want to hear them anymore, as a way of testing reality. These questions may not make sense to adults, but they do make sense to the child asking them. On the other hand, these children may turn away from the loss and information about it. This may be because of a short attention span or a temporary defense against the overwhelming nature of the loss (Deveau, 1997).

There is a great deal of variation among children and a large number of factors influencing development. In addition to normal variation, children under stress may regress to an earlier level of development. Adolescents, and even adults, may do the same. Children may adopt a variety of coping techniques that are developmentally appropriate but are, nevertheless, distressing to adults and/or may lead to later problems in relationships with others (Cook & Oltjenbruns, 1998; Oltjenbruns, 2001).

Development of the family will be affected by loss far after it has occurred. Later life transitions or other stressors may bring family members back to the pain and memories of earlier losses. Ordinarily happy family events, such as birthdays, holidays, or dates uniquely meaningful to the family, may also cause a revival of such feelings.

Relationships in the Family

Relationships within the family system are complex and multifaceted. With the loss of someone significant to us, we may feel that the relationship with that person has ended, yet work on the "continuing bond" with the deceased counters that view (Klass, Silverman, & Nickman, 1996). What continues is an internal relationship with the deceased and *that* relationship evolves and changes. The bereaved must also contend with changes in their relationship with others, both within and outside the family. Surviving siblings are faced with changes in the parent–child relationship, those between other siblings, and that which they observe between parents.

The sibling bond is a complex relationship, in which children may experience both love and hate and see each other as allies or rivals, or sometimes both. These sibling ties are fluid and changing. Loss of that sibling may bring a similarly fluid emotional response. Each surviving sibling will have a redefinition of their relationship with their deceased sibling. At the same time, their relationship with their fellow surviving siblings will be redefined. Because siblings relate to each other, at least in part, in terms of their relationship with their parents, relationships between surviving siblings may be altered by the parental response. For instance, an older child may take on increasing responsibility as a "little parent" towards younger children in order to alleviate pressure on the parent (Wender & Committee on Psychosocial Aspects of Child and Family Health, 2012). If the deceased sibling has become a "perfect" child in the eyes of their parents, surviving siblings may find an ongoing triangulated relationship in which they must compete for their parents' attention, always at a disadvantage.

Although less common than often thought, some parents will have another child as a replacement for the deceased. In this, the new sibling will provide a connection to the deceased child (Ainsfeld & Richards, 2000; McGoldrick & Walsh, 2004). Another way in which the "replacement child" phenomenon occurs is when already living siblings are placed, or place themselves, into the role of the child who has died (Ainsfeld & Richards, 2000; McGoldrick & Walsh, 2004). While this often refers to parents who pressure children into being more like their sibling (or have further children in an effort to "replace" the one who has died), it can be self-inflicted. Children may take it on as a way of staying connected to deceased siblings. It may be a form of penance as a result of survivor guilt. It may also be a way of comforting parents. By taking on their siblings' characteristics, they hope to relieve the grief of the loss (McGoldrick & Walsh, 2004).

Although the natural tendency of family members is to turn to others in the family for support after the loss (Gilbert, 1995, 1996), support may be difficult to maintain. This may take place with even young children, but the demands may exceed the capacity of those involved. Members of the families will experience their grief at different times, in different ways. At the same time, one or more of them may feel they *should* grieve in the same way, may compete with each other, may feel a need to protect each other, or may feel the best way to cope with loss is to withdraw (Gilbert, 1996). The end result may be that they grieve the original loss *and* the loss of the family system they knew and believed they could depend on (Rosenblatt et al., 1991).

One common result of a loss is the isolation of the bereaved, which can occur with both parents and siblings. In some cases, this is a self-isolation, as they may pull back, feeling overwhelmed. In other cases, the bereaved will be isolated by others. This isolation may, in fact, be unintentional, a byproduct of people, unsure of how to respond, attempting to respect the privacy of the bereaved (Wender & Committee on Psychosocial Aspects of Child and Family Health, 2012). They may also find their grieving behavior to be odd and off-putting. An irrational fear of contagion may also contribute to the isolation.

Parents grieving the loss of a child are likely to undergo significant behavioral changes of their own, including an inability to carry out normal tasks or meet the needs of their surviving children. Parents may struggle to support and care for their children when they, themselves, are in significant need of support (Buckle & Fleming, 2011). Children may exhibit increased levels of acting out or rejection after the death of their sibling (Archer, 1999), and parenting these children may be increasingly challenging (Buckle & Fleming, 2011).

Children may hide their grief or pretend they are doing well when they are not in an effort to protect their parents from further pain. Children also may experience survivor guilt or feelings of responsibility for the death (Archer, 1999; McGoldrick & Walsh, 2004; Wender & Committee on Psychosocial Aspects of Child and Family Health, 2012). The form that this guilt takes will vary developmentally and parents may find it challenging to deal with. Young children, before the age of 6, are developmentally egocentric, believing that they have far greater effect on events in the world around them than they actually do. A pre-schooler, for instance, may believe that a sibling died because they wished it to happen. Older children may experience guilt that they are alive and their sibling is not. Children may also experience a new understanding of their own frailty or mortality, leading to either excessive caution or risk-seeking behaviors which challenge that knowledge.

Summary

The loss of a child has profound and long-lasting effects on the entirety of the family system. Understanding how the members of that system respond to a loss is crucial – individuals cannot be pulled out of the system, nor can the system function in the same way when one of its members is lost. With a better understanding of the family system, the needs of the members can be addressed more effectively.

References

Anisfeld, L. & Richards, A.D. (2000). The replacement child. *The Psychoanalytic Study of the Child*, 55, 301–18.

Archer, J. (1999). *The nature of grief: The evolution of psychology in reaction to loss*. New York: Routledge.

Buckle, J.L. & Fleming, S.J. (2011). *Parenting after the death of a child: A practitioner's guide*. New York: Routledge.

Cook, A.S. & Oltjenbruns, K.A. (1998). *Dying and grieving: Life span and family perspectives* (2nd ed.). Fort Worth, TX: Harcourt Brace and Co.

Deveau, E.J. (1997). The patterns of grief in children and adolescents. In J.D. Morgan (Ed.), *Readings in thanatology* (pp. 359–89), Amityville, NY: Baywood.

Gilbert, K.R. (1995). Family loss and grief. In R.D. Day, K.R. Gilbert, B.H. Settles, & W.R. Burr (Eds.), *Research and theory in family science* (pp. 305–18). Pacific Grove, CA: Brooks/Cole.

Gilbert, K.R. (1996). "We've had the same loss, why don't we have the same grief?" Loss and differential grief in families. *Death Studies*, 20, 269–83.

Klass, D., Silverman, P.R., & Nickman, S.L. (1996). *Continuing bonds: New understanding of grief*. Philadelphia, PA: Taylor & Francis.

McGoldrick, M. & Walsh, F. (2004). A time to mourn: Death and the family life cycle. In F. Walsh & M. McGoldrick (Eds.), *Living beyond loss: Death in the family* (2nd ed.) (pp. 27–46). New York: W.W. Norton.

Oltjenbruns, K.A. (2001). Developmental context of childhood grief and regrief phenomenon. In M.S. Stroebe, R.O. Hansson, W. Stroebe, & H. Schut (Eds.), *Handbook of bereavement research: Consequences, coping and care* (pp. 169–97). Washington, DC: American Psychological Association.

Rosenblatt, P.C., Spoentgen, P., Karis, T.A., Dahl, C., Kaiser, T., & Elde, C. (1991). Difficulties in supporting the bereaved. *Omega*, 23, 119–28.

Schaefer, J.A. & Moos, R.H. (2001). Bereavement experiences and personal growth. In M.S. Stroebe, R.O. Hansson, W. Stroebe, & H. Schut (Eds.), *Handbook of bereavement research: Consequences, coping and care* (pp. 145–67). Washington, DC: American Psychological Association.

Shapiro, E.R. (1994). *Grief as a family process: A developmental approach to clinical practice*. New York: Guilford Press.

Stryker, S. & Burke, P.J. (2000). The past, present, and future of an identity theory. *Social Psychology Quarterly*, 63, 284–97.

Walsh, F. & McGoldrick, M. (1991). Loss and the family: A systemic perspective. In F. Wash & M. McGoldrick (Eds.), *Living beyond loss: Death in the family* (pp. 1–29). New York: Norton.

Wender, E. & Committee on Psychosocial Aspects of Child and Family Health (2012). Supporting the family after the death of a child. *Pediatrics*, 130, 1164–9.

White, J.M. & Klein, D.M. (2008). *Family theories* (3rd ed.). Thousand Oaks, CA: Sage.

chapter 22

The Impact on Siblings When a Parent Dies

Howard R. Winokuer

Grief is the intrapersonal response that occurs when an individual experiences a loss. Although the expression of one's grief is unique to each person, grief is often influenced by such factors as age, culture, and previous experiences with loss (D'Antonio, 2011; Winokuer & Harris, 2012). Although the focus of this book is on sibling loss and the impact that the loss of a brother or sister has on the surviving siblings, it is critical to understand that when a parent or parents die, the potential impact on the surviving sibling can also be devastating.

In the introduction to this book, Theoretical Models Guiding Our Understanding of Sibling Bereavement, Kissane and Kasparian provide a theoretical framework to help us understand sibling loss. In looking at the different types of family systems, one type of system identified is an *uninvolved* family. This is a type of family where it is common for the siblings to not be supportive to each other. One of the factors that has the ability to further fracture the relationship between siblings is associated with finance and inheritance (Carbo, 2014). In many situations, siblings who are uninvolved, in order to get their aging parents to change their wills or leave them money or property, may often do some unethical or underhanded things to influence their parents. And, the greater the loss of independence of the parents, and the greater control by one or more of the siblings, the greater the potential for increased conflict with the adult siblings. The issue of sibling rivalry is another theme that can arise when a parent dies. This rivalry, even if it was not active for many years, has the potential to tear a family apart. The sad consequence of this situation is that it has the potential to cause a rift between siblings that might not ever be able to be resolved.

The following set of events occurred in my family that led to the end of the relationship between me and my two siblings, my brother and sister. It began with the dying of my father. He died on May 6, 2000. Leading up to his death, he had been diagnosed with kidney disease; given that news, he scheduled an appointment with a nephrologist where he was informed that he would have to begin dialysis. The day he was scheduled for surgery to have a port inserted into his body, he had a major setback. That was the beginning of the end. He was admitted to the hospital after the procedure, and although we had no idea of what was to happen next, he never left. The first few days in the hospital he was relatively stable. While in the hospital, a series of tests were run to determine his health status. Besides having a problem with his kidneys, it was discovered that his arteries were once again occluded even though he had previously had quadruple bypass surgery. It was also determined that he had bilateral stomach cancer. It appears that my father's body was shutting down. As you might imagine, my mother, my siblings, and myself were all concerned. On his third day in the hospital, a Wednesday, he started having difficulty breathing. I spoke with him about the fact that he had signed a living will. I told him that, if he liked, we would honor his living will, have them administer medicine so he would be comfortable, and allow him to die peacefully. He looked at me and said, "Howard, I understand that I have a living will, however, in spite of that I would like for them to do everything that they can to keep me alive." It is interesting to note that, even though one might have a living will, when directly confronted with the imminence of death, one may change their mind. However, to honor my father's request, my siblings and I had my father brought to the ICU for further treatment. My father was intubated and put on a respirator. The first few days in the ICU seemed to go well. My father seemed to be improving and by Friday we had a sense of hope that he would leave the ICU, and possibly return home. Unfortunately, that was not meant to be. Friday night he had a major setback. Since I had been working in the hospital, I had a wonderful relationship with the doctors and the staff in the ICU. That morning, the doctor called me and said, "Howard, your father had a very bad night and I believe that he will probably die today." At this point in my father's decline, two important points need to be introduced: first, my mother had Alzheimer's disease; so therefore, she really couldn't be involved in making decisions about my father's healthcare; and second, an agreement was made between me and my siblings that no unilateral decision would be made regarding his care. So, given the news I received that morning from my father's doctor, I drove to my parents' home, where my siblings were staying, and informed them of my father's condition and prognosis. Between the three of us, we, and that's an important fact, made the decision to remove the ventilator and move my father downstairs to the hospice unit. We made that decision so that we, as well as some of my father's friends, could be with him when he died. Since I was working in the hospital, I was able to be in the ICU with my father and help the nurse prepare him in order to move him downstairs to the hospice unit. (On a personal note, it was such a privilege to be there to help the nurse prepare my father for transport.) During the process, the nurse and I cleaned his body, talked about his life, and talked about the topic of death. Imagine me doing that? Prior to our moving my father down to the hospice unit, the nurse said to me, "Dr. Winokuer, thank you for allowing me to be part of this experience; we are so busy in the ICU that we never really have this kind of time with our dying patients and a family member."

It was now noon on Saturday and my father was ready to be moved to the hospice unit. He was settled in his room by 12:25pm, at which time my mother, brother, sister, and some of my father's friends joined us in the room for the "death watch." I believe that this was the beginning of the end of my relationship with my siblings. At approximately 2:00pm, my brother stated the following: "there is nothing more we can do for dad, we now have to focus our energy on the future and on taking care of Mom." At that point my mother, brother, and sister left the room and went home; leaving me and my father's friends to be with him until he died. Prior to his death, he had been in a coma; however, just before his death, he awakened and sat up in his bed. At the time I was holding his hand. When he awakened, he looked at me directly in my eyes. I said, "Dad I love you and it is okay for you to let go and die." He looked at me, smiled, and said "I love you too." He lay back down, took his last breath, and died. He died at 4:21pm. There was an interesting side note I'd like to share at this time. The hospital has a tradition that, whenever a new baby is born, the Brahms Lullaby is piped through the hospital through the public address system. The moment my father died, I heard the lullaby; it reminded me of the refrain from a song by the musical group Blood, Sweat and Tears that stated, "and when I die, and when I'm gone, there will be one child born in this world to carry on." In retrospect, I wished that I had taken the time to find out who that baby was that was born at the moment of my father's death.

Back to the issue of my relationship with my siblings; after my father's death, in the spirit of our doing everything together as a family, I arranged with the funeral home to set up a meeting with the funeral director to plan my father's funeral. Given my experience in working in the field of dying, death, and bereavement, I was able to prepare my siblings for everything that was about to occur at the meeting with the funeral director; from the questions that would be asked, the decisions that had to be made, and the process of preparing for his burial. After the meeting, my brother stated, "I could never have imagined it would have gone so smoothly." The funeral went smoothly and the family seemed to be doing as well as could be expected. The next few weeks were difficult, but we survived.

It was a few weeks later that problems began arising. It started at the reading of my father's will. My father had designated me to be the executor of the will. I believe that he made me the executor because I was the only child who had not filed for bankruptcy. Although my father's will was clear, it appeared that my siblings were not happy with how the will read. Basically, the will stated that, at the time of my father's death, the entirety of his estate would go to my mother. And, when my mother died, the balance of the estate would be divided equally in thirds between me, my brother, and my sister. This seemed equitable to me and I was honored to be able to execute his will. As I mentioned previously, I don't believe that my siblings were happy with my father's decision to make me the executor of the will. It was about three weeks later that the first bomb exploded. I received a call from my brother telling me that he wanted me to meet with him, my mother, and my sister. At the meeting he informed me that he and my sister had taken my mother to an attorney, had rescinded my father's will, and changed it so my mother would be the executrix of the will. I asked my siblings the following question: "Do you really believe, with her Alzheimer's disease, that she has the cognitive ability to manage the will?" My sister responded, "Don't you think Mom should have the ability to manage her own affairs?" My response was a resounding "no." My sibling stated that I was being out voted and that the change would stand. I considered contesting it and had retained my attorney to do so. However, I asked myself, "Do you really want to subject your mother to a psychiatric evaluation in order to have her declared incompetent?" I decided against it.

My siblings then informed me that I could no longer come visit my mother, who they were caring for at my parents' residence, unless I made an appointment. They also changed the locks on the doors so that my key did not work. It seemed pretty clear to me that they didn't want me involved in either my mother's care or their lives. After the incident with the will and new guidelines about visitation, I decided that it was in my best interest to not have contact with them. My father died on May 6, 2000 and I have had no contact with them since that time.

Time had moved on and it was now November 2005. It had been over five years since I had been in contact with my siblings. One time in discussing this issue with my rabbi, he said something profound: "Although you may not have a relationship with your brother and sister, you have something that they don't have, your mental health." On Saturday, November

19, 2005, I received a phone call from my sister. She said, "I have to tell you something." I said, "Mom died." She said yes. I was not very involved in the planning of my mother's funeral. They handled all of the details. I did, however, go over to their home after the burial. We actually had, what I thought, was a healing time. They said that they would like me to come by and visit. I thought that would be nice. The following day I called to tell them that I would like to come by after attending a *shiva* service that evening at the temple. I was taken aback when they said, "Given all that's happened in the past, we're not quite ready to let you back in our lives, we need some more time and we'll call you in two to three weeks." I'll be honest, I didn't expect a call. However, approximately two and a half weeks later I received a call from the both of them. The call started out with them venting and accusing me of not being there during my mother's dying. However, after they vented, they stated that they wanted to let bygones be bygones and wanted to move forward and be a family again. I felt very hopeful. Then they informed me of the following: in order for us to be a family again, I would have to show them a sign of good faith that I wanted to be part of the family again. When I questioned them as to what the sign of good faith would be, they informed me that they wanted me to write them a check for $50,000. I told them that I would need some time to think about it. They asked how much time I would need. Based on the fact that they needed two to three weeks to make their decision, I thought it was reasonable for me to take that amount of time for me to make my decision. My sister said that I had to make the decision the next day. Below is the letter I wrote the next day as my response to them.

December 7, 2005

To my siblings

Charlotte, NC

Dear L.N. and D.M.,

This is a very difficult letter for me to write. I want you to know how nice it was to be with you at Mom's funeral (even though it was painful) and how hopeful I felt, that in spite of what's happened in the past, that we might be able to reconnect and be a family again. Unfortunately, that didn't last long. It started the next day when I was told that you weren't quite ready to have me back in your lives. It got worse when we spoke last Friday.

I was really taken aback when I was told that in order to be accepted back into the family, I needed to show a sign of love and caring. That act of kindness that you were asking for appeared to be my willingness to help pay off part of your $50,000 debt. Had that been approached a little differently, for example, after some healing had taken place, I might have been open to considering the proposal. However, I felt that the request was asking me to buy your love and that was the only way I would be accepted back into the family. If I can't be accepted for who I am, rather than what I can give, I don't need to be back in the family. I want you to know that I'm really sorry that you are in such debt. I would have been more than willing to have helped you with Mom's finances during these last years had I been asked, however, it was made clear to me, through your changing of Dad's wishes for me to be the executor and your having me call before I could come by and see Mom, that you guys wanted to be in charge of Mom's care and Dad's estate. Well, I backed off and allowed you to do what you felt was necessary. I am thankful that, with you in charge, Mom had the best of care she could have had.

I had hoped that Mom's death might be the catalyst for us to be a family again. In regard to your asking me to help with the debt, I'm not willing to help. I'm not willing to pay money in order to buy back your love. I want you to know that I hope that the two of you can continue to love and support each other and work through this financial difficulty and the pain of Mom's death. I also want you to know that I will always love you and care about you. I will always be your brother.

Howard

Unfortunately, sometimes when a parent or both parents die, it can cause a fracture in the relationship between siblings that can't be healed. I think that the root of this issue was money. It is my belief that my siblings believed that I was already successful and did not need to inherit anything from my parents' estate. And as was stated previously in this chapter, one of the factors that has the ability to further fracture the relationship between siblings is associated with finance and inheritance (Carbo, 2014). That was the case in my family. In conclusion, I think it is helpful to understand that we have two types of families: families of origin and families of choice (Ackendorf, 2011). Although I do not have my family of origin, I am blessed to have a family of choice that provides me with love, support, and comfort. Remember, if your family is fractured due to the death of your parents, you can still have very meaningful relationships with your family of choice.

References

Ackendorf, J. (2011). Families of choice vs. families of origin. Retrieved from: http://www.examiner.com/article/family-of-origin-vs-family-of-choice.

Carbo, D. (2014). Family feud over inheritance and uninvolved siblings. *Caregiver Relief*. Retrieved from: http://caregiverrelief.com/family-feud-inheritance/.

D'Antonio, J. (2011). Grief and loss of a caregiver in children: A developmental perspective. *Journal of Psychological Nursing and Mental Health Services*, 49, 10, 17–20.

Winokuer, H.R. & Harris, D.L. (2012). *Principles and Practices of Grief Counseling*. New York: Springer.

chapter 23

Disappearance, Not Death

The Ambiguous Loss of a Missing Sibling

Pauline Boss and Patty Wetterling

> People kept asking, "How are your parents doing?" What about me? Don't they want to know how I'm doing?
> (Trevor; US Department of Justice, 2007, p. 11)

On October 22, 1989, Jacob Wetterling of St. Joseph, Minnesota, and his brother and a friend were bicycling home from a convenience store at dusk. A half mile from home, they were confronted by a masked man with a gun. He told the boys to lie down in a ditch or he would shoot. He asked their ages. Trevor was 10, Aaron 11, and Jacob 11. He told Trevor to run into the woods or he would shoot, so Trevor took off. He said the same thing to Aaron and Aaron took off, but as he was leaving he saw the man put his hand on Jacob's shoulder, and when Aaron caught up to Trevor and they looked back, they were gone. The boys ran home and told the babysitter to call 911. "Somebody took Jacob," Trevor screamed.

Within six minutes police were at the scene and Trevor, Jacob's brother, began a journey of not only missing his brother but also being a key witness to this horrific crime.

Joining Forces

In this chapter, a family therapist (Pauline Boss) joins forces with the mother (Patty Wetterling) of a missing son in order to raise awareness of the impact of kidnapping on siblings. To guide professionals, we describe the unique stress and grief that follows such loss, especially for left-behind siblings. We also address why closure is impossible, why the effects may be similar but unlike those of PTSD, and why families of the missing understandably continue to hope.

While Boss offers theoretical underpinning of Family Systems Theory, Wetterling addresses the effect on siblings from first-hand observations and experience with families she has worked with and with her own children – Jacob, who remains missing after 25 years, and two daughters and a son who live nearby today. Wetterling, the co-founder of the Jacob Wetterling Foundation, was chair of the National Center for Missing and Exploited Children, and is recognized today as a US advocate for children's safety. The ripple effect of kidnapping affects the entire family system, but the piece of the system that has had insufficient study is the siblings. Exceptions are Clark, Warburton and Tilse (2009) and Greif and Bowers (2007).

Most professionals have been trained in grief and trauma therapies, but these are insufficient after kidnapping and often harmful when loved ones go missing. We need to learn more about what works. Our assumption is that parents and siblings of the missing hold an untapped "expertise of experience" from which we can learn. For example, Boss has developed the theory of ambiguous loss from her decades of listening to families of the missing (Boss, 1999, 2002, 2004, 2006; Boss, Beaulieu, Wieling, Turner, & LaCruz, 2003; Boss & Carnes, 2012; Boss & Ishii, 2015).

What Is Ambiguous Loss?

> Not knowing is probably the worst thing. In the end, it takes control… Your control is lost. You have no control when you don't know.
> (Beth; Clark et al., 2009, p. 275)

When a child is kidnapped, the other siblings face a unique experience – that of ambiguous loss. An ambiguous loss is a loss that remains unclear and thus defies closure. There is no verification of the missing child's status as dead or alive, so parents and siblings are immobilized in an indeterminate state of "not knowing." Unlike with death, there is no finality, and no community ritual for easing the pain.

In Their Own Words: Uncharted Territory for Siblings

Wetterling's daughter, now 32, writes:

> When I was in second grade, my brother was kidnapped...While most second graders were learning to add and subtract, I had to learn how to press "record" on our telephone [in case someone called with a lead]. I had to learn how to go to sleep with so many people in our house. I had to learn how to live with one less person in our family.

Wetterling writes:

> People can't possibly understand what the siblings of a missing child go through on a daily basis. They hate seeing their parents in pain and so constantly sad. They need some semblance of order, some of the routine back in their lives. They need friends and, depending on the age, that can be challenging. When our youngest was in second grade, Jacob's story was all over the news. Our family was suddenly "famous." She would go to school and everyone wanted to be her best friend. They wanted to sit by her; everyone wanted to be by her...but she just wanted school to be normal. She wanted one place in her life that was solid, the same as it had been before.
>
> The opposite happened to our oldest daughter who was then 13. Nobody knew what to say so there were many days when she would go to school and except for her best friends, nobody would talk to her, especially at the beginning.

Yet, her daughter writes, "For me, it was good to go back to school because it gave me structure and routine and it felt normal." Wetterling continues: "There was no part of their lives that was untouched. Family gatherings, their birthdays, holidays, and especially their brother's birthday were changed because the loss grows bigger. It was softened only a little over time. There remains a hole in their hearts – and lives – that few can really understand.

Clark et al. (2009) also found that most participants in their Australian study said "they thought about their missing sibling *all the time*" (p. 275). "Not knowing is probably the worst thing. In the end, it takes control...Your control is lost. You have no control when you don't know" (Beth) (p. 275). Wetterling adds:

> Siblings often share with each other because they don't want to burden their parents. They may grow up faster than their peers or they may regress to earlier childhood behaviors or both. They walk in uncharted territory and have to live with everyone's thoughts on what it must feel like, all the while knowing that no one else really knows.

Hoping and the Myth of Closure

Why do parents and siblings of the missing keep on hoping? This may seem like a legitimate question, but to families who live with ambiguous loss and "not knowing" the whereabouts or fate of a loved one, this is an inane question. Simply put, families keep hoping because there is no proof that they should not. "Closure" is impossible.

Hope, however, changes over time. It transcends into something bigger. A mother in Kosovo searching for her son first hoped for his return, then years later, to have his remains returned, and even later, to put flowers on his grave wherever that was. In the end, she may not have achieved any of those hopes, but meanwhile, she worked hard to be a good mother to her remaining children while also helping other families of the disappeared. Hope motivates families of the missing to move forward which allows them to imagine new hopes and dreams, often for a greater good (Boss, 2006).

Wetterling writes: "Our family has lived on the hope that one day our son, our brother, our grandson, our cousin, will be found and come home to us. As a parent, that was what I needed to do. Jacob's brother and two sisters have lived on that hope as well. Not everyone understands that hope, but we do."

How right she is! People in more mastery-oriented and can-do societies are eager to find closure after loss; they want the aggrieved to "get over it." It may be uncomfortable to witness long-term suffering and problems we cannot fix, but more patience is needed for those who, through no fault of their own, must live with the pain of unanswered questions.

Wetterling found that "Left-behind siblings hate the term 'closure.' Their lives are forever changed – they will never go back to being who they were – so 'closure' doesn't work for them, or any of us. We need 'answers,' not closure. That word is better." She continues: "On a Mother's Day some years ago, my oldest daughter framed a special verse for me that she had found. It is still comforting to me because it defines hope in a way that is right for me."

> HOPE
> is not pretending
> that troubles don't exist...
> it is the trust
> that they will not last forever,
> that hurts will be healed,
> and difficulties overcome...
> it is the faith
> that a source of strength
> and renewal lies within
> to lead us through the dark
> to the sunshine

In the absence of facts, there are no absolute answers. To think so is hubris. The least we can do is to allow parents and siblings their sliver of hope, because it sustains their resilience and motivation to live a good life. To tell them to give up hope is at the least misleading, and at the most cruel.

Both-And Thinking

Intervention and therapy for ambiguous loss is paradoxical. The more we tell family members to give up hope and find closure, the more they resist moving forward. Instead, we propose *both-and thinking*. Parents and siblings learn to hold two opposing ideas in their minds at the same time, e.g., continuing to hope for a good outcome while also moving forward with life. We support their hope for reunion while encouraging them to hope for something new. This is both-and thinking. Siblings may hope for a missing brother or sister to return and simultaneously work on a project to honor them. Such both-and thinking lowers the stress and anxiety that lingers with ambiguous loss.

The Wetterling family continues to both hope for Jacob's return and hope that fewer children will be kidnapped in the future as a result of their tireless work with the Jacob Wetterling Resource Center and the National Center for Missing and Exploited Children. Starting a foundation is a good example of both-and thinking as well as memorializing Jacob.

Culture

More research is needed to discern cultural differences in sibling effects, but Wetterling states:

> I believe that often huge challenges exist culturally. I have worked with families where language is a barrier and the children in the family become translators for the parents, which is a terribly difficult role for siblings of the missing child. Language barriers may also delay response from law enforcement.
>
> Recently in Minnesota, there was a 12-year-old boy, who had emigrated from Liberia, reported missing. He had told his friends on the school bus, as they neared his home, that he could see his uncle there outside his apartment. The boy disappeared a few hours later. After that, there was great discussion about who is an "uncle" in their culture. It was deemed to be any adult male. To this day, no one knows who this "uncle" was or is. This boy was missing for 24 days and was then found dead in the Mississippi River. After investigation, his father was arrested. The "uncle" remains a mystery.

Wetterling tells of other cultural challenges:

> I first learned about cultural challenges when I worked with an Hispanic family whose 12-year-old daughter went missing. She was thought to be with a 26-year-old man. The parents had been granted a restraining order against that man, but when I spoke to police [on their behalf], they suggested there wasn't really a problem because this man had the same address as the missing girl. I basically screamed, "It's an apartment building!" They told me that I had gotten entangled in a "cultural situation." The police said, "That's what 'they' do – these Latina young girls – they often have older boyfriends." Needless to say, there was little effort to find this young girl – initially.
>
> Also, in some cultures, I noticed that the extended family can be very tight so cousins can feel almost like siblings especially if they are all living in the same household. The loss then is almost as painful as the loss of a sibling.
>
> Finally, there can also be big challenges with trusting law enforcement in different cultural communities. Family members are often afraid to share what they know. This makes it difficult for families and also for the police.

Cautions for Professionals

In this chapter, professionals mean not only medical and mental health clinicians, but also clergy, teachers, counselors, police officers, journalists, attorneys, and judges. Wetterling writes:

Our family had regular family "meetings" to sort through some of the investigation, the news coverage, and challenges that we were facing. We were lucky to have extended family step in and help us out. My oldest daughter went to a therapist years later who said she must have felt abandoned. My daughter and her siblings talked about it and said, "No." They never felt abandoned but that is what everyone keeps projecting on them. It's still a challenge 25 years later for them to be understood.

Recently, we were shocked by the miraculous escape of three young women abducted and held captive for ten years in Cleveland. The sister of Amanda, one of the kidnapped women, told the judge: "The impact of these crimes on our family is something that we do not want to discuss with people we do not know…Even if I wanted to talk about it, it is impossible to put into words. For me, I lost my sister for all those years and thought it was forever" (Berry, DeJesus, Jordan, & Sullivan, 2015, p. 282).

Common Themes among Siblings of the Missing

Although more research is needed with larger and longitudinal samples, researchers Greif and Bowers (2007) suggest common themes among left-behind siblings – trust, parental reactions, communication patterns, unexpressed emotions, finding meaning, moving forward with life, and learning healthy coping mechanisms (pp. 214–17). But we must also listen to questions (also thematic) asked by left-behind siblings in their own voice. For this, we highly recommend the guidebook, *What About Me? Coping with the Abduction of a Brother or Sister* (US Department of Justice, 2007). Noting their directness and specificity, here are some questions siblings asked:

- Is home still "home" without my sibling there?
- Do we still sit at the same places at the table?
- Can I still borrow my sibling's clothes or toys?
- What do we do on my missing sibling's birthday? Do we just ignore it?
- How do I answer the phone if it's for my missing brother or sister?
- What about his or her room? Can I still go in there to find something? What if the police have blocked it off? Will it upset my parents if I go in there like I usually would?
- The police took some of the things that we shared – the computer, clothes, even a hairbrush. Will we ever get them back?

(US Department of Justice, 2007, p. 5)

These questions may differ from what we might ask, but siblings who posed them emphasized, "We are not trained mental health professionals. We are compassionate brothers and sisters" (p. 2). Their guidebook has resulted in a national family-like community of siblings who stay in touch with each other regularly by Facebook, chat rooms, and annual reunions. Wetterling's children were also part of the group. She says, "My kids no longer felt alone. They could be with others their age that understood what they were going through. They didn't have to explain."

Clark et al. (2009) state that while there is inadequate social response about "missingness," there is almost no information or social response about siblings of the missing. Yet, the sibling relationship is typically the longest human relationship (Bank & Kahn, 1982; Sanders, 2004; White, 2001), and its rupture by kidnapping destroys the normal expectation of growing old together. Left-behind siblings thus have a longer time to carry the pain of ambiguous loss. For this reason alone, there must be more study and more social awareness of left-behind siblings. Longitudinal research is needed to reveal not only the long-term individual effects of ambiguous loss, but also the systemic effects of a ruptured relationship that was expected to continue into adulthood and old age.

Implications for Future Research, Therapy, and Intervention

Research shows that peer groups are highly effective in easing stress for individuals and families experiencing various losses. Based on the success of peer groups using the guide *What about Me?* (US Department of Justice, 2007), we propose that peer groups are also highly effective for left-behind siblings. While we acknowledge that therapy is needed for some siblings of the missing, we submit that peer groups will be more helpful to the majority because they provide a family-like community of siblings who understand, like no one else, the experience of having a missing brother or sister.

An important point for professionals and researchers is that responses to ambiguous loss differ from ordinary loss and should not automatically be assessed as pathological (Boss, 2006; Boss & Carnes, 2012; Boss & Ishii, 2015; Boyden & Mann, 2005). It is the type of loss that is problematic, not the family system.

Nevertheless, the term *PTSD* is overused with siblings of the missing. Indeed the term *trauma* "indicates an emotional wound or shock resulting from exposure to an event or situation that causes substantial, lasting damage to the psychological development of a person" (Boyden & Mann, 2005, p. 13), but it does not always lead to pathology such as PTSD. In fact,

PTSD is the wrong diagnosis for left-behind siblings because there is nothing "post" about their traumatic event. Their stressor is chronic and may last a lifetime. If we have been trained to see only symptoms of pathology, we may not see the resilient majority.

Summary

There are many people who do well in life even though they have a missing sibling. While we must attend to those who actually need medical help, we must not forget the majority who need only psycho-educational interventions – e.g., informational support, emotional support, and peer-group support. Professionals may organize such groups and be available, but left-behind siblings need the company of peers who understand their unique loss. Family- and community-based systemic approaches focus less on pathology and more on how to live with the ambiguity of "not knowing."

Clark et al. (2009) write: "Individuals and families have experienced, and continue to experience, unremitting frustration. A more adequate response is long overdue" (p. 276). We agree and propose that the system of support and intervention in which left-behind siblings thrive is broader than just their own family or clinicians. It must include their peers and a collaborating team of support, focusing less on individual symptoms and PTSD, and more on resilience and the use of systemic interventions.

As this chapter goes to press, Patty Wetterling and her family are dealing with the discovery of Jacob's remains.

References

Bank, S. & Kahn, D. (1982). *The sibling bond.* New York: Basic Books.
Berry, A., DeJesus, G., Jordan, M., & Sullivan, K. (2015). *Hope: A memoir of survival in Cleveland.* New York: Penguin.
Boss, P. (1999). *Ambiguous loss: Learning to live with unresolved grief.* Cambridge, MA: Harvard University Press.
Boss, P. (2002). Ambiguous loss: Working with families of the missing. *Family Process,* 41, 14–17.
Boss, P. (2004). Ambiguous loss research, theory, and practice: Reflections after 9/11. *Journal of Marriage and Family,* 66(3), 551–66.
Boss, P. (2006). *Loss, trauma, and resilience: Therapeutic work with ambiguous loss.* New York: Norton.
Boss, P., Beaulieu, L., Wieling, E., Turner, W., & LaCruz, S. (2003). Healing loss, ambiguity, and trauma: A community-based intervention with

families of union workers missing after the 9/11 attack in New York City. *Journal of Marital and Family Therapy*, 29(4), 455–67.

Boss, P. & Carnes, D. (2012). The myth of closure. *Family Process*, 51(4), 456–60.

Boss, P. & Ishii, C. (2015). Trauma and ambiguous loss: The lingering presence of the physically absent. In K. Cherry (Ed.), *Traumatic stress and long-term recovery: Coping with disasters and other negative life events* (pp. 271–89). New York: Springer.

Boyden, J. & Mann, G. (2005). Children's risk, resilience, and coping in extreme situations. In M. Ungar (Ed.), *Handbook for working with children and youth: Pathways to resilience across cultures and contexts* (pp. 3–27). Thousand Oaks, CA: Sage.

Clark, J., Warburton, J., & Tilse, C. (2009). Missing siblings: Seeking more adequate social responses. *Child and Family Social Work*, 14, 267–77. doi: 10.1111/j.1365-2206.2008.00593.x.

Greif, G.L. & Bowers, D.T. (2007). Unresolved loss: Issues in working with adults whose siblings were kidnapped years ago. *American Journal of Family Therapy*, 35(3), 203–19.

Sanders, R. (2004). *Sibling relationships: Theory and issues for practice*. London: Palgrave Macmillan.

US Department of Justice, Office of Justice Programs (2007). *What about me? Coping with the abduction of a brother or sister*. Washington, DC: US Department of Justice.

White, L. (2001). Sibling relationships over the life course: A panel analysis. *Journal of Marriage and Family*, 63, 555–69.

chapter 24

The Dirt on Sibling Grief
A Look at Bereavement Camps

Tina Barrett and Molly Murphy

> Walk away quietly in any direction and taste the freedom of the mountaineer. Camp out among the grass and gentians of glacier meadows, in craggy garden nooks full of Nature's darlings. Climb the mountains and get their good tidings. Nature's peace will flow into you as sunshine flows into trees. The winds will blow their own freshness into you, and the storms their energy, while cares will drop off like autumn leaves.
>
> (Muir, 1992, p. 481)

The journey of grief has been compared to a venture through an internal wilderness. This path through uncharted territory can feel lonely, intimidating, and ominous. The grief journey may be even more pronounced for bereaved siblings who have unique needs. Whether a death occurs suddenly, prematurely, and/or after a pervasive illness, the impact on a child can be wrenching with numerous and life-changing effects (Busch & Kimble, 2001; Trozzi, Massimini, & Brazelton, 1999).

Nature-based camps and retreats can be ideal settings for bereavement programs (Schachter & Georgopoulos, 2008). Outdoor-based grief support programs can be tailored for the unique needs of bereaved siblings providing opportunities to foster connections with understanding peers, develop a wider repertoire of constructive outlets, and reflect upon natural metaphors. The casual, non-clinical setting is appealing (Fletcher & Hinkle, 2002).

Highlighting the voices of children and families who have participated in grief camps and retreats, this chapter explores the healing qualities of nature-based grief support for young people following the death of a brother or sister. Words of wisdom of bereaved siblings and their parents from *A Camp to Remember* grief camp exit interviews, compiled between 1998 and 2014, illuminate the benefits of the great outdoors in healing. Their comments are interspersed throughout the chapter.

Benefits of Grief Camps

> Talk counseling alone with bereaved children does not help them reconcile death loss into their young lives. It doesn't create wellspring of hope for healing and a sense of belonging in the world. It doesn't heal the wound of grief that comes with the death of someone loved. Yet something even simpler than talk counseling often has these desired effects: experiencing nature.
>
> (Wolfelt, 1996, p. 190)

The benefits of placing a bereavement program within a natural setting are plentiful. Supervised wide-open space and inviting lakes are conducive for fun as well as for letting off steam. Natural metaphors abound and can facilitate understanding and insight. Unique fallen logs and green meadows become natural gathering spots – places to build support networks with understanding peers. Favorite rock outcroppings or a nook under the pines may create an inviting space for self-reflection and contemplation. As campers and staff allow themselves to relax into the rhythm around them, camp pace provides a respite from the busyness and disparate energy in city life.

Kids grieving the death of a brother or sister describe distinct ways grief camps can be beneficial. A qualitative analysis (Barrett, 2003) blending multiple years of camp evaluations with extended interviews illuminated the following five valuable themes.

Connections with Understanding Others

Though we can't take the pain away, we are stronger together. The intimacy of the multiday camp setting – sharing bunk beds, engaging in new adventures, and exchanging stories – inevitably brings people together. This camaraderie, or connections with others who "get it," is a strong component to healing. Multiple campers shared the value of meeting others who have also experienced the death of a sibling. In the words of one camper, "I love everyone here. The best part of camp is being able to talk about it with people who understand. I have made new friends and memories." Another camper shared, "I lost my brother to suicide two years ago and camp has helped me so much... [It] helped me meet new people that have experienced a loss in their lives."

Group work with children can foster feelings of trust, safety, and joy; support the development of positive coping strategies; and provide opportunities for verbal and non-verbal reflection and self-expression (Sommers-Flanagan, Barrett-Hakanson, Clarke, & Sommers-Flanagan, 2000). Camps help bereaved siblings feel less isolated in their experience.

> My brother died when I was in 3rd grade, and my family is extremely sad about it. Support programs have helped me by letting me talk freely about my loss and not feel judged. Also by just being there for support. It helps that I could talk about his death and help my other brother through it. Knowing I am not the only one going through it makes it easier to express my feelings.
>
> (Camper)

Opportunities to Honor and Remember

Campers articulate the value of sharing stories, asking questions, and exploring how the life and death of a sibling continue to shape personal identities, values, and priorities. One child shared, "You might want to come to *A Camp to Remember* because you can light a candle for your sister or person." Another camper grieving the death of her sister offered the following reflection:

> You have to go on with your life and just because one balloon popped, the rest don't have to. They will always be with you and you can always say they are not totally gone, that they are still with you. They are in your heart and it is just really good. It was just really wonderful how you guys were so caring and so loving and stuff.

Immersion in the Natural World

Wild landscapes are ripe with natural metaphors, which can facilitate insight (Santostefano, 2004). Weaving metaphors together with personal experience and self-observation can foster self-discovery, hope, and strength along the grief journey. Evident are the life cycles of living plants and animals in different stages of the life cycle; examples of the resiliency of living things amidst adverse conditions and severe trials; and different ways of adapting and persevering. Some metaphors arise naturally: watching an ant carry an enormous load or marveling at a tree growing out of a crack in the rocks. Other metaphors arise from ways individuals or groups respond to natural challenges or more structured activities. One camper created a memory boat out of natural objects that symbolized his deceased sister, including small sticks arranged in a heart, a jagged pebble, and a flower.

Our grieving hearts and brains benefit from soothing moments and relaxed bodies. Learning to relax and center (self-regulate) our systems decreases suffering (Baranowsky, Gentry, & Schultz, 2011). Relaxation and self-regulation skills are important components to a child's healing. Campers allude to the splendor, calm, tranquility, and ease of the natural setting. One child shared, "It was peaceful where we were. It was pretty and you could just go sit and be alone and be with the water or be with the trees or be with anything" (Barrett, 2003, p. 194).

Freedom to Be

Permission to experience a range of emotions, thoughts, and reactions without judgment is a theme amongst campers. One young girl explained,

> There are times when you want to laugh the rest of the day and there are times when you want to do nothing but sit down and cry. There's so many different feelings. There are times when everyone wants to be funny and hilarious and times when people want to be serious or times when people feel like laughing or just talking or being quiet and shy. And everyone is good with it. Everyone is fine with how you feel…That's what helped me – just to know that I wasn't alone and there was gonna be people who were going to cry and I could cry if I wanted to and if I wanted to laugh I could laugh.
>
> (Barrett, 2003, p. 192)

Fun

When a household is caring for a terminally ill child, the routine is often strongly influenced, even dominated, by medical appointments and treatment protocols, or special needs and changing abilities. Following the death of a young person, the adults in the household often understandably express extreme distress. Guardians are likely to experience increased emotion, volatility, difficulty concentrating and following routines, and find themselves with less energy, motivation, and joy. One child explained,

> The loss of my sister in my family has been a long and windy road. Watching my sister struggle and fight leukemia was tough and after a few weeks she lost her battle and it took her away from my family and I. With the help of family and programs through *A Camp to Remember* and Tamarack Grief Resource Center, I have been able to cope with my losses and the changes in my life.

Parents expressed similar sentiments:

> Everyone gets so wrapped up with that it is important to cry and the anger and this and that, but they overlook the laughing. The fun. The spontaneity...People will think, "Well you must be all better because you laughed," or "are you crazy? All this just happened and you are having a good time?" But the important part is to have fun. Being with other kids in the same boat, that all have the same problems, that can all laugh. It is going to be all right.
>
> (Barrett, 2003, p. 286)

> My hope was that the emphasis be how to have fun. All these kids there know how to mourn. They do it day in and day out. They've lived with it, sometimes for years, and the important thing is that they again learn that doesn't stop you from having a life and enjoying things and that the person you lost would not want you to not have a wonderful camp experience.
>
> (Barrett, 2003, p. 265)

Indeed, campers echo the value of sheer delight in healing programs. In exit interviews, when asked about the best part of grief camp, the majority of campers reference "fun" in their response:

"It was fun."
"It was really fun."
"It is a lot of fun."
"I would do everything the same. It was a lot of fun and I thought it was perfect."
"It was pretty fun."
"It was just really fun."
"It is something fun to do."
"It will be one of the funnest experiences, one of the best experiences."

A Look at Reconciliation Needs in a Grief Camp Context

Worden outlined reconciliation needs for grieving children, or "tasks of mourning" (Worden, 2009, p. 39). These tasks are congruent with the themes identified by campers in interviews (Barrett, 2003). Not surprisingly, grief camp can be an ideal setting for addressing these tasks.

Task I: To Accept the Reality of the Loss

Gently confronting the reality that a significant person has died and will not return is important to healing. A child's ability to acknowledge the reality of the death is supported by opportunities to talk, play, and engage in rituals in the camp setting.

Task II: To Process the Pain of Grief

Children need permission to grieve and experience the range of emotions surrounding their experience. Hilliard (2001) points out that children not only experience grief differently than adults, they also may lack the verbal skills necessary to express their feelings and thus begin developing alternative coping strategies. Care professionals illuminate the importance of play and creative expression in meaning making and healing with children. Young people express their feelings through play (Fitzgerald, 1992). Camps can provide ample opportunity to learn and play, practicing safe, appealing, dynamic, and effective outlets for a variety of emotions.

Task III: To Adjust to a World without the Deceased

Bowlby (1973, 1980) dedicated his career to researching the tendency in human beings to form strong, affectionate bonds with others. He also observed the intense emotional reaction following a break in attachment bonds including behavioral changes marking protest, despair, and detachment. When the bond is restored, the protests stop and the distress decreases. Bowlby's work suggests a sequence that parallels the response of young children following the death of a family member.

The internal, external, and spiritual adjustments following the death of a sibling can be eased at camp by opportunities to explore self-identity, build adaptive strategies, experience feelings of competence, and create new meaning and memories.

Task IV: To Find an Enduring Connection with the Deceased in the Midst of Embarking on a New Life

Albom (1997) reminds us, "Death ends a life, not a relationship" (p. 174). That being said, relationships can be darn tricky, and deserve time and attention. As a child shifts a relationship from one of presence to one of memory, camps can be a place to share those memories, ask questions, and explore new ways to honor the relationship with someone who is no longer alive.

Implications for Counselors

The camp setting allows for healing opportunities throughout the entire experience.

Constructive Outlets

"After my brother was shot and killed, I became unsocial...Camp has benefited me by helping me learn to talk about it...*A Camp to Remember* has been a tremendous opportunity to help me open up, and I would like to be able to help others try and overcome some of the obstacles they may have struggles with" (Camper). Campers deserve opportunities, without pressure, to share stories about the death and life of their deceased siblings. Through structured and informal interactions with others, young people discover and offer parts of their own grief journey. Because words and verbal expression are not necessarily a child's most prominent way of processing, creative opportunities become a valuable avenue for self-expression. Options may include jewelry making, memory books, decorating picture frames, painting rocks, constructing worry dolls, or decorating flags of honor and remembrance.

We store tension related to trauma in our bodies (Levine, 1997; Van Der Kolk, 2014). Wide-open meadows and playing fields are fantastic venues for structured release. Natural landscapes can also allow for opportunities for relaxation. Campers benefit from understanding where stress is stored in their bodies and practicing ways to release that energy.

Rituals

Rituals serve many purposes. Shrines may be created to honor the significance of an event. Memory boats or spirals can help release painful parts of an experience (Barrett, 2012). Other rituals honor continued bonds or help reconcile difficult emotions (Doka, 2008). A burning ceremony is one example of a ritual of reconciliation allowing bereft individuals to express or receive forgiveness, or to express a message to the deceased. As campers gather around a stable foundation for the camp fire, each camper may add a letter or drawing to the fire pit and share bits of their story. As it is set ablaze, accompanied by camper-selected songs, the result is a unified chorus of very different voices holding similar experiences coming together for strength, shared sorrow, hope, and new growth.

Summary

Bereavement camps provide time to honor and remember, connect with peers with similar loss histories, and enjoy traditional camp experiences. Grieving siblings are often immersed in a house full of sorrow. Blending grief activities with camp recreation recognizes that children are still "kids" first and foremost, while honoring the fact that each child holds a unique grief experience that is ever present. Camp offers a variety of outlets for grief responses and for exploring self-identity. Days balance time to honor and remember as well as time to be silly and to experience joy and delight.

Immersion in an outdoor setting, surrounded by the wonders and trials of the natural world, fosters a sense of interconnection, a different look at life and death, and opportunities for meaning making.

References

Albom, M. (1997). *Tuesdays with Morrie: An old man, a young man, and life's greatest lesson.* New York: Doubleday.

Baranowsky, A.B., Gentry, J.E., & Schultz, D.F. (2011). *Trauma practice: Tools for stabilization and recovery* (2nd ed.). Cambridge, MA: Hogrefe Publishing.

Barrett, C. (2012). The grief spiral. In R.A. Neimeyer (Ed.), *Techniques of grief therapy: Creative practices for counseling the bereaved* (pp. 347–50). New York: Routledge.

Barrett, T. (2003). *Bereavement camp: A qualitative analysis of a therapeutic program for grieving youth.* Unpublished doctoral dissertation, University of Montana, Missoula, MT.

Bowlby, J. (1973). *Attachment and loss, Volume II: Separation, anxiety and anger.* New York: Basic Books.

Bowlby, J. (1980). *Attachment and loss, Volume III: Loss, sadness and depression.* New York: Basic Books.

Busch, T. & Kimble, C.S. (2001). Grieving children: Are we meeting the challenge? *Pediatric Nursing, 27,* p. 414.

Doka, K.J. (2008). The power of ritual: A gift to children and adolescents. In K.J. Doka & A.S. Tucci (Eds.), *Living with grief: Children and adolescents* (pp. 287–95). Washington, DC: Hospice Foundation of America.

Fitzgerald, H. (1992). *The grieving child: A parent's guide.* New York: Simon & Schuster.

Fletcher, T. & Hinkle, J.S. (2002). Adventure based counseling: An innovation in counseling. *Journal of Counseling and Development, 80,* 277–85.

Hilliard, R.E. (2001). The effects of music therapy-based bereavement groups on mood and behavior of grieving children: A pilot study. *Journal of Music Therapy, 38,* 291–306.

Levine, P. (1997). *Waking the tiger: Healing trauma: The innate capacity to transform overwhelming experiences.* Berkeley, CA: North Atlantic Books.

Muir, J. (1992). *John Muir: The eight wilderness discovery books.* Seattle, WA: Mountaineers.

Santostefano, S. (2004). *Child therapy in the great outdoors: A relational view.* Hillsdale, NJ: Analytic Press.

Schachter, S. & Georgopoulos, M. (2008). Camps for grieving children: Lessons from the field. In K. Doka & A. Tucci (Eds.), *Living with grief: Children and adolescents* (pp. 233–51). Washington, DC: Hospice Foundation of America.

Sommers-Flanagan, R., Barrett-Hakanson, T., Clarke, C., & Sommers-Flanagan, J. (2000). A psychoeducational school-based coping and social skills group for depressed students. *Journal for Specialists in Group Work, 25,* 2, 170–90.

Trozzi, M., Massimini, K., & Brazelton, T.B. (1999). *Talking with children about loss: Words, strategies, and wisdom to help children cope with death, divorce, and other difficult times.* New York: Perigee Books.

Van Der Kolk, B. (2014). *The body keeps the score: Brain, mind, and body in the healing of trauma.* New York: Penguin Group.

Wolfelt, A. (1996). *Healing the bereaved child: Grief gardening, growth through grief and other touchstones for caregivers.* New York: Routledge.

Worden, J.W. (2009). *Grief counseling and grief therapy: A handbook for the mental health practitioner* (4th ed.). New York: Springer.

chapter 25

Epilogue

Brenda J. Marshall and Howard R. Winokuer

"What would it have been like without brothers and sisters?" asked the psychologist. "I would have been lonesome – very, very lonesome. We were always close. We always had a wonderful relationship. We always shared. There were always ties."

(Bank & Khan, 1982, p. 3)

When we approached potential contributors for this book, we were struck by how excited each was to be part of the project. "Such a needed resource" was something we heard over and over. People genuinely wanted to participate and without exception were gracious in making accommodations to their chapters to fit both our time frame and format. Even colleagues who were not part of the project, but knew of it, were generous with their feedback and encouragement. Clearly we had landed on a topic that evoked genuine interest.

I (B.M.) have always gravitated to work where there is an intersection of the personal and professional – fused in a way that captures reader interest and yet provides an opportunity to glimpse a grander narrative than one story could tell. And I (H.W.) have gravitated to finding the balance between research and practice. With that in mind, we sought contributors who had a special connection to this topic – either through their research, practice, or personal loss story. By design, we provided few guidelines, trusting that the combined perspectives would provide a lens that was both academically sound and compelling to readers. A reading of our contributor list hints at the wide-ranging backgrounds and interests of each, and their resultant chapters provide a considerable variety of viewpoints, theories, practices, and disciplines.

Our intention with this final chapter is not to distill one single message or summarize the wide-ranging perspectives contained within the text. Instead, we offer some reflections about emerging themes we feel may inform further directions for both support and education about this loss. I (B.M.) like to speak with pictures, so include a few from my collection to help illustrate.

My Parents' Grief

> The importance of parental support cannot be underestimated in mediating surviving children's experiences of a sibling's death.
> (Packman, Horsley, Davies, & Kramer, 2006, p. 826)

From childhood through to late adulthood, when a brother or sister dies, the loss is profound and the life of the surviving sibling radically shifted in ways that continue to evolve and change with each passing year. Common across all age groups, with perhaps the exception of later adulthood, is the presence of grieving parents. And how those parents respond to the needs of their children in the midst of their pain greatly influences the grief experiences of surviving siblings.

Irrespective of age, bereaved siblings see and feel their parents' distress and universally respond in ways to "protect" them from further pain. The "protecting" behaviors are remarkably similar across age groups. There is often a silencing of their own outward displays of grief, in an effort to shield their parents from further sadness. This privileging of a parent's grief is reinforced in the comments of well-meaning friends and family. "You need to be strong for your parents" is a phrase so many bereaved siblings hear. As Lourenco remarked in his personal story (Chapter 4), "I am pretty sure if I had a dollar for every time someone asked me 'How's your mother?' I would be a rich man and never have to work again."

Recognizing that this narrative exists is a key component in understanding the experience of a bereaved sibling. Young or old, bereaved siblings live and respond to parents who are in tremendous pain. And the sibling's loss is always situated within the societal expectation that it is their parent who is most impacted by the death of their child.

Figure 25.1 *Umbrella*, B. Marshall (2012). Cartoon created for Conversations with Siblings Collection, Solacium Group, Uxbridge, Ontario, Canada.

I Am Alone with My Grief

"I can't talk to any of my friends about how I feel about Sophie," confided Isabella. "They just don't understand. They ask me how many brothers or sisters I have, and I don't know what to say."

(Goldman, Chapter 2)

Where do siblings turn for support? Society has no narrative for this loss. The death of a brother or sister is never "THE" story in media accounts or movies and so there is no baseline from which to draw inferences about impact. Friends, family, and co-workers are left ill-equipped to offer support or validation. For the grieving sibling, it is easy to infer "my loss doesn't matter." This is further reinforced by the absence of visible and easily accessible formal support mechanisms specific to siblings. It's not unusual for siblings to be offered a place in a generic loss group or a "friends" group

Figure 25.2 *Who Am I?* B. Marshall (2012). Cartoon created for Conversations with Siblings Collection, Solacium Group, Uxbridge, Ontario, Canada.

(Marshall, 2013). For years, I (B.M.) tried to generate interest amongst several bereavement organizations in my community to run a sibling-specific support group. "There are not enough of them," I was repeatedly told. And yet, when I recently ran a one-day sibling-specific workshop for a distant organization, participants drove from hours away simply because it was the first time their loss was "THE" loss. The absence of visible and easily accessible resources further contributes to the narrative that this loss is not as significant as others. No matter when in the lifespan a sibling dies, the loss is disenfranchised (Doka, 2002). This too represents another important dimension common to all sibling groups – they are accustomed to being outsiders.

I Am Alone in My Life

> I could never fully understand the trauma my parents experienced when Michelle died. However, I felt alone in the sense that they could not fully comprehend my suffering. My only sibling was dead. I had to now face the world without an automatic best friend.
>
> (Planer, Chapter 7)

A read through the personal stories contained within each section reveals a consistent thread – sadness over the loss of a future with their sibling. Whether it was teaching a younger brother to ride a bike (Part I), caring for older parents together (Part IV), or simply missing out on growing old together (Part V), the recognition of a future life lived without a beloved brother or sister is another common element across all age groups. Goetting's (1986) framework for understanding this relationship from a life-cycle perspective provides a helpful lens for articulating these additional losses. In the framework she articulates specific tasks or roles siblings play for one another during key developmental transitions. And while some of these tasks/roles differ by age, she notes a common link. "Perhaps the most important task of siblingship throughout the life cycle is that of providing companionship, friendship, comfort, and affection" (p. 704). Irrespective of age, bereaved siblings live with the knowledge that they will miss sharing key milestones with their brother or sister. In childhood and adolescence an easily accessible playmate is lost. In adulthood, a companion to offer support through illness and family changes is lost. And in late adulthood, someone with whom to share and reminisce about a life lived together is absent. One might see links between the bereaved parent who wonders

Figure 25.3 *Alone*, B. Marshall (2012). Cartoon created for Conversations with Siblings Collection, Solacium Group, Uxbridge, Ontario, Canada.

"what might my child have become?" and the bereaved sibling who wonders "what might we have done together?"

My Sibling Is Still Here

> More than his death and my grief, the hallmark of my experience has been his continued presence in my life. Our narrative encompasses how we remain connected and how our sibling bond never wavers. We are brother and sister still. We are brother and sister always.
>
> (Godfrey, Chapter 12)

The personal stories within this text offer a retrospective view of a life lived without a beloved sibling. Within each, the author describes how their sibling remains present in their life today. No matter the length of time that

Figure 25.4 *Still with Me*, B. Marshall (2012). Cartoon created for Conversations with Siblings Collection, Solacium Group, Uxbridge, Ontario, Canada.

has passed since their death, the relationship endures. Some dedicate their work to their deceased sibling. Some have written books about them. Some name their own children after them. And while each misses their brother or sister and wonders at how their life might have been different had they lived, there is a gentleness in the way they write that is tangible. They are still here. This too is another important piece of the sibling grief experience. Helping siblings remain connected with their deceased brother or sister seems to offer some comfort across all age groups.

Looking Ahead

> Over separations of time and distance, as they come to share fewer and fewer of life's circumstances, brothers and sisters persist in caring for one another...Their common heritage binds them in a truly unique relationship.
>
> (Goetting, 1986, p. 712)

One of the hidden narratives in this project is that the majority of contributors are themselves bereaved siblings. Beyond the personal stories, several of the research and clinical chapters are also authored by those who have lost brothers and sisters. And while many who work in the grief and bereavement field do so because of a connection to personal loss, to have so many in one project united by the *same* loss is unique.

In closing, we hope our readers have made some connections with the text that will prompt further reflection on how best to serve this grieving population. As with any work, there are limitations and gaps. Much of the work currently available (and indeed this text as well) focuses on very loving sibling relationships. One wonders how the grief experience might be different in relationships that were troubled or difficult. There is also room to explore how relationships *between* surviving siblings are impacted by the death of a brother or sister. Attempting to navigate birth order, gender, and family size in order to tease out such information is likely a challenging task but perhaps one worthy of further exploration. And finally, we acknowledge and appreciate that a more multicultural examination of both the importance of the sibling relationship and grief experience of siblings would add considerably to this conversation.

We hope our approach has helped to draw attention to this loss in a way that will resonate at multiple levels. The word that comes to mind through every chapter is validate. I want people to validate that the death of my brother or sister matters. With that in mind, education seems an easy entry into expanding support services to bereaved siblings. For every child that dies, young or old, very likely there are surviving siblings. In other words, for every support organization targeting bereaved parents, the opportunity to extend the reach to bereaved siblings seems a natural avenue to explore. And the more we discuss siblings and bring them into the conversation, the more likely we are to see additional research. We hope this text is just the beginning.

References

Bank, S. & Kahn, M. (1982). *The sibling bond*. New York: Basic Books.

Doka, K. (2002). Introduction. In K. Doka (Ed.), *Disenfranchised grief* (pp. 5–21). Champaign, IL: Research Press.

Goetting, A. (1986). The developmental tasks of siblingship over the life cycle. *Journal of Marriage and the Family*, 48, 4, 703–14.

Marshall, B.J. (2013). *Adult sibling loss: Stories, reflections and ripples*. New York: Baywood Publishing.

Packman, W., Horsley, H., Davies, B., & Kramer, R. (2006). Sibling bereavement and continuing bonds. *Death Studies*, 30, 817–41.

Index

9/11 terrorist attack 110–16

AAS (American Association of Suicidology) 92
acceptance 130, 189
accidents *see* traumatic deaths
Adams, D. 60
adaptation: in adolescence 54, 55; after suicide 152, 155, 156; and Attachment Theory 4, 5; and developmental life cycle 7, 8; and grief camps 189; Family Systems Theory 5, 6, 7, 160; in life crises 52; and Two-Track Model of Bereavement 84, 85, 87
adjustment 10, 84, 131, 189
adolescence, sibling loss in 49–71; core issues 50–1; as crisis 51, 52; empathy 61–2; empirical studies 52–4; family dynamics 53–4; and independence 50, 59; key points 62, 63; literature 58–60; recommendations to adults 63; self-concept 52, 53; and social media 51, 54, 55, 56
adult–child interactions 20–1, 22, 23
adulthood, sibling loss in 101–25; 9/11 110–16; protection of parents 105, 106
aggression 51, 60
Ainsworth, Mary 2
Albom, M. 190
alliances, family 114
ambiguous grief 11

ambiguous loss 174–82
ambivalent attachment 2, 3
American Association of Suicidology (AAS) 92
anger: in adolescence 51, 52, 54, 66; in uninvolved families 6; at medical profession 119; parental 78; and projective drawing 32; and psychotherapy 88–9; and shared grief 115
assumptive beliefs 7, 8, 50, 153, 161, 175
Attachment Theory 2–5, 7, 61, 84, 85, 130
authenticity 88–9
avoidance 60, 84, 86, 88
avoidant attachment 3

Babits, M. 62
Balk, D.E. 50, 53, 58
Bank, S. and Khan, M. xxx, 193
Barrett, C. 187–8
bereavement camps 184–91
"bereavement overload" 131
Berry, A. et al. (2015) 180
biopsychosocial functioning 84, 85, 86, 87
birth order 33, 44, 199
Blos, P.A. 59
both-and thinking 178
Bowenian theory 113
Bowlby, John: and adjustment 189; 189; "Attachment and Loss" 2, 111; Attachment Theory 2–5, 7, 61, 84, 85, 130; "Processes of Mourning" 2

Boyden, J. and Mann, G. 181
Buckle, J.L. and Fleming, S.J. 106
burning ceremony 190, 191

A Camp to Remember 185–91
cancer: impact on siblings 10, 37–41, 118–22, 123–5, 132, 133, 145; parental 145
caregiver and attachment 2–5
caretaker role 33, 43, 105, 106, 112, 162, 194
Carter, E. and McGoldrick, M. 113
child development 2–3
childhood sibling loss 17–45; bereavement programs 60–1; characteristics of bereavement 33–4; clichés 28, 29; developmental understanding 26, 27–8; grief process 189; memorialization 29, 30–1; projective play 31, 32, 33; recommended books 35; Shadows in the Sun model 17–23; support 34, 35
Cicirelli, V.G. 111, 130
Clark, J. et al. (2009) 176, 181, 182
clichés 28, 29
closure 54, 116, 175, 177–8
cognitive theory of development 26, 27
The Compassionate Friends (TCF) 43–5
complicated grief 2, 6, 130, 133, 135; assessment tools 134; risk factors 8–9
comprehension, lack of 19, 20
Connidis, I.A. 103
constructive outlets 190
continuing bonds, adaptive 33, 60, 115, 116, 163, 186, 190, 198–9
cultural influences 9, 10, 23, 178, 179
cumulative loss 9

death, understanding of 26, 27–8
Degriefing® 120
"delayed mourning" 106
dependence in child development 3
depression: and avoidance 60; in older adulthood 130, 135; and the Two-Track Model 84, 85; and uninvolved families 6
Developmental Life Cycle theory 7, 8
DeVita, Elizabeth (later Devita-Raeburn) 11, 33

DeVita, Vincent 11
disappearance 174–82
"Disenfranchised Grief" 11, 111, 112
disorganized attachment 3, 4
Doka, K.J. and Martin, T.M. 60
Dougy Center, Portland 60
dual-process model of bereavement 134, 136

egocentrism 59
elevated complicated grief 130
Elkind, D. 59
emerging adulthood, sibling loss in 75–97; forced maturity 78, 79; and identity 79; *Ordinary People* 83–90; sibling relationships 76–8; sibling suicide 91–3; worldview 79, 80
emotional security, childhood 2
empathy 10, 22, 61, 62
empowerment 2, 6, 31, 35
empty chair work 135, 136
environmental factors 20
Erikson, E.H. xxxi, 58, 59
ethnicity and bereavement 133

faith: questioning of 79, 80; support of 93 *see also* Judaism
families: of choice 172; coherence 53, 54; communication 20, 53, 54, 153; conflict-resolving 6; conflictual 5, 6; development 161–2; dynamics 53, 54, 106, 107, 111; family-level interventions 23; life-cycle framework 161–2; loss of contact 145, 146; low-communicating 6, 7; of origin 171; relationships 163–4; roles 19, 21, 114, 160, 161; supportive families 6; uninvolved 6, 167
Family Focused Grief Therapy 7
family planning 40
"family projection process" 113
family system, impact of sibling loss 87, 159–65
Family Systems Theory 5, 6, 7, 116, 153, 175
family therapy 6
Flomenhaft, D. 114
Ford Sori, C. 106
"forgotten bereaved" 111
freedom to be 187
Freud, Anna 52
fun 187, 188

funerals: adolescents' involvement in 52; adults and 105, 106, 125; children's involvement in 19, 20, 21, 40, 43; late adulthood and 142; and parental death 169, 170, 171; and suicide 153

gender 5, 8, 60, 133
"genetic resonance" 120
"ghost family" 107
global shared experience, 9/11 115
God and clichés 28
Goetting, A. 103, 105, 197, 199
Goldman, L. 27, 29, 34, 35
good death 133
Greif, G.L. and Bowers, D.T. 180
grief: in adolescence 161, 162; in children 161, 162; expression thorough play 189; hierarchy of 28, 33, 43, 69, 112, 154; responses 34
grief environment 26
grounded theory approach 18–23
group therapy 62, 107
guilt *see* survivor guilt

Hays, J.C. et al. (1997) 131
"heaven" 27, 38, 125
Henshelwood, L. 62
Hilliard, R.E. 189
Hogan, N.S. 53, 54
Hogan, N.S. and Greenfield, D.B. 53
honoring 187
Hooghe, A. 7
hope and disappearance 177–8
"The Human Knot" 62
hypothalamic-pituitary-adrenal hormonal axis 4

ICG (Inventory of Complicated Grief) 134
idealization of deceased 33, 34, 40, 59, 163
identity: loss of 70, 114, 160; new 38, 39, 44, 59, 79, 92, 93, 161; and older adulthood 130, 131, 134
illness 68–71, 79, 80, 141
immune mechanisms 4
inadequacy, feelings of 19, 33
individual approach, medical 10
inheritance 167, 170
insecure attachment 4
insecure-avoidant pattern 4

interpersonal interactions, importance of 22
Inventory of Complicated Grief (ICG) 134
irreplaceability 120, 151
isolation: and difference 59; in *Ordinary People* 84, 87; and peers 62; within family 6, 39, 164

Jacob Wetterling Foundation 175
journaling 66
Judaism 66, 67, 142

keys to surviving sibling loss 147
kidnap 174–82
King, C.A. and Merchant, C.R. 84

language, age appropriate 25, 26, 35
language barriers 179
Lawrence, E. et al. (2005) 60
life crises 51, 52
life cycles and nature 187
life expectancy calculations 132
life-review 134, 135
Linn-Gust, M.: *Conversations with the Water: A Memoir of Cultivating Hope* 93; *Do They Have Bad Days in Heaven? Surviving the Suicide Loss of a Sibling* 92
literature review 10–11
living wills 168

Madden, M. et al. (2013) 55
magical thinking 27, 28
Main, Mary 2
masculine models of grief 10, 60, 62
maturity 78, 79
Maynard, L. 104
meaning-making 152
medical profession 28, 168
memorial cards 102fig
memorialization 29, 30–1, 35
mental health issues, sibling suicide 8, 9, 103–1, 152
milestones 39, 162, 176
mindfulness 61
morbidity, sibling 6, 7, 10–11
mortality, sibling 10–11, 130, 132, 135
Moss, E. and Raz, A. 107
Moss, S.Z. and Moss, M.S. 130, 133
moving away 9, 38, 39, 44, 76, 78, 79

Muir, J. 184
multigenerational transmission process 113
murder 107, 110–16

narrative approach 104
National Alliance for Grieving Children 60
National Center for Missing and Exploited Children 175
National Institutes of Health (NIH) 68–9
nature 184–91
Neimeyer, R.A., Harris, D.L., Winokuer, H.R. and Thornton, G.F. xxxi
Neubauer, P.B. 114
NIH (National Institutes of Health) 68–9
Noppe, I.C. and Noppe, L.D. 59, 60

O'Bryant, S.L. 131
Offer Self-Image Questionnaire for Adolescents (OSIQ) 53
older adulthood, sibling loss in 129–37; assessment tools 134; clinical strategies 134, 135; cognitive function and 131; ethnicity and 133; and gender 133; loss of family contact 145, 146; and mental health 130–1; and mortality 130, 132, 135; and physical health 131, 132; risk and protective factors 132–3, 134; roles 142
Oltjenbruns, K.A. 59
"only children" 33, 78, 114, 142, 160
open-ended groups 60
Ordinary People (novel and film) 83–90
OSIQ (Offer Self-Image Questionnaire for Adolescents) 53
outdoor-based grief support programs 184–91

Packman, W. et al. (2006) 33, 35, 194
parent support groups 23
parental death 167–72
parental grief 105, 114, 194; as failure to protect 161; as more important 28, 33, 43, 69, 112, 154; and role reversal 106
parents: behavioral changes 164; inaccessibility of 5; protection of 33, 43, 105, 106, 112, 162, 194; and reassurance 21, 33
Parkes, C. 7
peer-based programs 62
peer groups: and adolescents 60; and disappearance 181; support groups 35

permission to grieve 96
personal fable 59
Pew Internet study, 2013 55
Piaget, Jean 26, 27–8
play 2, 18, 35, 189; projective play 31, 32, 33
post-traumatic stress disorder (PTSD) 10, 85, 179, 180, 181, 182
preoperational stage of development 27
Pretorius, G. et al. (2010) 106, 107
privacy 51, 54, 55, 56, 86, 164
private memorials 116
"prohibited mourning" 112
projective play 31, 32, 33
psychic containing 62
psychoanalytic approaches 22
psychodynamic psychology 53
psychoneurobiological model of development 4
psychosocial theory of development 58, 59; *Identity versus Identity Diffusion* 59; *Intimacy versus Isolation* 59
psychotherapy, in *Ordinary People* 86, 87–9
PTSD *see* post-traumatic stress disorder

realizations of loss, sequence of 105
reconciliation needs 189, 190
Redford, Robert 83
reflective capacity 3, 4
relational themes 152
relaxation 187, 190
religion *see* faith; Judaism
remarriage of surviving partner 111, 113
risk-taking behaviors 59
rituals 8, 96, 116, 190, 191
Rosen, Helen xvii
Rosenblatt, P.C. 105

"safe box" 29
safe spaces 60, 96, 155
school response 34, 35
second individuation process 59
secure attachment 2, 4
self-regulation 155, 187
self-awareness, adult 22, 23
self-concept 52, 53
self-harm, survivor 89
sensorimotor stage development 26
Shadows in the Sun model 17–23
shrines 39, 40

siblings: as mirror 59; new 163; and older adulthood 131; and relationships 5; as special 113
sibling rivalry 114, 168
sibling-specific support groups 196
Silverman, P. et al. (1992) 32, 33
situational factors 19, 20
social functioning 10
social learning theory 52
social media 50, 51, 54, 55, 56, 103
Strange Situation paradigm 2
stress and emotion regulation 4
suicide 89, 91–3, 151–6; of bereaved sibling 84, 85, 132
support network, assessment of 9
survivor guilt 113; and adolescents 70; after suicide 154, 155, 156; and children 19, 27, 28, 163, 164; and older adults 134, 135, 136; psychotherapy and 89; and sibling rivalry 114; and the Two-Track Model 85
symbolic nurturing 32

TCF (The Compassionate Friends) 43–5
therapeutic metaphor 62
therapy 26–8, 62, 96, 107, 112–16, 135–6, 178, 181
theoretical models 2–10

traumatic deaths (accidents) 42–5, 65–7, 77, 78, 79 94–7, 102; "compulsive inquiry" 8; in *Ordinary People* 83–90
Turner, K. 61
Two-Track Model of Bereavement 84–90

unfinished business 134
unpreparedness 133

validation of loss 115
Van Riper, M. 107
Vaught Godfrey, R. 103, 198
verbalization 35, 189

walking in the shoes model, suicide bereavement 151–6
Webb, N.B. 35
Wetterling, Patty 175, 176, 177, 179, 180, 181
What About Me? Coping with the Abduction of a Brother or Sister 180, 181
White, L. 103
Wolfelt, A. 185
Worden, J.W. 189
World Trade Center Memorial Commemoration 111
Wright, P.M. 104

youth interventions 61

For Product Safety Concerns and Information please contact our EU
representative GPSR@taylorandfrancis.com
Taylor & Francis Verlag GmbH, Kaufingerstraße 24, 80331 München, Germany

www.ingramcontent.com/pod-product-compliance
Lightning Source LLC
Chambersburg PA
CBHW050533300426
44113CB00012B/2070